AQUINAS'S *SU*

MW01196645

Alone among Thomas Aquinas's works, the *Summa Theologiae* contains well-developed and integrated discussions of metaphysics, ethics, law, human action, and the divine nature. The essays in this volume, by scholars representing varied approaches to the study of Aquinas, offer thorough, cutting-edge expositions and analyses of these topics and show how they relate to Aquinas's larger system of thought. The volume also examines the reception of the *Summa Theologiae* from the thirteenth century to the present day, showing how scholars have understood and misunderstood this key text, and how, even after seven centuries of interpretation, we still have much to learn from it. Detailed and accessible, this book will be highly important for scholars and students of medieval philosophy and theology.

JEFFREY HAUSE is Michael W. Barry Professor at Creighton University. He has published widely on the work of Thomas Aquinas and is the editor of *Debates in Medieval Philosophy: Essential Readings and Contemporary Responses* (2013).

CAMBRIDGE CRITICAL GUIDES

AQUINAS'S
Summa Theologiae

A Critical Guide

EDITED BY

JEFFREY HAUSE
Creighton University, Omaha

CAMBRIDGE
UNIVERSITY PRESS

University Printing House, Cambridge CB2 8BS, United Kingdom

One Liberty Plaza, 20th Floor, New York, NY 10006, USA

477 Williamstown Road, Port Melbourne, VIC 3207, Australia

314-321, 3rd Floor, Plot 3, Splendor Forum, Jasola District Centre, New Delhi - 110025, India

79 Anson Road, #06-04/06, Singapore 079906

Cambridge University Press is part of the University of Cambridge.

It furthers the University's mission by disseminating knowledge in the pursuit of education, learning and research at the highest international levels of excellence.

www.cambridge.org
Information on this title: www.cambridge.org/9781107521438
DOI: 10.1017/9781316271490

© Cambridge University Press 2018

First published 2018
First paperback edition 2019

A catalogue record for this publication is available from the British Library

Library of Congress Cataloging in Publication data
Names: Hause, Jeffrey, editor.
Title: Aquinas's Summa theologiae : a critical guide / edited by Jeffrey Hause, Creighton University, Omaha.
Description: New York : Cambridge University Press, 2018. | Series: Cambridge critical guides | Includes bibliographical references and index.
Identifiers: LCCN 2017059346 | ISBN 9781107109261 (hardback)
Subjects: LCSH: Thomas, Aquinas, Saint, 1225?-1274. Summa theologica.
Classification: LCC BX1749.T6 A73 2018 | DDC 230/.2--dc23 LC record available at https://lccn.loc.gov/2017059346

ISBN 978-1-107-10926-1 Hardback
ISBN 978-1-107-52143-8 Paperback

Contents

Contents

Contributors

MARILYN MCCORD ADAMS was Emerita Professor of Philosophy at University of California, Los Angeles, and Senior Fellow, Center for Philosophy of Religion at Rutgers University. Prior to her appointment at Rutgers, she was Regius Professor of Divinity at the University of Oxford. She is the author of *Horrendous Evils and the Goodness of God* (2000) and the magisterial *William Ockham* (1987), as well as many classic articles in medieval philosophy and the philosophy of religion.

STEPHEN L. BROCK is Ordinary Professor of Medieval Philosophy at the Pontifical University of the Holy Cross, Rome. He is the author of *Action and Conduct: Thomas Aquinas and the Theory of Action* (1998) and *The Philosophy of Saint Thomas Aquinas: A Sketch* (2015).

BRIAN DAVIES is Distinguished Professor of Philosophy at Fordham University and Honorary Professor at Australian Catholic University. He is the author of *Thomas Aquinas's Summa Theologiae: A Guide and Commentary* (2014) and *Thomas Aquinas's Summa Contra Gentiles: A Guide and Commentary* (2016).

MICHAEL GORMAN is Professor of Philosophy at The Catholic University of America. He is the author of *Aquinas on the Metaphysics of the Hypostatic Union* (2017) and many articles on contemporary metaphysics as well as medieval philosophy.

TOBIAS HOFFMANN is Associate Professor of Philosophy at The Catholic University of America. He is co-editor of *Aquinas and the Nicomachean Ethics* (2013) and the author of many articles on medieval philosophy.

NICHOLAS E. LOMBARDO, O.P. is Associate Professor of Historical and Systematic Theology at The Catholic University of America. He is the author of *The Logic of Desire: Aquinas on Emotion* (2011) and *The Father's Will: Christ's Crucifixion and the Goodness of God* (2013).

THOMAS M. OSBORNE, JR. is Professor in the Department of Philosophy and Center for Thomistic Studies at the University of St. Thomas (Houston, TX). He is the author of *Love of Self and Love of God in Thirteenth-Century Ethics* (2005) and *Human Action in Thomas Aquinas, John Duns Scotus, and William of Ockham* (2014).

JT PAASCH is Adjunct Professor of Philosophy at Georgetown University. He is the author of *Divine Production in Late Medieval Trinitarian Theology* (2012) and co-editor of *The Routledge Companion to Medieval Philosophy* (forthcoming).

ROBERT PASNAU is Professor of Philosophy at the University of Colorado Boulder. He is the editor of *Oxford Studies in Medieval Philosophy* and *The Cambridge History of Medieval Philosophy* (2010), and the author of *Metaphysical Themes 1274–1671* (2011).

MATTHIAS PERKAMS is Professor of Philosophy at Friedrich-Schiller-Universität Jena. He is the editor and translator of Thomas Aquinas's *Kommentar zur Nikomachischen Ethik I und X* (2014) and co-editor of *Aquinas and the Nicomachean Ethics* (2013).

JEAN PORTER is John A. O'Brien Professor of Moral Theology at the University of Notre Dame. Her most recent books include *Nature as Reason: A Thomistic Theory of the Natural Law* (2005) and *Justice as a Virtue: A Thomistic Perspective* (2016).

JACOB SCHMUTZ is Lecturer in the Philosophy Department at Paris-Sorbonne University. He is co-editor of *The Legacy of John Duns Scotus* (2008) and *Juan Caramuel: The Last Scholastic Polymath* (2008).

Abbreviations

Works by Aquinas

De Subst. Sep.	*De Substantiis Separatis*
DM	*Quaestiones Disputatae de Malo*
DP	*Quaestiones Disputatae de Potentia Dei*
DSC	*Quaestio Disputata de Spiritualibus Creaturis*
DV	*Quaestiones Disputatae de Veritate*
DVC	*Quaestio Disputata de Virtutibus in Communi*
DVCard.	*Quaestio Disputata de Virtutibus Cardinalibus*
In Sent.	*Scriptum super libros Sententiarum*
In BDT	*Super Boetium De Trinitate*
In De An.	*Sententia libri De Anima*
In Ethic.	*Sententia libri Ethicorum*
In Met.	*Sententia super Metaphysicam*
In Meteor.	*Sententia super Meteora*
In Post. an.	*Expositio libri Posteriorum*
DA	*Quaestio Disputata De Anima*
SCG	*Summa Contra Gentiles*
ST	*Summa Theologiae*
I	First Part of the *Summa Theologiae*
I-II	First Part of the Second Part of the *Summa Theologiae*
II-II	Second Part of the Second Part of the *Summa Theologiae*
III	Third Part of the *Summa Theologiae*

In references to Aquinas's works, "c" refers to the body or main response of an article, "s.c." to the *sed contra* or considerations "on the other hand," while "ad" picks out responses to initial objections. Unless otherwise stated, all references to Aquinas's works are from the critical Leonine edition. Line and paragraph numbers are taken from that edition.

Works by Aristotle

Cat.	*Categories*
De An.	*De Anima*
Met.	*Metaphysics*
NE	*Nicomachean Ethics*
Phys.	*Physics*
Pol.	*Politics*

Introduction
Jeffrey Hause

0.1 The *Summa Theologiae*: A Demanding "Introduction"

Thomas Aquinas (1224/5–74) lived to be no more than 50, yet in his short career he wrote dozens of philosophical and theological works spanning multiple genres. Among these, the various *Quaestiones Disputatae*, or disputed questions, contain focused treatments of such specialized topics as truth, evil, virtue, and spiritual creatures. As revised transcripts of sophisticated graduate-level classroom exercises, these works presume familiarity with both time-honored and contemporary discussions of the relevant topics, as we see from contributions made by student participants in the exercise. By contrast, Aquinas composed the *Summa Theologiae* for students at the outset of their theological studies. In fact, his target audience for the *Summa* was not the highly educated few who succeeded in studying theology at such elite institutions as the University of Paris, where he conducted many of his disputations. Rather, they were friars from his own Dominican order – bright enough for studies but not the intellectuals who would be scholars and academics. Hence, Aquinas made sure to compose the *Summa* in clear, plain Latin, as free from jargon as any work of scholastic philosophical theology could be, and he takes pains to present topics in the order he finds most sensible for beginners. The *Summa* is the work of a master teacher.[1]

Knowing Aquinas's pedagogical intentions, we might wonder why an introductory-level work written in plain, lucid prose, itself a guide for students of modest capabilities, would require a critical guide for readers to grasp its teachings. It is no secret that philosophical works written in approachable, inviting language may nevertheless contain confoundingly difficult arguments or systems of thought. Hume's *Enquiries* still demand

---

[1] For discussion of Aquinas's pedagogical plans for the *Summa Theologiae*, see Boyle, "The Setting of the *Summa*."

study, despite their admirable transparency. Few philosophers could write such entrancing prose as Plato or Wittgenstein, yet there has been no shortage of struggles to comprehend the *Republic* and *Philosophical Investigations*. It is the same with the *Summa Theologiae*, whose plain and straightforward expression shows us all the more clearly the difficulty of the topics Aquinas treats. In introducing students to the subject of his study, which Aquinas called "Christian religion" in the prologue to the *Summa*, Aquinas also introduces them to a stupefying number of debates and complexities in fields we would now describe as metaphysics, moral psychology, ethics, philosophy of religion, and theology. For Aquinas, the study of "Christian religion" requires both depth and breadth across these many areas.

As several of this volume's chapters make clear, the lessons Aquinas means to teach us in the *Summa* stretch our human capacities to their utmost, as we see most evidently in his treatment of the existence and nature of God. God is, as Brian Davies argues in Chapter 3, unknowable and inevitably mysterious. God is not a being like any other, is not a member of any kind; we can therefore not grasp God by any system of classification. Nor can we understand what God is like on the model of what creatures are like. If Socrates is just, then Socrates has a property – a virtue – of justice. His human potentiality for justice has been actualized. God's justice cannot be like this, however. God is complete actuality with no admixture of potentiality, and so must be absolutely simple. God must therefore be identical with perfect justice. Aquinas therefore expresses a powerful skepticism that human beings are able to form a positive conception of God.

Even familiar beings infinitely easier to grasp than God, such as ourselves, can be recalcitrant to accurate conceptualization. For instance, as Marilyn McCord Adams explains (Chapter 5), Aquinas's philosophical commitments lead him to the conclusion that the intellectual soul carries out activities without the body's participation, which in turn shows that the soul subsists per se and will survive the body's death. But if the intellectual soul is functionally independent of the organic body in this way, then how can Aquinas argue against Platonic dualism in favor of the view that the human being is unified by a single substantial form – the soul – that is the element in us explaining our essential characteristics, the constellation of structures, potentialities, and powers that characterize human being? In resolving these puzzles, Aquinas draws on both his metaphysics and psychology to offer answers that are as ingenious as they are controversial.

0.2 Reading the *Summa Theologiae*

The arguments of the *Summa* turn out to be no less challenging than those in works Aquinas writes for more sophisticated audiences. What makes the *Summa* a more introductory work is its more straightforward style and its meticulously plotted ordering of ideas. Aquinas's pedagogical sensitivity is evident throughout the work, as it had to be for Aquinas to achieve his goals. He means to discuss Christian religion in such a way that his students would grasp all they need to know to serve as moral and spiritual guides. That in turn requires him to treat a dizzying variety of topics in the course of hundreds and hundreds of pages. He asks the reader to study the entire work in order, bearing in mind the interconnections these many discussions bear to one another. Aquinas's thoughtful ordering of topics makes it easier for us to grasp these interconnections. For instance, as Michael Gorman explains (Chapter 11), the treatment of Christ, who has both divine and human natures and whose efforts redeem us from the wages of sin, comes after the discussion of divine nature, human nature, and sin. Nevertheless, it is a rare scholar who has studied every word of this text as Aquinas had intended. To help us see the *Summa* as Aquinas meant us to, most of this volume's chapters, such as Robert Pasnau's (Chapter 1), Stephen Brock's (Chapter 2), and Nicholas Lombardo's (Chapter 6), draw connections across the vast regions of this text rather than focusing on just a few of its questions.

In fact, the *Summa* often *appears* less daunting than it really is, precisely because readers treat it as a collection of individual treatises on discrete topics rather than as an interconnected whole presented in a carefully plotted order. That approach also makes it look far less theological than it really is, as we see from Jacob Schmutz's exposition of the *Summa's* reception (Chapter 12). After all, the massive Second Part concerns ethics (human action and passion, virtue and vice, wrongdoing), and much of the First Part treats human nature and created being more generally. That leaves just the unfinished Third Part, which investigates Christ and the sacraments, and the opening units of the First Part, which focus on God. Nevertheless, Aquinas did not write the *Summa* as a work of Christian humanism, since he means for us to understand creatures as products of God, dependent on him for their existence, reflecting him in their natures, and striving toward him so as to imitate him insofar as they can. The work is therefore deeply theological throughout. Even so, there is also considerable truth to the claim that the work's focus is on human beings. As Aquinas notes at the work's outset, his purpose is to convey "what belongs to the Christian religion in a way suitable for the education of beginners." By "Christian religion," Aquinas does not mean a sort of catechism or statement of creed, but rather a way of life responsive to the distinctive truths of Christianity and expressing its characteristic virtues. As a work intended to guide us toward what Aquinas takes to be a flourishing life, which includes the right use of our cognitive and appetitive powers, the *Summa* must offer a detailed account of human nature that captures the ways in which our intellect, will, senses, and sensory appetite function. Aquinas finds it pedagogically useful to reach that goal by comparing and contrasting human beings with other intellectual beings (God and the angels) as well as non-rational animals. The treatments of God and the angels, then, serve not merely as treatises on these discrete topics; rather, they provide important background for the account of human beings, which will occupy the bulk of the *Summa*.

0.3   Human Nature

In one such discussion, Aquinas points out that human beings live in the metaphysical borderland between purely spiritual beings – God and the angels – and non-human animals. As with other animals, humans come to be when our soul informs matter, organizing it into the sort of body that lives the characteristically human life. The result is not a joining of two independent, or potentially independent, substances. Rather, as Marilyn McCord Adams points out, the soul as "the substantial form is the source of the *esse* and constitution of the whole composite" (Chapter 5, p. 91). Nevertheless, unlike the souls of other animals, which are the first principles only of organic functions, the human soul has intellectual cognition and so performs an activity that the body does not participate in. Therefore, our souls are incorporeal and incorruptible, continuing to exist even after separation from the body. Nevertheless, even in this state of separation, souls are different from angels. Since a separated soul cannot think by turning to phantasms, which requires the bodily power of imagination, God or angels must infuse the separated soul with the sorts of intelligible species through which angels cognize even particulars without need for phantasms. Our more limited minds, naturally suited to thinking by appealing to abstracted species supplemented by phantasms, will inevitably fail to reap as much cognitive benefit from these infused species as angels do.

Likewise, Aquinas explains, because the angels are entirely spiritual creatures, they can have only intellectual emotions or "affections," such as intellectual joy or love. Like other embodied animals, humans also experience passions, which have a bodily expression. However, because of the ways in which our rational capacities interact with our sensory capacities, human passions are not simply reactions to sensory cognitive input, as Nicholas Lombardo argues (Chapter 6). The way our intellects conceive of an object influences the way our sensory cognitive powers grasp and present it. One might look at the Coliseum in Rome and see an architectural marvel, a place of massive animal slaughter, or the fruits of Vespasian's ransacking of the Temple in Jerusalem. Which perspective one takes will determine the sort of passion one will feel on contemplating the Coliseum.

0.4 Human Happiness

Aquinas intended the Dominican students studying his *Summa* to use it as a guide to human happiness or flourishing both for themselves and for those in their spiritual and moral care. It might seem odd, then, that he does not treat the subject of human happiness in detail until the beginning of the Second Part, after the 119 questions discussed in the First Part. Those 119 questions, however, contain important preliminary considerations that Aquinas will draw on in his arguments about the nature and attainment of human happiness.

Like God and the angels, human beings are intellectual: We understand the natures of things and see how they are ordered and interconnected with each other. For this reason, we are able to pursue those fields of study that Aquinas considers sciences. In addition to our ability to use our intellect theoretically, we can also use it practically. We do not simply grasp particular good things and pursue them. Rather, we have a general conception of a good, flourishing life, and we are able to deliberate about and determine for ourselves what would constitute such a life and what steps we should take to attain such a life. This intellectual element is what is highest in us and makes us God-like.

Therefore, when Aquinas explores what happiness consists in, he argues that it is an activity of our theoretical intellect, which is the highest activity of our highest capacity. In fact, as Tobias Hoffmann explains (Chapter 7), it must be an activity that makes our lives self-sufficient, so that we lack nothing fulfilling, as well as final, so that it is an end in itself and not a means to some further end. In this life, however, we can never reach perfect happiness because we will never be able to gain complete understanding. We find that perfection, Aquinas argues, only in the vision of the divine essence itself, which is reserved for the blessed in heaven (I-II 3.8). Nevertheless, we can achieve an imperfect happiness in this life by contemplating the theoretical sciences, such as physics or metaphysics (I-II 3.5). Because, as we learn from the First Part, all creatures are in a way reflections of the divine essence, when we contemplate science we are united in our intellects with these reflections and are thereby assimilated to God. In addition, Aquinas admits that even the virtuous exercise of practical reason affords us a measure of happiness in this life, even though it makes us God-like in a less robust way: We are related to what we know through our practical intellect as God is related to what he knows, namely, as their cause. Nevertheless, for the long remainder of the Second Part, Aquinas will focus on just this sort of virtuous practical activity. That is because human beings merit the perfect happiness of the next life through practical activity informed by the virtue of charity. Because our eternal happiness depends on it, the virtuous activity of the practical intellect takes on enormous importance in Aquinas's guide to the moral and spiritual life.

0.5   Happiness Won and Lost

We have already seen that the perfect happiness of the next life, as well as one sort of this-worldly happiness, is gained through virtuous activity. Although Aquinas contends that virtuous human action will conform to universal moral rules, those rules do not dictate our virtuous choices in any straightforward way, as both Jean Porter (Chapter 9) and Matthias Perkams (Chapter 8) explain. Practical reasoning for Aquinas is not simply a matter of subsuming a particular case under a general rule and straightforwardly deducing the right course of action. For one thing, we must judge which rules are salient in the conditions in which we find ourselves and then determine which rule is best applicable here and now. Even then, moral reasoning does not follow a simple algorithm. Rules must be interpreted and applied in concrete circumstances. For instance, if a student determines that she ought to express gratitude for a scholarship she receives from a donor, she must still think carefully about how to do so appropriately. She must consider the right means (a handwritten letter or an email?), the right content (evidence of academic success or simply an expression of thanks?), the best tone (steering a course between too fawning a display, which would be demeaning to her, and too meager an articulation, which would be ungracious). In particular, she must bear in mind who her donor is (a kindly neighbor or a public figure?) and who she herself is (a student with her particular plan of study and career goals). So, although practical reasoning is always grounded in universal rules, those rules may lead to different judgments about how to proceed, even in very similar situations, because of importantly different circumstances. This is an especially important lesson for moral and spiritual advisors, who must learn that there is no such thing as a life of simply following moral rules. The moral life requires sensitivity to detail, imagination, sympathy, and a robust self-knowledge, without which universal moral rules may be very dangerous indeed.

By repeatedly performing virtuous activity, we develop virtues, that is, dispositions or habits (*habitus*) that incline us to good activities. The virtues dispose us to attend to morally salient considerations, keeping us focused on the right goals as well as increasing our sensitivity to relevant circumstances. Because they render our sensory appetite more responsive to reason, we experience fewer and less powerful wayward passions that would render our actions unpleasant and therefore make us sluggish. Instead, those with virtue have the resolve to carry out what they have determined to do, even if it turns out to be difficult, and they find pleasure in leading morally good lives.

These so-called "acquired" moral virtues enable us to achieve imperfect happiness in this life. To attain the perfect happiness of the next life, people need special, divinely infused virtues that enable them to merit union with God. Chief among these virtues are what Aquinas calls the "theological" virtues of faith, hope, and charity. Faith disposes humans to assent to what is revealed by God. Aquinas does not deny that philosophical reasoning can lead us to at least some truths of faith. (As JT Paasch argues in Chapter 4, Aquinas might even have the resources to provide a philosophical argument for a triune God, though Aquinas himself says otherwise.) However, as Thomas M. Osborne, Jr. explains (Chapter 10), faith inclines people to believe on different grounds from those employed in philosophical arguments. The assent of faith is a response to divine authority expressed in revelation, and it is divine grace that enables one to make such a response. Through faith, one can be confident in what one believes because it is God's teaching, even if the truth of what one believes is not evident. Through the virtue of hope, people rely on God's power to help them attain a future good that is exceedingly difficult to attain: the happiness of the next life. Counting on God's power gives the hopeful person the confidence to pursue a morally virtuous life. Anticipation of that future good in turn rouses them further to persevere in that life. Finally, the virtue of charity moves its possessors to love God above all and to love their neighbor as themselves. In addition, charity directs all the other virtues to its own end: If a person of charity acts generously or courageously, that is not simply because she values generosity or courage. That is also because she sees those she is helping through these virtues as brothers and sisters, fellow children of God.

Eternal happiness is merited through virtuous acts motivated by charity, but it is lost through sin, which is a barrier to the grace needed for the infused virtues. We sin when our activity is defective. Sometimes we fail to will and carry out activity we should, and sometimes the activity we do will and carry out fails to live up to moral standards as determined by reason or divine law. Aquinas upholds the view, widely accepted by medieval thinkers, that in either case, the evil we are responsible for is not a positive element or quality but is rather a privation. The evil of sin is the defect in our activity.

On the one hand, it seems plausible to think that if we lose the relationship with God that is the source of meritorious activity, that would be due to defective activity on our part. However, this view is also puzzling in obvious ways. How can the evil of sin, which strictly speaking is not something that really exists, have any causal consequences at all? Likewise, how can any field of study explore the evil of sin if evil does not really exist? Stephen Brock (Chapter 2), drawing on metaphysical, psychological, and moral theses from Aquinas, argues that the *Summa* helps to answer these questions by explaining the ways in which even positive things can be denominated evil. For instance, we call acts evil when they fail to live up to the standards required by morality. The failure may be a privation, but the act is a positive item. Likewise, if acts are evil, that is not because they aim at nothing at all, but because they aim at objects that reason finds to be unfitting. These objects are positive items, but pursuing them means failing to pursue a fitting end. These positive concomitants of evil allow Aquinas to subsume sin into his rational study of philosophical theology, detailing its causes, effects, and remedies – crucial topics for any work dedicated to moral and spiritual direction.

0.6   Charity

Even this brief introduction to Aquinas's *Summa Theologiae* should give readers an idea of the exceptional breadth and complexity of his thought, which not only spans nearly every subfield of philosophy but draws on all of them to teach his Dominican beginners what is important for them as moral and spiritual guides. However, I do not want to leave readers with the idea that the most impressive characteristic of the *Summa* is its complexity. Equally impressive, and evident to anyone who reads the work, is its deep charity, which we see most clearly in the way Aquinas treats those philosophers and theologians, whether his predecessors or contemporaries, with whom he carries on a discussion. He treats them always as colleagues in the same enterprise of searching for and teaching the truth. When he presents their ideas, he strives for fair and plausible ways of understanding their views. In fact, such fairness stems from one of Aquinas's most noteworthy moral considerations: Judging mere things, and judging people, are importantly different (II-II 60.4). When we judge mere things, we aim for the greatest accuracy possible. When we judge humans, however, we must also be mindful that we harm others when we think ill of them without sufficient reason. Therefore, when a person's reputation is at stake, we should try, whenever evidence allows it, to judge him or her in a positive way. It is not simply in Aquinas's *teaching* that we find a guide to life. We can also find it in the charitable spirit that animates his work.

CHAPTER I

On What There Is in Aquinas

Robert Pasnau

Since Quine, it has become common to distinguish between ideology and ontology. The first concerns the conceptual framework in which a theory is articulated. The second concerns what entities the theory postulates. Suppose we apply this distinction to the familiar metaphysical framework of Thomas Aquinas, couched in terms of potentiality and actuality, matter and form, substance and accident. From this Quinean point of view, the Aquinian theory can be examined to discover how much is mere ideology, and how much is ontology. My suggestion will be that the theory is more ideological, and less ontological, than is ordinarily supposed. But this is not to say that it is mere ideology, because the ideology serves to map the modal structure of reality.

1.1 Cosmology

Before diving into the metaphysical details, it will be useful to locate ourselves within the cosmological worldview that Aquinas embraces. First and foremost, there is God, there has always been God, and there will always be God, necessarily. This, Aquinas famously thinks, can be proved in at least five different ways (I 2.3).

Might there *only* have been God? Well, before the world's creation there *was* only God. Indeed, to be precise, that was the situation for an eternity, though not of course for *all* of eternity, but only for that eternal part of the universe's history that predates God's initial creative act. One might then wonder: If God existed alone for an eternity, could God have chosen to exist alone for *all* of eternity? Scholars have disagreed on this question, but on the most straightforward reading of Aquinas's words, the answer is yes: God might have chosen not to create, in which case there never would have been anything other than God:

> Since God's goodness is perfect, and he can exist without other things (since none of his perfection comes to him from others) it follows that

there is no absolute necessity that he will things other than himself. (I 19.3c)

Given that God, considered alone, is perfectly and infinitely good, a world with only God in it would necessarily be as good as any world could be.[1]

Nothing could be added to such a world to make it better. Still, nothing created by a perfectly good God could make the world any worse, else God would not be perfectly good. This suggests that God had a great deal of latitude in choosing to create this particular world rather than another: "Speaking in absolute terms, for everything made by God, God can make another that is better" (I 25.6c). There was, then, no decisive, sufficient reason why our world was chosen. Aquinas thus has an explanation for why it took so long – an eternity! – for God to get around to creating, and why God created only this one earth, with only so much space for creatures. God could have created more and larger earths, without limit, but more would not have been better, just as less would not have been worse.

Focusing on earth gets the cosmology right as far as the material world goes, but the material world is only part of creation. Indeed, it is both less numerous and less exalted than the immaterial part of creation, the angels, which "exceed in number, incomparably, material substances" (I 50.3c). The number of angels is "maximal, exceeding every material multitude" (ibid.), which seems to mean that the angels outnumber anything physical that one might care to count. How does he know this? His basis is the general principle that "to the extent things are more perfect, to that extent they are created by God in greater measure" (ibid.). Aquinas has no doubt that the immaterial angels are more perfect than we mere mortal animals, but still he has to admit that his conclusions about the angels are speculative, because "immaterial substances are of an entirely different nature from the quiddities of material things" (I 88.2c).

Details aside, it is the overall cosmic system that is the primary object of God's attention: "God principally wills the good of the whole of his effects rather than any particular good" (SCG I.85 par. 3). So Aquinas supposes that, however the details are filled in, the universe is at any rate a well-ordered collection of things of different kinds, ranging from the simplest of corruptible bodies to the most elevated of immortal intellects. "If only one grade of goodness were found in things, the

---

[1] For the case that God's goodness requires creation, see Kretzmann, *The Metaphysics of Creation*, pp. 130–6. I have argued otherwise in Pasnau, *Thomas Aquinas on Human Nature*, pp. 394–404.

universe would not be perfect" (I 47.2c). The angels contribute to this story not just in virtue of their lofty minds, but in virtue of Aquinas's surprising view that each angel belongs to its own discrete species (I 50.4). Indeed, Aquinas is so focused on the contribution of species-level diversity to the goodness of the whole, that he feels it necessary to offer some explanation of why there are multiple individuals within a single species:

> For things that are incorruptible, there is only one individual in each spe-
> cies, because the species is adequately preserved in that one. But for things
> that are generable and corruptible, there are many individuals in each spe-
> cies, so as to preserve the species. (ibid.)

This focus on the species level has to be qualified when it comes to human beings, the only corruptible beings that are also rational. Our ability to love and understand God gives us special worth as individuals beyond the contribution we make to the well-ordered hierarchy of species. Thus, "rational creatures have as their end God, whom they can attain by their own operation, in knowing and loving him" (I 65.2c). Such considerations lead us into the domain of psychology and ultimately theology, and so lie beyond the scope of this chapter. For our purposes what warrants attention is the overarching design of the created world, which divides into material and immaterial domains, and then into further distinctions among species and individuals. These are the basic structural features that Aquinas's metaphysics ought to be able to explain.

1.2   Dependence and Distinctness

When Aquinas turns his attention in the First Part of the *Summa Theologiae* from God to creatures, the very first conclusion he reaches is that "it is necessary to say that everything that exists in any sort of way exists from God" (I 44.1c). God is the limiting case of this principle, because God has already been *identified* with existence (I 3.4). Since Aquinas has proved already that there can be only one being like that (I 11.3), everything else must merely *have* existence or, as Aquinas puts it here, must "participate in existence" (I 44.1c). The language of participation signals that we have come to one of the most Platonic moments in the *Summa Theologiae*, where the critical argument turns on the familiarly Platonic principle that where many things have F in common, this commonality must be explained by some one thing that is F intrinsically.

This is made most explicit in a later parallel discussion of whether corporeal creatures come from God, in which Aquinas reasons as follows:

> If distinct things are unified in something, it is necessary for there to be some cause of this union, since distinct things are not unified in virtue of themselves. And so it is the case that, whenever in distinct things some one thing is found, those distinct things must receive that one thing from some one cause, just as distinct hot bodies have their heat from fire. But *existence* is found to be common to all things, no matter how distinct. Therefore it is necessary that there be one principle of existing from which whatever exists in any sort of way has existence – whether it be invisible and spiritual or visible and corporeal. (I 65.1c)[2]

Let us refer to this, as Aquinas himself does (DP 3.5c), as "Plato's argument," the *ratio Platonis*. The trouble with Plato's argument is that it threatens to yield an absurd inventory of primary Fs – i.e., the "some one cause" in virtue of which other things are Fs. Not even Plato believed that there is a Form for every way in which things are. As *Parmenides* 130c puts it, "What about things that might seem absurd, like hair and mud and dirt, or anything else totally undignified and worthless? ... Surely it is too outlandish to think there is a form for them." But how then does one decide where Plato's argument does and does not apply? And if this *ratio Platonis* is indeed sound, how can one avoid applying it to *every* case where "distinct things are unified in something"?

For Aquinas, an answer to these questions requires noticing that the argument does not require that distinct Fs must be made F by some sort of common *proximate* cause that is itself intrinsically F. This *is* something like how the story goes for the example he offers, where everything that is hot is so in virtue of the elemental quality of Fire, which is essentially hot and is a constituent of everything that is hot. But in most cases the explanation of F-ness will not be so straightforward. Although many things are *rough*, for instance, there is no quality of roughness that all the rough things share. The argument, however, does not require this; it requires only that, at some level of explanation, there be some common cause. And for Aquinas there turns out to be only one cause, God, that is truly common to all things. Hence he offers this *ratio Platonis* only in the context of establishing that God is the cause of all things, because here it so happens that the deeper explanatory structure neatly tracks the surface appearances. All things have existence because they participate in the one

---

[2] Aquinas offers more extended versions of arguments along these lines at DP 3.5 and SCG II.15. For a careful analysis of the latter version, see Shields and Pasnau, *The Philosophy of Aquinas*, Section 5.1.

thing, God, who just is existence. Because the argument is sound, it can be generalized to other cases, but in most other cases the story is too messy to be very illuminating. To trace roughness back to its ultimate cause, for instance, would be an extremely convoluted and unrewarding project.

Even in the paradigm case of heat, the *ratio Platonis* does not work in quite the way one might suppose. For although everything that is hot can be explained in terms of the elemental quality of Fire, there is no *single* thing (other than God) that accounts for the heat of each individual. Rather, this flame has its elemental qualities and that flame has its elemental qualities. Aquinas makes it very clear that he thinks there are no universal properties *in re*. For instance, he writes that "no commonness is found in Socrates; rather, whatever is in him has been individuated" (*De Ente* 3.80–2).[3] Aquinas also does not countenance any sort of separate entity that would intrinsically be hot, analogously to the way that God is existence itself. He does imagine the possibility of such Platonic entities, remarking for instance that "if whiteness were subsistent, it would have to be one thing, since whitenesses are multiplied in virtue of their receptacles" (I 44.1c). But he sees no need to postulate this higher domain of entities. As far as the *ratio Platonis* is concerned, God alone does all the necessary explanatory work.

So the problem of the one and the many, for Aquinas, ultimately reduces to the problem of God and creatures. From a cosmological perspective, as we have seen, there are many creatures because God wills there to be a universe like that, richly diverse in kinds. From a metaphysical perspective, there are many kinds of beings because all beings other than God merely participate in existence. Whereas God's nature *just is* existence, creatures *have* existence as something additional to their own nature. Hence God's existence is infinite, whereas in creatures "their existence is received and contracted to a determinate nature" (I 7.2c). Thus there are many ways of participating in the divine being, so as to exist in this way or that way.

Within a given kind (whiteness, say, or humanity) there are many particulars insofar as such natures are instantiated within different receptacles or subjects. There are many whitenesses, for example, because there are many white bodies, and each body has its own distinct sensible qualities. Similarly, there are many human souls, because each is individuated by the body in which it is received. In general, "the natures of created things are individuated through the matter that is subjected to that specific nature" (I 39.1 ad 3). Without such matter, there can be no individuation, meaning that there can be no diversity beyond the diversity of kinds. And so it is, as noted earlier, that Aquinas thinks each angel must be a species

[3] See Leftow, "Aquinas on Attributes," and Brower, "Aquinas on the Problem of Universals."

unto itself. Because angels lack bodies, the only way they can be individuated is by having an existence that is delimited by a distinct nature.

Matter's status as the principle of individuation raises various perplexing questions, such as *What individuates the matter?* This is not a question to which Aquinas has a clear answer. In other respects, however, the theory is well suited to his needs. Because he thinks of individuation as a one-time event, taking place at the moment a nature first comes to exist in matter, he need not suppose that a nature's ongoing existence depends on material sameness. Matter individuates the form that it receives, and that form then goes on to individuate the enduring entity: "Distinct individuals have distinct forms made distinct by their matter" (I 85.7 ad 3). This two-step explanation helps account for identity through the perfectly ordinary sorts of material change that plague other descriptions of sameness over time. Aquinas also has room to account for some of the theological oddities that the Christian faith requires. Whiteness can be separated from the bread, for instance, in the sacrament of the Eucharist, without losing its individual identity. Similarly, the human soul, at death, can be separated from the body. These are unnatural occurrences, but they are not metaphysically impossible.[4]

We thus have at least a sketch of how a multitude of distinct things arises from, and depends upon, a single God. But the sketch presupposes various bits of ideology: the idea of natures, and the idea that these natures at least sometimes exist in material subjects. So now we need to extend this story to account for these notions. To do this, we need the idea of actuality.

1.3   Actuality and Composition

Aquinas's youthful primer on what there is, *On the Principles of Nature*, begins like this:

> One should know that some things can be, although they are not, and some things are. That which can be is said to be in potentiality; that which is now is said to be in actuality. (1.1–2)

---

[4] On the separated human soul, see Pasnau, *Aquinas on Human Nature*, Chapter 12. On the Eucharist, see Adams, *Some Later Medieval Theories of the Eucharist*. As Aquinas conceives of accidental being (see Section 1.4 below), an accident can exist apart from its subject only if it changes its mode of being, i.e., the way in which it exists, so as to go from a way in which a substance exists to being a subsistent entity in its own right (see Pasnau, *Metaphysical Themes*, Section 10.3). To some this may seem metaphysically impossible, and indeed it did seem impossible to many later scholastics. I regard it as a virtue of my account that it explains why Aquinas's account of the Eucharist was so widely regarded as untenable.

What there is, is actual. God, as usual, manifests this principle *in excelsis*, being purely and perfectly actual (I 4.1) without even the constraints that come from having a determinate nature that participates in existence (I 3.4). Everything else is actual in a more limited way, having received its actuality – its existence of one sort or another – from God: "everything created is in actuality, but not in pure actuality" (I 44.2 ad 3).

Creatures are never purely actual, because they are always composite in one way or another, and "in every composition there must be potentiality and actuality" (I 3.7c). An angelic nature has the potential to exist – it can exist – but it does exist only when actualized by the existence it receives from God. A certain sort of body – an embryo – has the potential to become a human being, but the human being comes into existence only when the embryo's matter is actualized by a human soul, giving rise to a soul–body composite. To mark such composition, Aquinas relies on the Aristotelian terminology of matter and form: "Just as everything that is in potentiality can be called *matter*, so everything from which something has existence ... can be called *form*" (*Principles of Nature* 1.36–9). When these terms are used as broadly as this, even the angels can be said to have matter, simply inasmuch as they are a composite of potentiality and actuality.

This broad usage is not standard for Aquinas, since he ordinarily prefers to say that the angels are wholly immaterial (I 50.1–2), but the broad usage is helpful in highlighting several important features of the theory. First, the concepts of *potentiality* and *actuality* are the bedrock of Aquinas's metaphysics and are to be understood in modal terms, as ways in which things are possible or actual. God is actual in all respects, and at all times and places. Some finite natures are merely possible, whereas some natures are actual, which is to say that they have been actualized by participating in existence. Second, although Aquinas accepts the familiar distinction between material and immaterial entities, and draws the line roughly where one might expect – with bodies on one side and minds on the other – his metaphysics is not fundamentally dualistic. Fundamentally, the created world is all of one kind, finitely actual, and as a result Aquinas faces fewer of the notorious difficulties over mind–body causation and mind–body union that confront more categorical forms of dualism. Minds, for Aquinas, are just a certain kind of actuality, and are just as well suited to act on bodies, and be joined with bodies, as are any other sorts of actualities.

Still, there is a principled distinction here between immaterial substances (the angels) and material substances. We had a glimpse of this already, in the way that angels are not individuated within a species. They are not individuated, because they do not actualize bodies. Aquinas holds that "everything existing in act has some form" (I 7.2c). In this sense, the angels are forms, but they are not forms that actualize matter, now speaking of matter in the strict sense. But what is this strict sense? The question is complex, because there are various kinds of matter in play here. For starters, there is one kind of matter that serves as the prior materials for something new (like the ingredients in a recipe), and another kind that serves as the subject that individuates the forms it receives. (The surface of a wall, for instance, is potentially white, and becomes actually white by taking on *this* whiteness.) Angels have no matter of the first kind, but in a way they do have matter of the second kind, inasmuch as an angel's mind serves as the potential subject for virtue, knowledge, and other mental qualities (I 55.1). This, however, does not preclude the angels from being strictly immaterial, because there is yet another kind of matter that they lack: matter as the stuff that is potentially a body of some kind. The angels are simply minds, without bodies, and so they lack the sort of matter that characterizes our earthly domain.

To get a clearer sense of this domain, we need to distinguish between two kinds of forms. One kind makes a thing be a substance of a certain kind, and so is known as *substantial form*. Another kind makes a substance be a certain way, and is known as *accidental form*. Aquinas writes:

> Matter is contracted through form to a determinate species, just as a substance of some species is contracted through an accident inhering in it to a determinate mode of being, as a human being is contracted through white. (I 44.2c)

So here we have two levels of matter (or potentiality), and two levels of form (or actuality): a first matter that takes on a substantial form, and then a second matter – a substance – that takes on various accidental forms. When that first matter – what we call *prime matter* – takes on a substantial form, the result is a body of a certain kind. To say that it is a *body* is to say that it is spread out with part outside of part, in three dimensions (I 18.2c). To say that it is a body *of a certain kind* is to say that it has a *nature*, or an *essence* or *quiddity*. The angels, then, are actualized natures but they are not bodies, because they do not inform prime matter.

The two levels of hylomorphic (i.e., matter–form) composition just described raise a great many puzzling questions, first and foremost questions about how such composites are unified. That there must be unity is taken for granted by Aquinas, because he takes for granted that a thing exists only insofar as it is a unity:

> *One* (*unum*) does not add to *being* (*ens*) any thing (*res*), but only the denial of division. For *one* signifies nothing other than *undivided being*. From this it is plain that *one* converts with *being*. For every being is either simple or composite. Something simple is undivided both actually and potentially. Something composite, in contrast, has existence not while its parts are divided, but only once they constitute and compose that composite thing. Hence it is clear that the existence of any thing consists in undividedness. And so it is that any given thing, as it maintains its existence, so it maintains its oneness (*unitatem*). (I 11.1c)

To say here that "*one* converts with *being*" is to assert a biconditional: A thing exists if, and only if, it is one thing. As this passage makes clear, to say that a thing is one is not to say that it is simple: Only God is wholly simple, and so there is composition throughout the created world. Still, there are different kinds of composition, and Aquinas thinks that the things that exist in the primary sense have a special sort of unqualified unity: They are one thing *simpliciter*.

Of the two sorts of hylomorphic composition described above, only the first level yields unqualified unity. At the second level, Aquinas is unconcerned with securing unity in this strong sense. Here "matter, as it is under one substantial form, remains in potentiality to many accidental forms" (I 7.2c), and Aquinas is happy to allow that such unions are merely accidental: "From an accident and its subject results not something one per se, but one per accidens" (*On Being and Essence* 5.43–4). The implication of this doctrine, when conjoined with his views about the convertibility of *one* and *being*, is that a substance joined with its accidents is not, strictly speaking, a being at all. Of course we talk about the pale man, and the speckled hen, just as we talk about a stack of wood or an army of soldiers. We can speak of these as *things* if we like, since they all have, after all, one or another *kind* of unity. But in each case their unity is accidental, and so none of them is a *being* in the proper sense of the term.

The true hylomorphic unities, then, are unities of substantial form and prime matter. Among material creatures, these are the substances, the things that Aristotle (*Categories*, Chapter 5) had marked as the primary beings on which all else depends. Composites that have such substances as ingredients do not have the same kind of unity, because in these cases the ingredients are liable to preexist and outlast the composite. The textbook definition of an accident, after all, is that "accidents are items that come and go without the destruction of their subjects."⁵ So the conjunction of a substance with an accident, or the conjunction of two substances, cannot be a unity in the unqualified sense. And because of the tight connection between unity and existence – "something is a being in just the way that it is one" (I 76.1c) – Aquinas is committed to concluding that such conjunctions do not have unqualified existence.

This commitment to the primacy of substance becomes particularly vivid when Aquinas considers what it is, strictly speaking, that God creates. His answer is that God creates the substances:

> Creating is a kind of making, as was said, and making is directed at a thing's existing. Hence making and creating are properly suited to the things to which existence is suited, and existence is properly suited to subsistent things, whether they are simple, like the separate substances [viz., the angels], or composite, like material substances. (I 45.4c)

Existence is properly suited to subsistent things, Aquinas says here, because such substances are the things that are true unities and so truly exist. In a broad sense, as we saw in Section 1.2, God creates *everything* that there is, and that includes things like armies and woodpiles, speckled hens and pale men. But these things come for free with creation, as it were, because in creating substances God creates all of the rest. God can create the substances and then take a day off, because the substances exhaust the things that truly exist.

So we have now made some progress in distinguishing between Aquinas's expansive ideology and his much more minimalist ontology. But these results yield a puzzle. It is easy to see the appeal in supposing that God creates only the basic building blocks and gets the rest for free. But, as we have seen, humans and hens and trees are not themselves entirely simple; they are composites of prime matter and substantial form. So why not suppose that when God created, what he created, strictly speaking, was the matter and its forms, and then he got the substances for free out of those ingredients? What gives the substances priority? Moreover, what about the man's paleness? What about those speckles on the hen? If they are among the things that exist, then do they not need to be created too? To answer these questions, we need to take up Aquinas's doctrine that things have different ways of being.

---

⁵ Porphyry, *Introduction [Isagoge]*, Section 5.

1.4   Ways of Being

Where I have been urging a distinction between ideology and ontology, Aquinas talks only of ways of being. We have seen this repeatedly already in how he characterizes creation – for instance when he concludes "it is necessary to say that *everything that exists in any sort of way* exists from God" (I 44.1c), or "it is necessary that there be one principle of existing from which *whatever exists in any sort of way* has existence" (I 65.1c). Such expressions hearken back to Aristotle's dictum that "being is said in many ways."[6] But when one looks to see how exactly Aquinas understands this dark saying, it turns out that he does not mean that there are different manners of existence, as if existence were a determinable property like a color that comes in various determinate shades. Instead, his point is that when we speak of the various elements of his metaphysics – the various kinds of form and matter under discussion – we inevitably describe them as things or beings or entities. We can hardly help but talk that way, since these are indeed ineliminable features of the metaphysics. But we should not thereby conclude that the theory is ontologically committed to such things. Beyond the theory's ideological expansiveness lies a surprisingly parsimonious ontology.

Since this is an unorthodox way to understand Aquinas, it requires strong textual support. Let me return, first, to his discussion of what it is that God creates (I 45.4c). We saw at the end of the previous section that what God creates, strictly speaking, is substance. The immediate lesson drawn from this was that various sorts of higher-level composites – speckled hens and woodpiles – are not, strictly speaking, created. They are not the things created because they are not the things to which "existence is properly suited" (as above). That led to a question about the metaphysical ingredients of substances, and how they fit into this story. And in fact Aquinas immediately goes on to address this question:

> Forms and accidents, and other things of this sort, are called beings (*entia*) not because they themselves are, but because through them something is. Whiteness, for instance, is said to be a being because through it a subject is white. Hence, according to the Philosopher [*Met.* VII.1, 1028a18–20], an accident is more properly said to be *of a being* rather than *a being*. Therefore, just as accidents and forms and such things that do not subsist are more properly *coexistents* rather than *existents* (*entia*), so they ought to be called *concreated* rather than *created*. The properly created things, then, are subsistent things. (I 45.4c)

---

[6] See e.g., *Met.* IV.2, 1003b5 and VIII.2, 1042b25, and the discussion in Shields, *Order in Multiplicity*, Chapter 9.

The word "concreated" nicely captures the idea that, in creating the substances, God gets forms and accidents for free. These are not additional entities that need to be created on top of the substances, as it were, because they do not themselves have any proper existence. For them to exist just is for the substance to exist in a certain way.

This boldly sweeping claim is one that Aquinas regularly repeats, and not just in the context of creation but also when discussing the natural generation of forms. Here there was often felt to be a special problem for the Aristotelian about how a form (e.g., the soul of a dog) could come into existence anew, as if *ex nihilo*, something that is supposedly forbidden in natural processes.[7] Aquinas simply denies that we should think of substantial and accidental forms as entities that come and go in the world. Instead, the sense in which forms are beings is not univocal with the sense in which substances are beings:

> A natural form is not said to exist univocally with the thing (*re*) that is generated. For a natural generated thing is said to exist per se and properly, as if having existence and subsisting in its existence. A form, in contrast, is not said to exist in this way, since it does not subsist, nor does it have existence per se. Rather, it is said to exist or be a being because by it something is. In this way, accidents are called beings because a substance, by them, is either qualified or quantified – not that, by them, the substance unconditionally *is*, as it is through a substantial form. Hence accidents are more properly said to be *of a being* rather than *beings*. (DP 3.8c)

So "being" is said in many ways inasmuch as the term is non-univocal, although the term is not wholly equivocal either, since Aquinas thinks the different usages are analogical along the lines just described. Thus far, one might hesitate over the ontological implications of this doctrine, but the passage continues so as to leave no doubt:

> Any sort of thing that is made is said to be made in the way in which it is said to exist. For existence is the endpoint of the making. Hence that which is properly made, per se, is the composite. The form, in contrast, is not properly made, but is that by which something is made – that is, that through whose acquisition something is said to be made. Therefore, from the fact that, through nature, nothing is said to be made from nothing, there is no obstacle to our saying that substantial forms exist by the operation of nature. For that which is made is not the form but the composite, which is made from the matter and not from nothing. (ibid.)

[7] On the general consensus that generation *ex nihilo* is impossible, see Aristotle, *Phys.* I.4, 187a27–9. On the debate over the generation of forms within late scholasticism, see Pasnau, *Metaphysical Themes*, p. 664.

Aquinas's conclusion here must have ontological import; otherwise it will have no force against his opponent. If substantial and accidental forms are among the things that are, then they need to be generated, and then Aquinas faces the problem of where they come from, if not from nothing. Of course, one might try to evade this problem in various ways, but Aquinas's way is to insist that, among material things, only composite substances exist. If this is not really what he means here, and if substantial and accidental forms are themselves beings in any proper sense, then he fails to have a response to the objection.[8]

For still another text, consider this general discussion of existence:

> Existence (*esse*) is attributed to a thing in two ways. In one way, as to that which properly and truly has existence or is, and in this way it is attributed only to a substance that subsists through itself. Thus *Physics* I [186b4–8] says that a substance is what truly is. All those things, on the other hand, that do not subsist through themselves, but are in another and with another – whether they are accidents or substantial forms or any parts whatsoever – do not have existence in such a way that they truly are, but existence is attributed to them in another way – that is, as that by which something is – just as whiteness is said to be not because it subsists in itself, but because by it something has existence-as-white (*esse album*). Therefore existence properly and truly is attributed only to a thing that subsists on its own. (*Quodlibet* 9.2.2c)

Substances, again, are the only things that properly and truly exist. There is no indication here that Aquinas has in mind some sort of diminished manner of existence that might be ascribed to their metaphysical parts. Rather, substantial forms and accidents – and indeed "any parts whatsoever"[9] – are said here to exist only inasmuch as they are things "by which something is." Whiteness, for instance, does not exist, but yet in virtue of it a substance exists-as-white.

On the surface, all these passages look like as explicit a denial as one could want that such forms have any sort of ontological standing on their own. But there may seem to be an obvious problem here. For Aquinas seems to be saying, at once, both that substantial forms and accidents do not exist, and yet that it is in virtue of these forms that the substances

---

[8] On the analogy of being in Aquinas, see the recent skeptical discussion in Hughes, *Aquinas on Being, Goodness, and God*, pp. 7–20, and the more enthusiastic treatments in Klima, "Thomistic 'Monism' vs. Cartesian 'Dualism'" and Brower, *Aquinas's Ontology of the Material World*, Section 2.4.

[9] For the status of the integral parts of material substances – that is, bodily parts such as hands and arms – see my discussion in Pasnau, *Metaphysical Themes*, Chapter 26.

are a certain way. But if the forms do not exist, how can they play the role they are alleged to play? Consider, first, the case of substantial form. We have seen how the substantial form of a material substance actualizes prime matter and thus makes a substance with a nature of a particular kind (dog, stone, etc.). If such forms make substances, are they not obviously real? Aquinas sheds light on this question in the following passage:

> For something to be the substantial form of another, two things are required. The first is that the form be the principle of existing substantially for that of which it is the form. But by "principle" I mean not the efficient (*factivum*) principle, but the formal principle by which something exists and is called a *being*. And from this follows the second thing required, namely that form and matter come together in one existence, which does not arise from an efficient principle together with that to which it gives existence. And this is the existence in which subsists a composite substance, comprised of matter and form. (SCG II.68 par. 2)

Substantial forms would have their own existence if we were to think of them as extrinsic causes, making the material cause be a certain kind of thing in the way a mason makes bricks into a wall. It is very hard, in fact, to avoid this picture of the process. Even when Aquinas tries to warn us against it here, by saying that "form and matter come together in one existence" (*forma et materia conveniant in uno esse*), his language works against him, because talk of "coming together" suggests a picture of two independently subsisting things that merge into one thing. But this is precisely the sort of accidental unity Aquinas wants to avoid. The unqualified unity of form and matter is such that there is really and truly only one being there. Talk of substantial form's *doing something* to the composite does not entail that this form is an entity with its own causal agency.[10]

What about accidental forms? The painter Bridget Riley begins an essay on color with an insightful remark: "For all of us, colour is experienced as something – that is to say, we always see it in the guise of a substance which can be called by a variety of names."[11] Aquinas seeks

---

[10] The passage immediately goes on to make an exception for the human substantial form – the rational soul – which *is* subsistent and *does* exercise its own independent efficient causality. This creates an enormous problem for the unity of a human being, as Aquinas is well aware, because now he needs to explain how we can be one thing *simpliciter* and yet have an ingredient, the rational soul, which is a true entity in its own right. I take it to be a virtue of my account that it explains why Aquinas faces such difficulties here. His solution turns on the way in which, even though a human being consists of distinct substances, it still consists in just one substantial existence. A pale human being, in contrast, is not a true unity, and so not a true thing, because it is a composite of substantial existence and accidental existence.

[11] Riley, "Colour for the Painter," p. 31.

to escape this sort of naïve conception of color and other such forms: "Many err regarding form because they judge it as if they were judging substance. This seems to happen because forms are signified as substances are, in the abstract, as whiteness or virtue, and so on" (DVC 11c). This passage too goes on to make the same point as the earlier passages: "a form is said to be a being not because it exists – if we are to speak properly – but because something exists by it" (ibid.). Aquinas thus wants to allow that there is *being* associated with the color of the hen. This being is not the same as the being of the hen itself, because the one sort of being is accidental and the other substantial. But there is only one entity here, the hen, and it exists both as a substance and also in various accidental ways.[12] If we imagine God creating a hen, then we had better imagine God creating a hen of a certain size, shape, and color, since there can be no indeterminate hens. But there is only one thing here that God creates: a hen, existing like *that*. These various determinate features are not things in their own right but mere modes of the hen (to use a later idiom),[13] such that in creating a hen, these features come along for free.

1.5 Mere Ideology?

My conclusion is that what there is in Aquinas is only substance. The rest is ideology, not ontology. If this conclusion still seems doubtful, consider for a moment how else one might read the passages discussed in the previous section. One option is to treat *being* as a genuinely determinable concept, so that substances have one kind of existence whereas other sorts of beings have a different kind of existence. The difficulties with this way of proceeding, however, are considerable. In addition to the intrinsic obscurity of the notion of modes of being,[14] there is the further problem that Aquinas never offers the slightest help with characterizing any sort of lesser, sub-substantial existence. Even worse, as I have been stressing, he seems to make it pretty clear that he wants to understand modes-of-being talk differently: not that it is a lesser way in which forms exist, but that

---

[12] For comprehensive discussions of accidental being, as distinct from substantial being, see Wippel, *Metaphysical Thought*, pp. 253–65 and Brown, *Accidental Being*.

[13] As a first approximation, it is useful to think of Aquinas's theory of accidental forms as akin to the later theory of modes, as articulated by Suárez and then deployed by Descartes, Spinoza, and others. Aquinas's theory is quite unlike the standard scholastic theory of accidents, as developed first by John Duns Scotus, which is much more ontologically committing, and is the origin of the notorious doctrine of real accidents. See Pasnau, *Metaphysical Themes*, Chapter 13.

[14] For a recent attempt to clarify the notion, see McDaniel, "Ways of Being."

it is a way in which substances exist. So this line of thought ends up supporting the conclusion that what there is is only substance.

Another option would be to treat all of Aquinas's ideology as fully ontologically committing, so that all of it – substantial form, prime matter, accidents, accidental unities – exists in a perfectly ordinary sense of "exists."[15] One would then need to read the passages from the previous section as making the point that, while many things exist in a perfectly ordinary sense, substances have existence (*esse*) in some sort of special sense. But this just shifts the mystery, because now we need a story about what this special sense of substantial existence is. And although there are various familiar ways in which substances are special – their unity, their independence, their persistence – these do not seem to give rise to any difference in manner of *existence*. Moreover, even if some such alternative story could be developed, it would seem inconsistent with the passages examined in the previous section, which critically depend on Aquinas getting the result that substances, "properly and truly," are the only things that come into and go out of existence.

So I say that the famous apparatus of Aquinas's metaphysics – its forms and matter – is ideology rather than ontology. But this is not to say that it is *mere* ideology. For even if the hylomorphic framework is not *ontologically* committing, it had better serve some purpose beyond the merely decorative. And there is a quick argument to show that form and matter have to make some sort of difference to what there is, which is that Aquinas holds that only God is simple, and that all created substances are complex in various ways (I 50.2 ad 3). Given what I have said, I cannot allow that this complexity is ontological. But what other sort of complexity is there? The answer is that there can be a complexity of modal characteristics. Whereas God's simplicity is a consequence of his pure actuality, the complexity of creatures stems from their various admixtures of potentiality. Thus he says, as quoted already, that "in every composition there must be potentiality and actuality" (I 3.7c). I am the potential subject of whiteness, because I am potentially pale, which is to say that I *can be* pale (in a way that my chickens cannot). After a long, cold winter spent reading old books, I *am* pale, which is to say – using the familiar ideology – that the accidental form of whiteness inheres in me. But it is not as if there really is such a *thing*, a form of whiteness, that has sprung into existence within me. It's still just me and my books here (and my

---

[15] See Brower, *Aquinas's Ontology of the Material World,* who ascribes to Aquinas an extraordinarily rich ontology of prime matter, substantial forms, accidents, and even accidental unities.

chickens).[16] To be sure, I have taken on a different way of existing, and one might now want an explanation of what it is for a substance like me to take on a certain color. But this is a question for the natural philosopher, not for the metaphysician.

Modal complexity, on this story, does not rest on some further story about ontological complexity. Instead, for Aquinas, the different ways of being potential and actual lie at the ground-level of the theory. Nothing could be more familiar than to say that, for Aquinas, matter is potentiality and form is actuality. But we should resist reading these familiar formulations as ontologically committing. A substance does not have a certain potentiality or actuality *because* a certain thing (a form) inheres in a certain other thing (the matter); rather, Aquinas's talk of form and matter is just his way of talking about a thing's basic modal characteristics. As we have seen, such talk comes in various kinds. There is the sort of potentiality that the ingredients have to be something new, and there is the potentiality of prime matter, and there is the potentiality of a substance to take on accidents. Then there is the actuality of substantial form, by which a substance *is*, and the actuality of an accidental form, by which a substance is F. Actualities themselves carry further potentialities or powers, and such higher-order potentialities are actualized not by existence (since the substance already exists) but by operation. So Aquinas writes: "Just as existing itself is a kind of actuality of an essence, so operating is the actuality of an operative potential or power. Accordingly, each of these is in actuality: the essence in terms of existing, the potential in terms of operating" (*DSC* 11c). Consider, for instance, the soul of an animal. According to Aristotle, it is the actuality of a body potentially having life (*De An.* II.1). In addition, a soul carries with it various potentialities: nutritive, sensory, or rational. These are not parts of the soul in any literal, ontologically committing sense, but merely its modal features:

> It is true that the soul has various parts and powers, and that it thinks through one and senses through another. For the soul is a kind of whole potentiality and in this connection "part" is interpreted as a potentiality relative to the whole potentiality. (*De An.* Commentary I.14.65–9)

---

[16] Strictly speaking, the books may not count either, because artifacts in general are not substances. Aquinas has little to say explicitly, however, about what sorts of things do and do not count as substances. For an effort to sort this out, see Pasnau, *Thomas Aquinas on Human Nature*, Section 3.2.

If we want to know what a soul is, then, we should think not of some sort of mysterious entity that joins itself to matter, but rather as a set of potentialities and actualities that defines a thing as a living substance of one kind or another. What looks on its face like an ontologically promiscuous metaphysics is instead a theory that privileges, as fundamental, the modal features of reality.

The theory of prime matter makes for an interesting test of this approach. Until now, this discussion has not put much weight on that element of the theory, just because it is all too easy to make the case that prime matter lacks ontological standing. It is, after all, a purely potential element of a theory that treats existence as actuality, which is why God cannot make prime matter exist by itself (*Quaestiones de Quodlibet* 3.1.1). Still, it is an important part of Aquinas's ideology, and the *Summa Theologiae* even insists that prime matter is among the things created by God (even if, as we have seen, it is not properly created in the way composite substances are). Why concede that prime matter has been created at all? Aquinas's discussion runs quickly through some historical background, beginning with theories that postulated only bodies of one sort or another, then the introduction of substantial forms and accidental forms, and finally coming to prime matter. All he tells us at this point is that if God is "the cause of things inasmuch as they are beings" then he must be their cause "with reference to *all* that pertains to their existence in any sort of way" (I 44.2c). But this serves only to sharpen the real question: How does prime matter pertain to the existence of material substances? Elsewhere he is slightly more forthcoming: "Prime matter *is* in some way, since it *is* being in potentiality. God, however, is the cause of all things that are, as was shown above. Therefore God is the cause of prime matter" (SCG II.16 par. 12). This draws the needed connection to modality. To say that a substance contains prime matter is not to say that it has an ontological constituent, but rather to say something about its potential – about what the substance could become. It is to say, in short, that a material substance can become any sort of body whatsoever: "prime matter is that which is related to *all* forms and privations in just the way that bronze is related to *statue* and *unshaped*" (*Principles of Nature* 2.83–4). Just as I can become pale, so the bronze can become a statue. Aquinas's ideology of form and matter tracks modal features such as these. The point of talking about prime matter, then, is to highlight a distinguishing feature of

material substances: that, through substantial change, they can, eventually, become any sort of body whatsoever.[17]

By decoupling Aquinas's ideology from his ontology, we can take at face
value the plain sense of what he says there is in the world. The result is an
innovative metaphysics that treats actuality and potentiality as basic
modal facts rather than as the product of further entities from which
substances are composed. Having thus escaped the ontological extrava-
gance to which his ideology might seem to give rise, we can in turn save
the unqualified unity of substance, and so explain why only substances
truly exist. This is not how Aquinas's views are generally understood, but
it fits remarkably well with what he actually says there is.[18]

---

[17] In Pasnau, *Thomas Aquinas on Human Nature*, pp. 131–40, I argued against the "independent
ontological status" (p. 131) of prime matter in Aquinas. That discussion still strikes me as generally
correct, as far as it goes, but as less than wholly persuasive, because it fails to explain the purpose of
the ideology. The present discussion seeks to supplement that earlier treatment by explaining why
the theory needs prime matter. I would also no longer speak of the account as "reductive in the
direction of form" (p. 133). If it is reductive at all, it is so in the direction of substance.

[18] Thanks to Jeffrey Brower, Jeffrey Hause, and an anonymous referee for their very helpful
suggestions.

Dead Ends, Bad Form: The Positivity of Evil in the Summa Theologiae

Stephen L. Brock

As is widely recognized, Thomas Aquinas teaches that evil does not consist in any positive reality, but rather in a certain sort of absence or negation. He taught this throughout his career, and the *Summa Theologiae* is no exception. Thomas does hold that evil always belongs to a positive subject, and that its full explanation always involves a positive agent. These positions of his are also usually acknowledged. But here I wish to draw attention to other positive associates of evil, four of them, that Thomas identifies in the *Summa* and that get much less notice. In addition to their intrinsic interest, I think these points deserve attention for at least two reasons. One is that the so-called privation theory of evil is often criticized for failing to account for the role that evil plays in our lives and in the world. An adequate account, it is urged, requires assigning evil some positive status. So if Aquinas does just that, though without abandoning the thesis that evil is essentially something negative, the critics will surely want to take a look. The other reason is more general. This topic, it seems to me, offers a prime example of what we could call the agility or suppleness of Thomas's metaphysical thinking. His formulations of fundamental principles are extremely simple and definite, and yet his applications of them are anything but simplistic or rigid. I think we see this very clearly in his handling of evil. The devil really is in the details.

In what follows, the first two positive associates of evil that I shall discuss pertain to our experience of evil. The third plays a key role in morals and I will dwell on it longest, partly because it is rather complicated, and partly because I think it is of greatest general metaphysical interest. The fourth is a kind of extension of the third, into the natural domain, which Thomas apparently hit upon only around the time of writing the Second Part. To set the stage, I shall survey some of the chief elements of his doctrine of evil in general, as presented in the *Summa*.

2.1   The General Account of Evil in the *Summa Theologiae*

Evil is the subject of two questions in the First Part: q. 48, on evil in itself, and q. 49, on its cause. Their location is noteworthy. After one question (*quaestio*) on the science of theology and forty-two on God in himself, the rest of the First Part concerns the procession of creatures from God. This section is tripartite: the production of creatures by God (44–6), their distinction (47–102), and their governance (103–19). So evil stands almost at the start of the section on creaturely distinction. The one prior *quaestio* explains in a general way that God causes both material (or numerical) and formal distinctions, with the latter entailing inequality; and that his world is nonetheless one, with a unity of order. The first specific distinction treated, then, is good and evil.

Now, Thomas had already examined the good in general in question 5, as background for examining the goodness of God in question 6. Question 48 therefore centers on evil. But why is this distinction first? I suppose because Thomas likes to go from the more to the less universal. Thus, what comes next is the distinction of spiritual and bodily creatures: angels (50–64), purely bodily creatures (65–74), and humans (75–102). Good and evil run through all of these.

In fact, Thomas sees good and evil as "transcendental," in his sense of this term: They go beyond any single Aristotelian category of being and extend to all.[1] This is not to say that both are "convertible" with being; only good is. This means that whatever is good is a being, and vice-versa.[2] As we shall see, whatever is evil is also, in some sense, a being, and even a good; but not every being, or good, is in any sense evil. In this respect good and evil are like one and many. Both are transcendental, but only the first is convertible with being.[3]

So Thomas insists from the start that nothing is evil just insofar as it is a being.[4] Evil does not consist in any act of being (*esse*) or any real form or nature. His argument for this rests on the assumption that evil is the opposite of good. Everything desirable, as such, is good, and every nature desires its own being and perfection. Hence evil must consist in a certain absence of good and of being.

---

[1] He taught this already in *In II Sent.* d.34 1.2 ad 1. For the chronology of Thomas's works I follow Torrell, *Initiation.*
[2] See ST I 5.1–3; I 6.3 obj. 1.
[3] ST I 11.2 ad 1; I 30.3c.
[4] ST I 48.1.

So evil is not a real being, a thing in its own right. This does not mean, however, that it cannot be "found in" real things.[5] It can, in the sense that it can be truly predicated of things. Some things are truly said to *be* evil. In some sense, therefore, evil itself must be a being. It can be, because "a being" (*ens*) is equivocal. It can signify the real "beingness" (*entitas*) of a thing, according to the thing's own substantial or accidental nature. Evil has no such nature. But "a being" can also signify a mere truth, the agreement of predicate and subject in a proposition. So evil is not a real being, but it is what Thomas calls a being of reason. The mind can treat absences in the manner of real beings, naming them and ascribing them to things, as when we speak of blindness and say that it is in an eye. It may sound strange to say that an absence is "in" something, but we do after all say that there is a hole in the ground, a cavity in a tooth, and so forth.

Not every absence of good is evil. Being an elephant is a good, but your dog not being one, and your bedroom not containing one, are not evils. There is evil only if a good is absent from something in which it could be present and which naturally needs or ought to have it, as an eye can and ought to have sight. That in which a perfection can be present, and from which it can also be absent, is what Thomas calls a subject. He calls the presence of a perfection in a subject "possession"; the absence, "privation." Evil, then, is essentially privation of needed or due good.[6]

The subject, in itself, is always somehow positive and good. Either it is something in act and perfect in some other respect, or at least it is in potency to an act and so is good qua ordered to good.[7] But the privation of a due good can still denominate the subject, so that it can be termed evil or bad.[8] A blurry eye is a bad eye.[9] This is not merely a semantic point, about the range of the word "evil." Again, Thomas regards good and evil as opposites. But "good," in his view, signifies not only perfection, but also desirability. "Evil" therefore signifies not only privation, but also undesirability. Its essence is privation of due good, but other things connected with the privation can share in its undesirability. One of these is its subject. As we shall see, there are also others.

---

[5] ST I 48.2.

[6] ST I 48.3; I 49.1. For a helpful study of privation in general, see Oderberg, "The Metaphysics of Privation."

[7] This is how prime matter is good: ST I 5.3 ad 3.

[8] ST I 48.3 obj. 4; cf. DM 1.2 obj. 2. In this chapter I use the adjectives "bad" and "evil" interchangeably.

[9] ST I 5.3 ad 2.

Substances are not the only subjects of evil. The privation in sin, for example, is a disorder. Its proper subject, in a sin of commission, is an action; in an omission, its subject is the will.[10]

An evil may be the privation of something essential to a thing. Sight is essential to an eye; "with sight lacking, an eye does not remain, except equivocally."[11] This raises a question.[12] If it is not truly an eye, is sight truly due to it? If not, then its lacking sight is not bad for it. Or again, does a dead body have a nature to which life is due? If not, then its being dead is not bad for it. Blindness seems to be bad only for the eye that was; death, only for the living body that was. Hence, even if all evil is an absence of some thing's due good, is it always in that very thing?

Thomas's general answer to this, I think, would be that a privation's subject must be a real thing, but it might not be real at the time when it has the privation. For since the privation is only a "being of reason," its inhering in or belonging to a subject – the subject's "having" it – is only a being of reason too.[13] And so not even the subject itself need be real precisely when subjected to the privation. It must be real only when subjected to the corresponding possession. Socrates is truly dead, lacking life, even though he is not truly there. He was truly there when he had it, but when it was taken away, so was he.

However, we can also ask: Is sightlessness an evil in a presently existing orb? And is lifelessness an evil in a dead person's corpse? The chapter's last section will address this question.

Since evil has a positive subject and so is joined to some form and some good, it can in a sense play positive causal roles, those of active principle and end. But really it does so only by association. What plays those roles per se is the conjoined form or good.[14] Evidently evil cannot be either a formal or a material cause of a positive thing. In that case it would have to have something positive *in* it – some act or potency – and then it would be good.

As for causes of evil, its subject is a material cause. It has no formal cause, being rather a privation of form. Nor does it have a final cause, since then it would be good, at least in the sense of useful; it is rather a lack of order to a due end. But it must have an agent cause. This is because it is against a thing's nature. Things naturally tend toward their

---

[10] See ST I-II 75.1 ad 1; DM 2.1 ad 4.
[11] *In II De An.* 2.89–91. Translations in this chapter are mine.
[12] See Crosby, "Is All Evil," pp. 198–200.
[13] See *In V Met.* 14.964. Cf. ST I 49.3 ad 4: Beings are called evil, not by participation, but by lack of it.
[14] ST I 48.1 ad 4.

due good, and so they will have it, unless something acts to impede or remove it.[15] However, agents cause evil only per accidens. They do not aim at privation, at least not on its own account.

If the privation that an agent causes is evil relative to the agent itself, not just to what is acted upon, then it presupposes some absence of possible good in the agent. Often this absence is itself an evil, as when a horse limps because of a hoof injury. But sometimes the presupposed absence of good is not evil, because the absent good is not a strictly due good. This must be the case, Thomas argues, at the first origin of sin.[16] There the absent good is the sinner's consideration of the moral rule prohibiting the sinful act. Considering the rule would impede the act. Yet the first evil is in the act. Prior to it, there is no moment when considering the rule is strictly due, or when not considering it is sinful.[17]

God does not directly cause evil. What he directly causes is an unequal distribution of good.[18] This brings evil with it, because some good things are able to fail and sometimes do fail.[19] God does indirectly intend and cause corruptions of things, but he in no way causes sins. He wills neither the occurrence nor the non-occurrence of the sins that occur, but only his own permission of their occurrence.[20] He does so intending to bring good from them.[21] He is not an indirect cause of them, since he provides what is needed to prevent them, though in a measured way, as his justice and wisdom dictate.[22] Still, he is a cause of whatever there is of being and act in a sin.[23]

2.2 Evil as Cause of Suffering

One objection commonly urged against privation accounts of evil is that they do not explain evil's power to cause pain and suffering. Thomas

---

[15] ST I 49.1c.

[16] His account of sin's origin is presented summarily in ST I 49.1 ad 3, I 63.1 ad 4, and I-II 75.1 ad 3. The fullest versions are in SCG III 10.26a27–27b22 and DM 1.3; on these see Dewan, "St. Thomas and the First Cause."

[17] DM 1.3 ad 13. Barnwell, "The Problem," proceeds as though, for Thomas, not considering the rule is not evil so long as the agent is not yet contemplating the sinful act, but becomes a failure to fulfill a moral obligation – i.e., becomes an evil, sinful – when she is "about to commit" (p. 284) or "about to engage in" (p. 286) the act. If Thomas held this, his account would certainly fail, as Barnwell shows exhaustively; but he does not hold it.

[18] ST I 49.2.

[19] ST I 48.2.

[20] ST I 19.9 ad 3.

[21] ST I 2.3 ad 1; I 22.2 ad 2; I 48.2 ad 3.

[22] ST I 49.2 ad 3 (cf. I-II 6.3); I-II 79.1.

[23] ST I-II 79.2. On this see below, pp. 39–40.

himself says that nothing can be a cause except insofar as it is a being, and that therefore only a good can be a cause.[24] As we saw, he does say that causality can be attributed to evil by association with its positive subject. But surely it would be paradoxical to say that what really accounts for pain or suffering is not an evil but a good that accompanies an evil in the same subject. That would amount to saying that pain and suffering regard evil only incidentally. Thomas, however, explains an evil's power to cause pain and suffering differently. He finds another positive associate of it, besides its subject – one that is nearly identical with the evil itself.

He explains the point in the course of addressing this question: Which is more the cause of suffering (*dolor*), a good lost (*bonum amissum*) or an evil sustained (*malum coniunctum*)?[25] He begins by observing that the question might seem trifling. And it would indeed be so, he says, if privations stood in the soul's apprehension as they stand in real things themselves:

> For an evil ... is a privation of good, and in reality a privation is nothing but the lack of the possession opposed to it; so on this score it would be the same to suffer at a good lost and at an evil sustained. But suffering is a movement of appetite following apprehension. And in apprehension, a privation itself constitutes a sort of being, whence it is called a being of reason. And in this way evil, though it be a privation, functions as a contrary.[26]

Thomas is assuming that contraries, in the strict sense, are always positive.[27] In the soul, evil can function as a contrary of good, not a mere privation. He then explains that *delectatio* – delight or pleasure – is like a movement of pursuing or approaching a thing, while suffering is like fleeing or withdrawing. Things naturally approach the condition that suits them, and they withdraw from the contrary condition. But the object of delight is an attained good (*bonum adeptum*). So the object of suffering – what suffering is like a withdrawal from – is an evil sustained. Thus, he says, evil causes suffering, as its object.

Evil is negative in reality, but it is experienced as positive. What gives it this positivity, and the resulting power to cause suffering, is the very soul that experiences it. Evidently it need not be a rational soul. The

---

[24] ST I 49.1c.
[25] Actually in this discussion he speaks now of *dolor*, now of *tristitia*, indifferently; I use "suffering" for both.
[26] ST I-II 36.1c. As far as I know, this passage has no parallel in Thomas's other writings.
[27] See ST I 48.1 obj. 3 and DM 1.1 obj. 2; cf. below, p. 42.

sense-appetite also undergoes suffering. Even the senses can give rise to beings of reason.

Someone might object that on Thomas's account, insofar as what causes suffering is a being – even if only a being of reason – it should to that extent be understood as good, not evil. Thomas himself teaches that even sin, insofar as it is a being of reason, must be seen as a good; for in that respect, it is something true (*verum*), and truth is the good of the mind.[28] Still, not every good suits every nature.[29] The apprehended evil that causes suffering, insofar as it is an object of apprehension, does suit the cognitive power. And in fact it does not cause suffering by suiting the cognitive power. But it is apprehended as unsuited to the animal in some other respect, and that is how it causes suffering.[30]

Privation is something positive in the soul. From here on I wish to look at certain things that are positive in reality, which Thomas is willing to call evil, and whose evil is not that of a subject, or even an agent, of privation. Some of them are things that he judges evil without qualification.

2.3   Suffering Itself as Evil

Thomas calls suffering a movement of appetite. This means it is something positive. And although it is in or of the soul, it is not therefore a mere being of reason. What makes something a being of reason is its being apprehended by the soul. But movements of appetite are operations performed by the soul. They are quite real. Yet is not suffering, as such, evil?[31]

A first response to this might be that suffering is caused by evil, but in itself it is good. It is the soul's suitable reaction to evil. To this, however, one may reply that what is suitable in relation to something else may still be evil in itself.

Thomas's own treatment of suffering's goodness or badness is complex.[32] He asks whether it is all bad. To this his unqualified answer is no, some is good. For, indeed, supposing that a true evil is sustained, suffering is the suitable reaction; and since operations concern singulars, they are most appropriately judged in connection with the singulars that

---

[28] ST I 16.5 ad 3; cf. I 16.1, I 94.4.
[29] See ST I 6.2 ad 2; I 65.1 ad 2.
[30] Cf. ST I 78.1 ad 3; I 80.1 ad 3.
[31] Cf. Crosby, "Is All Evil," pp. 200–3; also Calder, "Is the Privation Theory," pp. 373–4.
[32] ST I-II 39.1.

they concern.[33] However, Thomas does allow for taking them abstractly, just in themselves, and for framing qualified judgments about them as so taken. And his judgment is that all suffering, considered just in itself, "is a certain evil" (*quoddam malum*). He explains: "This very thing, that a person's appetite be troubled over a present evil, has the aspect of evil; for through it, the repose of the appetite in the good is impeded."

By "repose of the appetite" Thomas means simply pleasure or delight.[34] To what delight is he referring? This is important. It is not just the delight in the particular good whose privation, as apprehended, causes the suffering. What impedes that delight is the privation itself. But the suffering, in turn, has a wider effect, on the sufferer's whole appetitive condition.[35] Just a few pages earlier, Thomas had said that, on the side of the subject, any suffering is a hindrance to any delight.[36] Suffering disturbs even the enjoyment of the goods that one has. It tends to spoil everything.[37] And so, quite generally, it can be called evil, at least in a qualified way. Again, this is not just a semantic point. It means that in some way all suffering is undesirable.

In sum: Suffering is something positive, a vital operation. Absolutely speaking, suffering over what is evil is good, and suffering over what is good is evil. But in a certain respect, all suffering is evil. To be sure, this is only because it is tied to a privation.[38] And yet it is not the privation's subject. Rather, it is a principle of privation in its subject, which is the appetite.

The psychological thesis is surely interesting. So is the broader implication, that subjects of privation are not the only positive things that can be denominated evil. Still, the denomination here is merely qualified. And the type of evil involved is not that which Thomas deems worst, namely, moral evil.[39] Our next group contains positive things that are denominated morally evil, in ways other than as subjects of privation; and in some cases, the denomination is unqualified.

---

[33] On the general point he cites NE III 1, 1110a4–19, b3–9, about how things done from fear are voluntary; cf. ST I-II 6.6.

[34] See, inter alia, ST I-II 26.2c; 30.2c; 31.1 ad 2; 31.8c and ad 2; 34.1c; 34.2c and ad 2.

[35] Murphy, *An Essay*, p. 110, seems to have something like this in mind.

[36] ST I-II 35.4 ad 2; cf. ad 3.

[37] For a similar account, see *In VII Ethic.*, 13.19–20, on NE VII 14, 1153b1–3. Very different is the early *In IV Sent.* d.49 3.4 qla.2c.

[38] As Grant points out, if something positive is evil because it excludes some other thing (e.g., conformity with the moral standard), then the core of the evil is the lack of that other thing; Grant, "The Privation Account," pp. 279 and 283.

[39] ST I 48.6.

2.4 Evil Formal Principles in Morals

The evils in this group are so positive that they can even be willed. For some readers this may bring to mind Thomas's treatment of malice, because he holds that malice involves willing evil.[40] But there, by "evil" he means something negative, the very privation of due good. He says that, in a way, this can be willed or intended, but only in view of something else, not on its own account.[41] My focus here, however, is on certain things that he thinks can be willed and intended on their own account. They are the things that specify morally evil kinds of action. The field is broader than malice. It extends to all the kinds of sin treated in the Second Part of the Second Part. Thomas calls evil both the intended object that specifies a sin and the intention of it. And both are positive.

Here once again, the essence of evil is privation. Like sin itself, these things are evil only by denomination. But it is not as subjects of privation. It is rather as formal principles that bring privation to some subject. What I mean by this should be clear once we see three key texts.

The first is back in the opening article on evil in the First Part, about evil's not being a form or nature. The second objection argues: A differentia constituting a kind is a certain nature, and in morals evil is such a difference; for evil habits differ in kind from good ones, as illiberality from liberality. Thomas's reply, which twists and turns in a way not typical of him, is as follows.

Good and evil are not constitutive differences except in moral things, which are specified by an end that is an object of the will, on which moral things depend. And since the notion of end belongs to the good, good and evil are specific differences in moral things; good is so per se, while evil is so insofar as it is the removal of a due end. But the removal of a due end does not constitute a moral kind except insofar as it is joined to an undue end; just as the privation of a substantial form is not found in natural things unless it is joined to another form. So the evil that is a constitutive difference in morals is a certain good joined to the privation of another good; as an intemperate person's end is not to lack the good of reason, but what delights the senses apart from reason's order.

---

[40] ST I-II 78.1c and ad 2.

[41] This is how Thomas takes Pseudo-Dionysius's saying, "none acts intending evil" (*De Divinis Nominibus*, IV.19.189, p. 163; cf. IV.31.243, p. 212): No one intends privation of due good on its own account. Again, evil can be an end only per accidens. See ST I-II 72.1c; I-II 78.1 obj. 2; I-II 79.2 obj. 2. Cf. ST I 48.1 ad 4; I 49.1c; I-II 75.1c.

Hence evil is a constitutive difference, not as evil, but by reason of the good joined to it.[42]

Let me paraphrase this. Moral things are voluntary things: actions, habits, etc. They can be compared to natural things, inasmuch as they come in kinds. What constitutes or specifies a natural kind is a substantial form. What specifies a moral kind is an end that is an object of the will. Now, good and evil do not specify natural kinds. But it is in the very nature of a good to be an end, and therefore a good, as such, can specify a moral kind. As for evil, or privation of due good, it specifies a moral kind insofar as it is the removal of a due end. This, however, cannot specify by itself. Consider natural things. None is utterly formless. The privation of one substantial form is never found in a thing except along with another form, and that other form is what specifies the natural thing. Likewise, in a moral thing, the lack of a due end is never without another end – nothing voluntary is utterly pointless – and that end, as the will's object, is what specifies the thing. By being the will's object, that end prevents the end that ought to be the will's object from being so. We might call it a dead end. But it is still some sort of good. We are thus led to the striking assertion, "the evil that is a constitutive difference in morals is a certain good."

This would be absurd if it meant that a privation of due good is a certain good. What it means is that the good that specifies a moral kind may, of itself, bring a privation of due good. The kind is denominated evil, as subject of the privation. But the specifying good is denominated evil too, as principle of the privation. The good and the privation are not identical; the one specifies the kind, the other makes the kind evil. But it is no mere coincidence. This good is an end that is contrary to a due end. The due end's removal follows on it necessarily and immediately.[43] It is an "undue end." It is a false or wrong good – an evil good.[44]

It seems clear that this good is not the specifying principle of the privation itself. In a sense, there is such a thing; it is whatever the privation is the privation of, as sight in a way specifies blindness.[45] But what the undue good specifies is the act that has the privation. Nevertheless the privation does follow on it per se. And on this basis, a positive reality,

---

[42] ST I 48.1 ad 2. Specification by ends is quite universal in morals; see ST I-II 1.3; I-II 72.3 ad 2.

[43] He says that the privation belongs to the act's kind "as a consequence" of its differentia: ST I-II 79.2 ad 3.

[44] It is a merely "apparent" good; see the closely related discussion in ST I-II 19.1c and ad 1.

[45] See ST I-II 72.1 obj.2; I-II 72.9 ad 1; II-II 10.5 ad 1.

functioning not as a mere subject, but as a formal principle of action, is called evil. This is surely rather surprising.[46]

Let me turn to my second text. It is from the section of the First Part of the Second Part on good and evil in human acts. Here the overall focus is not evil in general, but specifically moral good and evil. The question is whether an action has goodness or badness from its object. Of course Thomas says it does. But he considers an objection: "An object of an action is a thing (*res*), and as Augustine says, evil is not in things but in their use by sinners." Thomas replies:

> Exterior things are good in themselves, but they do not always have due proportion to this or that action; and so insofar as they are considered as objects of such actions, the notion of good does not apply to them.[47]

Notice that Thomas's formulation attributes privation to the very things that are objects of evil actions. They "do not have due proportion" to this or that action. For example, things that belong to someone else are unfit for the action of taking possession of them. Thomas is pressing to see the objects as genuine principles of evil in actions. Still, he seems to attenuate this attribution when he says these things lack goodness "insofar as they are considered as" objects of such actions. Being an object of moral action is a relation; and it belongs to a thing, not in itself, but in the soul that grasps it, intends it, and orders action to it.[48] It is a relation of reason. What is real is the action's relation to it – the order or tendency to it that is rooted in the agent's will. What truly lacks due proportion, then, is the action. The thing itself is not evil in itself or unqualifiedly, but only in comparison with the action. It is like what Thomas says about matter that has the form of water and lacks the form of fire.[49] This lack is evil, not unqualifiedly, but only for fire. A privation is unqualifiedly evil only if it is evil for the subject to which it is ascribed. Both fire and water are good in kind, and so are things that are objects of evil actions.

To digress for a moment: I think this point is important in view of the role that Thomas assigns to God in sins – the role of a cause of whatever there is of act and being in them. As Thomas grants, this implies that God is a cause of whatever is contained in the sin's kind. He is so even when the kind itself is sinful. To be sure, an act's being evil is not constitutive

---

[46] At least, Cardinal Cajetan thought it was; see his remarks on ST I-II 18.5 (especially ad 2) in the Leonine edition of the *Summa*. Also pertinent are his remarks on ST I-II 72.1.

[47] ST I-II 18.2 obj. 1 and ad 1.

[48] Cf. ST I-II 19.1 ad 3. On relations of reason, see ST I 13.7.

[49] SCG III 5/6.14b8–27. Cf. DM 1.1 ad 1.

of its kind, but only follows on the kind.[50] But how exactly is God a cause of the actuality in a sin? Certainly not as its proper agent. That is the sinner. The actuality in a sin, however, arises from that of certain principles, namely, the sinner's operative powers, the sinner's natural desire of universal good, and the sin's object; and all of these in turn do come from God as first being and first act and first cause.[51] But surely, then, these principles – the powers, the natural desire of the good, and the thing that is the sin's object – cannot in themselves have moral defect. I do not mean that this very act, consisting of the deliberate application of these very powers to this very object, could be without such defect. But the sinner could have chosen an act with a different, due object. God did not determine the sinner to one object rather than the other.[52] The sin, as such – the act with the defect – therefore arises solely from the sinner's will.

Returning to the main discussion: Evidently the object of an evil action may be evil only in a very qualified way. However, a sinful kind of action does also seem to have a formal principle that is denominated evil in an unqualified way. This principle is precisely the sinner's intention of the object. Thomas certainly regards intention as a formal principle of action.[53] Indeed, objects specify just insofar as they are intended.[54] And the intention informing a sin is itself sinful.[55] It may seem odd to speak of one act having two formal principles, the object and the intention. But actions, after all, are not substances. And besides, in a sense these function as one principle, since the thing that is an object is so only as intended, and the intention's own being is entirely relative to the thing intended.

Now let me turn to my third text, which comes only a few pages after the second.[56] The article to which it belongs offers a fuller treatment of the point addressed only in passing in ST I 48.1, that good and evil differentiate kinds of moral acts. The corpus explains that they do so insofar as the acts are good and evil by their objects. For their objects make them good or evil by being suitable or unsuitable to reason, which is a human being's form and nature; and this difference is per se and specific, not merely accidental, because reason is a principle of moral acts as such.

---

[50] ST I-II 79.2 ad 3.
[51] See ST I-II 79.2c; also very pertinent are ST I-II 9.6 ad 3 and I-II 79.1 ad 3.
[52] See ST I-II 9.6 ad 3.
[53] This is already explicit in *In IV Sent.* d.6 1.2 qla.1 sc2.
[54] See ST I-II 18.2 ad 3, together with I-II 1.3 ad 2; also I-II 72.3 ad 2, II-II 59.2, II-II 64.7.
[55] ST I-II 21.1 ad 2.
[56] ST I-II 18.5.

But what I want to highlight is the reply to the second objection. The objection invokes a very fundamental metaphysical principle: A non-being cannot be a differentia.[57] But what constitutes a kind is a differentia. Evil is a privation, a non-being, and so an action cannot be constituted in a kind by being evil. Thomas answers:

> Evil implies, not an absolute privation, but one that follows on some positing. For an act is called evil according to its kind, not by the fact that it has no object, but because it has an object not suited to reason, as in the case of taking possession of another's belongings. Hence insofar as the object is positively something, it can constitute an evil act's kind.[58]

Evil, privation, does not just have a positive subject. The subject must also have some positive determination upon which the privation follows. Why is this determination needed? I think the reason is the same as why evil needs an agent. The privation is against the subject's tendency. Something must obstruct the tendency. An agent is an extrinsic cause. How does it obstruct, if not by positing a contrary determination in the subject itself?

Now although the thought is quite similar, the formulation here is much simpler than in I 48.1 ad 2, which in fact was written years earlier. There, as we saw, to support the idea of morally evil kinds, Thomas invoked natural substances, wherein the privation of one specifying principle entails the possession of another. But here he simply asserts that all evil (moral or otherwise) follows on some positing. This is stronger support. For, again, in water, the privation of the form of fire is not unqualifiedly evil. Moreover, as Thomas recognizes, not all privations require a positing, e.g., darkness in air.[59] Darkness is not evil for air, and it needs no agent and no positing either.[60] As Santiago Ramírez has shown in detail, we have here the final step in a long development of the doctrine that moral things can be evil in kind.[61] Thomas always held the

---

[57] He cites *Met.* III 3 (998b22–27), where the principle is used to show that being cannot be a genus.

[58] ST I-II 18.5 ad 2. The words "some positing" render a textual variant reported in the Leonine edition, vol. VI, p. 131b: *quandam positionem*. According to the apparatus, instead of *positionem*, most of the codices used show *potentiam*, which the edition adopts (replacing *quandam* with *talem*). However, the last sentence's "positively something" (*aliquid positive*) surely favors *positionem*. Also, as Professor Robert Wielockx has observed in a private exchange, in comparison with *potentiam*, *positionem* would seem to be the *lectio difficilior* – that is, a reading that would have been less familiar to copyists, and hence less likely to be read into the text by mistake and more likely to be the original.

[59] ST I-II 18.8 ad 1.

[60] ST I-II 75.1.

[61] Ramírez, *De Actibus Humanis*, pp. 521–42. He finds the young Thomas already departing from the *Summa Fratris Alexandri* and from Albert and Bonaventure. The first pertinent text would be *In II Sent.* d. 34 1.2. Reichberg, "Beyond Privation," signals the doctrine in *De Malo*.

basic thesis, but his metaphysical account of it underwent considerable refinement.

He got special help from William of Moerbeke's translation of Simplicius's commentary on Aristotle's *Categories*. This appeared in 1266. Apparently Thomas was the first to cite it.[62] The key passage, for our purposes, concerns Aristotle's treatment of good and evil as contraries.[63] Simplicius tries to square this with their relating as possession and privation.[64] He distinguishes two types of privation, *in privando* and *in privatum esse*.[65] The latter is total lack of the corresponding possession. The former leaves something of the possession mixed in, and so it is only, so to speak, on the way toward unqualified privation. In this case, the positive remnant provides a certain contrariety. This is how illness is opposed to health. If no health at all remained, there would not be illness but death. An illness is a defective form of health – one contrary to unqualified health. Likewise an evil moral kind is a defective form of good. Not many pages before our text, Thomas explains that what the sinful will tends toward, although truly bad and against rational nature, is always apprehended as good and as in some respect suited to nature.[66] At later points in the First Part of the Second Part he uses Simplicius's idea to explain various things: e.g., there being a middle zone between moral good and evil, the specification of sins by objects, grades of sinfulness, and even original sin being a habit.[67]

2.5 Evil Forms in Nature

But I-II 18.5 also contains a further step in the development of Thomas's account of evil. It is in the reply to the first objection. According to the objection, how good and evil are in actions conforms to how they are in

---

[62] Chase, "The Medieval Posterity," pp. 9–10.

[63] *Cat.* 11, 13b36–14a25.

[64] Simplicius, *Commentaire sur les* Catégories *d'Aristote*, pp. 571.77–574.45.

[65] Ibid., p. 572.1–7. Instead of *privando*, Aquinas says *privari*: DM 1.1 ad 2; ST I-II 18.8 ad 1. For a clear example of his change of approach in this matter, compare DM 1.1. ad 2 with *In II Sent.* d.40 1.5.

[66] ST I-II 6.4 ad 3.

[67] ST I-II 18.8 ad 1 (cf. DM 1.1 ad 7); I-II 54.3 obj. 2 and ad 2 (this is especially akin to I-II 18.5 ad 2, defending the division of habits into good and evil kinds); I-II 72.1 ad 2; I-II 73.2c (cf. DM 2.9c); I-II 82.1 ad 1. In all these passages, the privation of evil is opposed to "pure privation" (*privatio pura*). This, I take it, is the same as the "absolute privation" of ST I-II 18.5 ad 2 (*privationem ... absolutam*). Notice "pure privation" also in *In I DGC*, 8.3 (see below, at n. 73).

things – i.e., in substances, the producers of actions[68] – and in things, good and evil do not diversify kinds. Thus, good and bad persons, however different morally, are the same in kind. So neither do good and evil diversify kinds of actions. Thomas replies:

> Even in natural things the good and evil that are according to nature and against nature diversify the natural kind, for dead body and living body are not of the same kind. And likewise good as according to reason and evil as against reason diversify the moral kind.[69]

Now, it might be tempting to say that since the form of a dead body, qua form, is a certain being and good in itself, it can be considered evil only in relation to the living body whose form (soul) it replaced. This would mean that it is evil only in the way the form of water is: for something else (fire), and hence only in a qualified way. Absolutely speaking, water and its form are not evil. But Thomas is saying that a dead body is evil, not just for the living body from which it came, but without qualification. It is evil in itself. It is unnatural.

To my knowledge, this is the only place where Thomas explicitly presents a natural thing as simply evil in itself. He comes closest, perhaps, in some remarks about monstrous offspring.[70] But even there the evil is relative to the intention of the generator. Here he is not relating the dead body to any agent. Moreover, in saying this within a discussion of things differing in kind, he seems to be suggesting that the dead body has a formal principle which is not only contrary to that of the living body but also fit to be called evil in its own right. This would flatly reverse the view he often expresses elsewhere, even in *De Malo*, that a positive contrary item can be called evil only in morals and that in natural things evil is solely privative.[71]

This reading is corroborated, I believe, by two other late texts, both from Aristotelian commentaries. Let me first present the one that Thomas probably wrote later.[72] In a very obscure passage, Aristotle makes

---

[68] See ST I-II 18.1c.
[69] ST I-II 18.5 ad 1.
[70] See e.g. ST I-II 18.2c; I-II 21.1 obj. 1, ad 1, and ad 2; SCG II 40.360a12–16. Cf. Mulligan, "Moral Evil," p. 18.
[71] See DM 1.1 obj. 4 and ad 4; 1.1 ad 12; 2.5 ad 3; Reichberg, "Beyond Privation," p. 754. For a detailed treatment see Ramírez, *De Actibus Humanis*, pp. 536–42. (Ramírez's discussion is not free of imprecisions. For instance, he accepts a very late dating for the *Compendium Theologiae*, whereas in fact it seems to date from around the time of SCG. But this mistake is offset, in my opinion, by another; Ramírez finds the view stated in *Compendium* 116 to be close to that of ST I-II, whereas I find it closer to SCG III 8/9. But space prevents treating this in more detail here.)
[72] *In I DGC*, 8.3. This unfinished commentary is one of Thomas's very last writings.

a distinction between unqualified modes of generation or corruption and merely qualified modes of them, and he offers what Thomas takes to be various possible ways of taking this distinction. What interests us is the first way of taking unqualified corruption. It would be the corruption of what is unqualifiedly a being into what is unqualifiedly a non-being. Such non-being, Thomas observes, cannot be sheer nothingness, since all natural corruption is by resolution into some matter. Nor can it be "pure privation."[73] That would leave mere formless matter, which is impossible. But it might be something that is only qualifiedly a being. Thomas's explanation of this is remarkable:

> The non-being to which unqualified corruption tends must be understood as a privation that is joined to some form ... But form is twofold. One is indeed perfect, which completes some natural thing's kind, as the form of fire or water or human or plant. But the other is incomplete form, which neither perfects some natural kind nor is the end of nature's intention, but is in the path of generation or corruption. For it is plain that, in the generation of composite beings such as animals, between the origin of generation which is the seed and the final form of the complete animal there are many intermediate generations ... which must terminate in some forms, none of which makes a being that is complete in kind, but only an incomplete being, which is on the way toward some kind. And likewise in corruption there are many intermediate forms that are incomplete forms; for, when the soul is separated, the animal body is not immediately resolved into the elements, but this happens through many intermediate corruptions, with many incomplete forms succeeding one another in the matter, such as is the form of the dead body, then that of the decayed body, and so forth. So when, through corruption, a privation is reached that is joined to such a form, it is an unqualified corruption.[74]

A corpse is no full-fledged kind of thing, and in that sense, it is a non-being. Yet it has its own form – evidently a substantial one. This is important. If it did not have its own form, then it would not be unqualifiedly one body. It would only be some sort of combination of bodies – of elements or (as we should say) of chemicals. These bodies would have their own forms, perfectly "normal" or natural ones, and it would be according to these forms that they should be judged. They would have to be judged good. Now indeed, Thomas thinks that it does not take long for a corpse to disintegrate into just such a combination of normal elemental bodies. But disintegration does not happen immediately upon

---

[73] Cf. above, n. 67.
[74] In I DGC, 8.3 (on DGC I 3, 318a35–b14).

death. For a while the corpse is truly one single body, one substance. It is not the same one as the organism from which it came, but it is still one, with one form. This form, nevertheless, is imperfect. It does not constitute a full-fledged kind. Thomas compares it to the intermediate forms that he thinks appear in the course of animal generation.[75] Now I hardly think he would call these latter forms, or their embryonic bodies, evil. For while they exist, the perfect animal form is not yet due. They serve to prepare the matter for its reception. But obviously the corpse-form does not prepare for the soul. Nor is it needed for the forms of the elements; these can, and normally do, come about in other ways. But why would a corpse-form be, not just imperfect, but downright evil? I think the other (probably slightly earlier) text explains why.

The topic is matter. Aristotle asks whether the matter of contrary forms is ordered or in potency to them equally. He says that in some cases it is, e.g., health and illness; in others it is not, e.g., wine and vinegar. Thomas explains:

> For the form of wine is as a certain possession and kind, while the form of vinegar is as a certain privation and corruption of wine. So the matter is chiefly ordered to wine, as to a possession and a kind, but to vinegar as to a privation and corruption of wine.[76]

In fact,

> The matter of wine is not related (*non comparatur*) to vinegar except through wine, insofar as it [vinegar] is the corruption of wine. It is likewise with dead and living, blind and sighted, etc.[77]

I take him to be saying that the matter of vinegar, as such, is properly or primarily wine-matter, and the matter of a corpse is primarily the matter of an organism. We still call it organic matter. Of course, for Thomas, it cannot continue to be an organism, a body having genuine organs. Nevertheless, just as (for him) a living body, which does not have the substantial forms of the elements, can still have qualities or dispositions like theirs, so too the corpse has dispositions like those of the organism that it came from.[78] But at the same time, whereas the soul of an organism enjoys a stable dominion over the elemental dispositions and orders them to the organism's life and vital activity, the corpse-form has no such

---

[75] See ST I 118.2 ad 2 and I 119.2c.
[76] *In VIII Met.*, 4.1749.
[77] Ibid., 1753; cf. *In X Met.*, 6.2052.
[78] On the "virtual" presence of the elements in the organism, see ST I 76.4 ad 4.

mastery over the corpse's dispositions; in fact it does not sit well with them at all. We can say that the corpse-form lacks "due proportion" to the matter in which it is found. And it excludes the form that does have such proportion, the soul.[79] Moreover, matter too is a sense of "nature."[80] In that sense, the corpse-form is against the nature of its own subject. It is an unnatural form – a bad form. And it is unqualifiedly bad, since it is bad for its own subject.[81]

Does this contradict I 48.1 ad 2, which says good and evil specify only in morals? Perhaps not quite. For really that teaching rests on the status, not of evil, but of good.[82] In morals, the formal principle specifies by functioning as an end, and to function as an end just is to function as a good. But the formal principle of a natural thing specifies by functioning, not as an end, but as a form. So the notion of good can be in the very definitions of some moral things, and that of evil, taken as undue good contrary to due good, can be in others. Neither notion is in the definition of a natural thing.

But either notion can be true of a natural thing, and this by reason of the thing's definition – that is, by reason of the formula of its nature. Every natural kind is good. But a natural thing may fall short of any natural kind. And its nature, in the sense of its form, may run against its nature in the sense of its matter. The thing is by nature evil. Yet the nature of evil itself is still privation.

---

[79] Obviously in this discussion the dispositions are seen as on the side of the matter. On the proportion between the human soul and the elemental dispositions of the human body, see ST I 76.5.

[80] *In II Phys.*, 2.1.

[81] This does seem to contradict, or at least to qualify, SCG III 5/6.14b8–18, where he treats matter as equally in potency to all forms.

[82] This is also clear in DM 1.1 ad 12, as well as in the roughly contemporary DVC 1.2 ad 3.

CHAPTER 3

The Summa Theologiae *on What God Is Not*

Brian Davies

In his introduction to *Summa Theologiae* I 3, Aquinas writes: "We cannot know what God is, only what he is not. We must therefore consider the ways in which God does not exist rather than the ways in which he does."[1] This might seem like an odd thing for a Christian theologian to assert, so one might suppose that Aquinas does not mean what he appears to be saying here. In this chapter, however, I shall explain how the *Summa Theologiae*'s teaching on God is shot through with the conviction that those who speak about God do not know what they are talking about regardless of whether they say "God exists" or "God does not exist."

3.1

We can begin by looking at I 2.3, where Aquinas presents arguments for the truth of the proposition "God exists." According to Aquinas, we can know that this proposition is true. Indeed, he thinks that we can *demonstrate* its truth. But only by using what we might call "nominal definitions" of the word "God."

Following Aristotle, Aquinas takes a demonstration to be an argument with evidently true premises that entail its conclusion, and he thinks that knowledge that God exists can only be gained from such a demonstration. More precisely, Aquinas takes a demonstrative argument to have the form: (1) "All X is Y" (e.g., "All human beings are mammals"); (2) "All Y is Z" (e.g., "All mammals breathe air"); (3) "Therefore, All X is Z" (e.g., "Therefore, all human beings breathe air"). And, I should add, Aquinas thinks that we can only know that "God exists" is true on the basis of a deductive *causal* argument.[2] He is aware that some have claimed that

---

[1] I quote from Davies and Leftow (eds.), *Questions on God*, p. 28.
[2] Aquinas, like Aristotle, holds that there are four kinds of cause: efficient, material, formal, and final. It is efficient causation that he has in mind when speaking of us knowing that God exists on the

"God exists" is self-evident, and he discusses this position in I 2.1 under the heading "Is it self-evident that there is a God?" (*Utrum Deum esse sit per se notum*). However, that "God exists" is *per se notum* (known through itself) as far as we are concerned (*quoad nos*) is a view that Aquinas rejects because of what he thinks concerning our ignorance when it comes to God. For example, in response to the suggestion that God has to exist given that "God" means "that than which nothing greater can be signified," he says "because we do not know what God is, the proposition is not self-evident to us and needs to be demonstrated by things more known to us ... that is, by God's effects."[3] Here Aquinas is arguing that we can know, as opposed to truly believe, that God exists only because we can reasonably claim that God produces effects from which we can reason to God as one who brings things about.[4]

With that said, however, we also need to note that Aquinas recognizes two kinds of causal demonstration: (a) from cause to effect, and (b) from effect to cause. In I 2.2 he writes: "There are two kinds of demonstration. One kind, *propter quid* ('on account of which' or 'of the reason for'), argues from cause to effect and proceeds by means of what is unqualifiedly first. The other, demonstration *quia* ('that'), argues from effect to cause and proceeds by means of what is first so far as we are concerned."[5] What is Aquinas thinking here? His distinction can be grasped by means of examples.

Suppose we reason thus:

1 Hydrogen is the element with atomic number one.
2 The element with atomic number one is the lightest gas.
3 So, hydrogen is the lightest gas.
4 Any balloon filled with the lightest gas rises in air.
5 So, any balloon filled with hydrogen rises in air.

---

basis of causal reasoning. For Aquinas, an efficient (or "agent") cause is something that acts so as to bring about the existence of something or a change in something. Hence, for example, Aquinas would take parents to be the efficient causes of their children. Again, he would take me to be the efficient cause of my dirty dishes becoming clean as I wash them. As we shall see, however, Aquinas thinks that we are using the word "cause" in a unique way when speaking of God as an efficient or agent cause – a way which goes beyond what we usually mean by "cause."

[3] Davies and Leftow (eds.), *Questions on God*, p. 21.
[4] Aquinas tends to distinguish sharply between knowledge and belief. He takes belief to involve conviction without seeing, and he takes knowledge to amount to recognizing that a proposition is true and *why* it is true. In the *Summa Theologiae*, this distinction surfaces particularly clearly in Aquinas's discussion of the theological virtue of faith (*Summa Theologiae*, II-II 1–7).
[5] Davies and Leftow (eds.), *Questions on God*, p. 23. We might translate *demonstratio propter quid* by "demonstration why" and *demonstratio quia* as "demonstration that."

Here we start from a definition of what something is, and we end up arguing syllogistically for the occurrence of a visible effect. Our procedure here is an example of what Aquinas has in mind by "demonstration *propter quid*," which he thinks of as an argument from cause to effect starting with a grasp of the nature of the cause.

However, suppose we reason:

1 This balloon is rising in the air.
2 Every rising balloon is full of something that makes it rise.
3 So, this balloon is full of something that makes it rise.
4 Everything that fills a balloon and makes it rise must be lighter than air.
5 So, this balloon is full of something lighter than air.

Here we make no appeal to what it is precisely that fills this balloon rising in the air; we do not claim to know what exactly that is. Is it hydrogen, helium, or just hot air? But we do try to account for what we perceive in terms of a cause of some sort. We reason from effect to cause. Our procedure here is an example of what Aquinas has in mind when he refers to demonstration *quia*, which he thinks of as a syllogistic argument from effect to cause.[6]

Now, according to Aquinas, if we know that "God exists" is true, that can only be by virtue of a demonstration *quia*. Demonstration *propter quid* is, he thinks, impossible when it comes to the truth of *Deus est*. Why? Because, says Aquinas, we lack an understanding of what God is, because we do not know God's nature or essence. The second objection in I 2.2 runs: "The middle term in a demonstration is what something is. But, as Damascene tells us, we do not know what God is, only what he is not."[7] The objection is arguing that one cannot demonstrate that God

---

[6] Aquinas does not think that we can never offer a demonstration *quia* that relies on some knowledge of what a certain cause is. His point is that a distinction can be made between demonstration *propter quid* and demonstration *quia* so as to flag the idea that we can reason causally while not understanding what a certain cause really is. For another example of *propter quia* reasoning as Aquinas understands it, consider the case of a door which normally opens as we push on it but gets stuck on some occasion since it is obviously meeting resistance of some kind from the other side. We would try to account for the door failing to open, but we might have little idea as to what exactly is resisting our pushing against it so as to allow us to open it. I mention this example since it fits in with the fact that Aquinas thinks that demonstration *quia* when it comes to God actually leaves us in a serious state of ignorance concerning God even though it can successfully be employed when arguing for the truth of "God exists."

[7] Aquinas is here appealing to St. John of Damascus (c. 675–749). The reference is to *De Fide Orthodoxa* (*On the Orthodox Faith*), Book 1, Chapter 4.

exists, and Aquinas denies that conclusion. However, he does not quarrel with what I have just quoted from the objection. Instead, he says that there are two kinds of demonstration, one of which does not presume a knowledge of what God is. Then he says that one can demonstrate that God exists by means of an argument from effect to cause. "When we demonstrate a cause from its effect," he observes,

> the effect takes the place of what the cause is in the proof that the cause exists, especially if the cause is God. For, when proving that something exists, the middle term is not what the thing is (we cannot even ask what it is until we know that it exists) but what we are using the name of the thing to mean. But when demonstrating from effects that God exists, we are able to start from what the word "God" means.[8]

So Aquinas's arguments for "God exists" in the *Summa Theologiae* presuppose that we do not know what God is. They rely on the idea that we do not have a grasp of God's essence or nature. In that case, however, why does Aquinas present them as arguments for it being true that God exists? Does not the question "Does God exist?" already depend on an understanding of what God is? In turning to this question we need to note how Aquinas distinguishes between nominal and real definitions.

According to Aquinas a real definition tells us what something is by nature or essence. So, in his view we can reasonably aim at a real definition of what, say, a cat or a rose is. For Aquinas, such things have *esse* ("existence" or "being"). Considered as such, they can be examined, and their nature or essence can, hopefully, be grasped – at least to some extent.[9]

In this chapter John emphasizes the incomprehensibility of God. He writes:

> It is clear that God exists, but what He is in essence and nature is beyond all understanding ... As regards what God is, it is impossible to say what He is in His essence, so it is better to discuss Him by abstraction from all things whatsoever. For He does not belong to the number of beings, not because He does not exist, but because He transcends all beings and being itself.

What Damascene says about the unknowability of God will strike many contemporary thinkers as strange. But it would not have seemed strange to Damascene's target audience. His emphasis on the mystery of God was commonplace among theologians of his day. My quotations from Damascene come from pages 170–2 of the translation of *De Fide Orthodoxa* provided in Chase, *Saint John of Damascus, Writings*.

[8] Davies and Leftow (eds.), *Questions on God*, p. 23.

[9] I say "hopefully" so as to flag the fact that Aquinas is not over-optimistic about our ability to arrive at a complete understanding of what various things in the world are. In his sermon-conferences on the Apostles' Creed, he observes: "Our knowledge is weak to such a point that no philosopher would be able to investigate perfectly the nature of a single fly." Here I quote from Avo (ed.), *Sermon-Conferences*, p. 21. The passage continues as follows:

> Thus one reads that one philosopher spent thirty years in solitude that he might know the nature of a bee. Therefore, if the human intellect is so weak, is it not foolish to be willing to

What, though, of wizards or hobbits or unicorns? Can these be defined? Since they do not exist, Aquinas would not speak of us being able to arrive at a real definition of them. Yet "wizard," "hobbit," and "unicorn" are words in the English language and it is possible to explain what they mean. So, as well as acknowledging that there are real definitions, Aquinas also agrees that there are nominal definitions, and in I 2.3 he is clearly offering arguments for the truth of "God exists" based on a series of nominal definitions.

Aquinas does not think that "God" signifies something unreal as is a wizard, a hobbit, or a unicorn. But, when arguing that God exists, and in line with what he says about the need to argue for "God exists" by means of causal arguments *quia*, it is nominal definitions from which he starts, not an understanding of what God actually is essentially or by nature. This is what accounts for the minimalistic understandings of the word "God" in I 2.3. In this text, all Aquinas claims to have shown is that there is (1) "a first cause of change that is not itself changed by anything," (2) "a first cause that is not itself caused in any way," (3) "something that owes its necessity to nothing else, something which is the cause that other things must be," (4) "something that causes in all other beings their being, their goodness and whatever other perfection they have," and (5) "something with intelligence who directs all natural things to ends."[10] Here Aquinas is only working with nominal definitions that he derives from what he takes to be traditional talk about God. Over and again in I 2.3 he refers to "what everybody takes God to be." Critics of Aquinas have often said that people mean more by "God" than Aquinas does in I 2.3. Yet Aquinas is fully aware of this fact. In the demonstrations *quia* that constitute the *Summa Theologiae*'s arguments for "God exists," Aquinas sticks to what he takes to be non-controversial nominal definitions of "God," ones that do not rely on an understanding of God's actually existing nature or essence. As I said above, Aquinas's arguments for "God exists" in the *Summa Theologiae* presuppose that we do not know what God is essentially.

3.2

Why, though, does Aquinas say that we do not know what God is? Here we need to note the drift of I 3, which is devoted to ways in which God lacks composition (*compositio*).

---

believe about God only those things that human beings are able to know by themselves? And in counterargument it is said "Behold God is great, overcoming our knowledge" (Job 36:26).
[10] Davies and Leftow (eds.), *Questions on God*, pp. 25–6.

Like Aristotle, Aquinas thinks that there are various senses in which something can be composite. On the other hand, Aquinas has a notion of composition that goes beyond anything that Aristotle presented. That is because he allows for composition of what he calls "essence" (*essentia*) and "subject" (*suppositum*) and because he also allows for composition of "essence" and "existence" (*esse*). His doing so is one of the many things that distances him from Aristotle, albeit that Aquinas is commonly referred to as an Aristotelian thinker.[11]

As it begins, I 3 remains on familiar Aristotelian ground since in I 3.2 and I 3.3 Aquinas employs the idea that some things are composite by being corporeal, by having both form and matter.[12] Aquinas argues that anything corporeal has potentiality or ability for change, a potentiality that must be lacking in God, given the reasoning of I 2.3. "The first being must of necessity be actual and in no way potential," he says. He continues:

> Although in any one thing that passes from potentiality to actuality, the potentiality precedes the actuality, actuality, absolutely speaking, precedes potentiality, for nothing can be changed from a state of potentiality to one of actuality except by something actual. Now we have seen that the first being is God. So there can be no potentiality in God. In bodies, however, there is always potentiality, because the extended is as such divisible. So, God cannot be a body.[13]

Armed with this conclusion, Aquinas thinks that he has no problem in going on to assert that God cannot be "composed" of matter and form. He says, "Since having dimensions is one of the primary properties of matter, anything composed of matter and form must be a body. As I have

---

[11] Aquinas repeatedly draws on conclusions and vocabulary favored by Aristotle. However, he frequently goes way beyond what Aristotle thinks. He does so in the First Part of the *Summa Theologiae* when he talks about God. He also does so in the Second Part of the *Summa Theologiae* when he talks about ethics. Aristotle is someone acknowledged by Aquinas as important when it comes to what he has to say about virtue and vice. In the Second Part of the *Summa Theologiae*, however, Aquinas makes it clear that he takes the virtues that Aristotle admired, and which Aquinas also admires, not really to be true or perfecting virtues since they are arrived at by human effort and not by divine grace. I elaborate on this point in Chapters 12–16 of my *Thomas Aquinas's 'Summa Theologiae'*.

[12] Roughly speaking, Aquinas takes a thing's form to be what we refer to when saying what kind of thing it is or what it is like in various ways. And (again roughly speaking) he takes matter to be what allows something to change either by passing out of existence or by being modified somehow. So, for example, being feline is a form had by my cat, and my cat being able to perish is due to it being material.

[13] I 3.1 (Davies and Leftow [eds.], *Questions on God*, p. 30).

shown, however, God is not a body. So, God is not composed of matter and form."[14]

So far, so good, with little to puzzle a card-carrying Aristotelian. In I 3.3, however, Aquinas goes on to argue that in God there is no composition of *suppositum* and nature, thereby taking us into highly non-Aristotelian territory. By *suppositum*, which I translated above as "subject," Aquinas really means "*this* individual thing as opposed to another one." So, he would say, for example, that Socrates is a *suppositum* and is, as such, an individual subject. He is Socrates and not another human being. Aquinas would also say that beings such as Socrates, like all material substances, are composites of *suppositum* and nature (*natura*) or essence *(essentia)* – meaning that they display or have a nature that is not to be identified with the individual subjects that they are. Socrates is a human being. Yet there are many human beings. As Aquinas would say, there are many things that have the same nature or essence as Socrates while not being Socrates. Such things, thinks Aquinas, are, like Socrates, not to be identified with the nature or essence that they have. Rather, they are a mixture (*compositio*) of *suppositum* and nature. Yet, Aquinas maintains, God is no such mixture. In God, he says, there is no distinction of *suppositum* and nature. So, God (the individual that God is) and God's nature (what God is) are one and the same thing, this being a wholly immaterial form. Or, in Aquinas's own words:

> Divinity bears the same relationship to God as life does to the living. So, God is divinity itself ... God is the same as his essence or nature ... Things composed of matter and form cannot be the same as their natures or essences. For essence or nature in these things includes only what falls within the definition of a species – as humanity includes what falls within the definition of human being, for this makes us to be human and is what humanity signifies (i.e., what makes human beings to be human beings). But we do not define the species of anything by the matter and properties peculiar to it as an individual. We do not, for example, define human beings as things that have *this* flesh and *these* bones, or are white or black, or the like. *This* flesh and *these* bones, and the properties peculiar to them belong indeed to *this* human being, but not to its nature. Individual human beings therefore possess something that human nature does not, and particular human beings and their natures are not,

---

[14] I 3.2 (Davies and Leftow [eds.], *Questions on God*, p. 32).

therefore, altogether the same thing. "Human nature" names the formative element in human beings; for what gives a thing definition is formative with respect to the matter that gives it individuality. However, the individuality of things not composed of matter and form cannot derive from this or that individual matter. So, the forms of such things must be intrinsically individual and themselves subsist as things. Such things are therefore identical with their natures. In the same way, then, God, who, as I have said, is not composed of matter and form, is identical with his own divinity, his own life, and with whatever else is similarly predicated of him.[15]

This somewhat dense text calls for some commentary. Let me, therefore, offer the following observations.

First, Aquinas is here saying that God is not an individual in the sense of "individual" that we have in mind when saying that an individual is one of a kind of which there is or could be more than one member. He is not, however, saying that God is the only individual of a kind as, say, the last surviving zebra would be the only individual of its kind. In the passage just quoted Aquinas is distancing himself from the suggestion that God is any kind of "such and such." He does not think it possible to classify God or to think of God as a countable being among beings. He does not think that God and the universe add up to two.

Our ability to add things up depends on them having some nature in common, even if only notionally. We can add to a collection of dogs because what we are adding is a dog. Or we can add things up under a description like "things that I asked for from Santa Claus" or "things I noticed on the way to work." Given what he says in the passage quoted above, however, Aquinas is denying that God can be listed together with anything else in these kinds of ways. He is denying that "God exists" is properly to be analyzed along the lines "For some X, X is divine," and he does so because he does not think that there is a real distinction between God and being divine, as there is a distinction between being a particular dog and being a dog. One might suppose that Aquinas would at least concede that God and everything other than God add up to a definite number of beings. Yet Aquinas believes that "is a being" does not tell us what something is. In this sense, he prophetically endorses Immanuel Kant's famous claim that "being is obviously not a real predicate, i.e., a concept of something that could add to the concept of a thing."[16] Or, as

---

[15] I 3.3 (Davies and Leftow (eds.), *Questions on God*, pp. 33–4).
[16] I quote from Kant, *Critique of Pure Reason*, p. 567.

Aquinas says in agreement with Aristotle, there is no such class of things as things that simply are.[17] Aquinas is not even willing to say that God is a substance. In I 3.6 he observes: "The word 'substance' does not mean baldly that which exists of itself, for existence is not a genus ... Rather, 'substance' means 'that which is possessed of an essence such that it will exist of itself, even though to exist is not its essence.' So, it is clear that God does not belong to the genus of substance."[18]

Second, the passage quoted above is telling us that God bears a more than passing similarity to a Platonic Form or Idea on the common understanding of what Plato means when he speaks of there being existing Forms or Ideas such as the Form or Idea of Horse and the Form or Idea of Dog.

Some authors have taken this fact to count heavily against Aquinas since they think that the traditionally received Platonic teaching on Forms is misguided. And in defense of such authors we can say that it is true that Aquinas holds that God is pure form and not form received in matter or displayed by something material. In this sense, he is prepared to countenance the idea of there being pure forms that somehow subsist. We should, however, note that Aquinas is generally critical of what he takes Plato to teach about Forms or Ideas. In I 6.4, for example, he says: "Plato believed that the Forms of things exist separately, and that we name individual things after these separate forms, in which they participate in some way – that, for example, we call Socrates a 'man' by reference to some separate Form of Man."[19] Aquinas goes on to observe that Aristotle "repeatedly proves" that this opinion is false. In Aquinas's view, two ducks are ducks not by standing in relation to a separate form of "duck" but by being identical in certain respects, ones which allow us to speak of what it is to be a duck – this not being some existing thing over and above what individual ducks are.

---

[17] Cf. *Summa Theologiae*, I 3.5:

> Since the genus of something states what the thing is, a genus must express a thing's essence. But God's essence is to exist ... So, the only genus to which God could belong would be the genus of being. Aristotle, however, has shown that there is no such genus: for genera are differentiated by factors not already contained within those genera, and no differentiating factor could be found that did not already exist (it could not differentiate if it did not exist). So we are left with no genus to which God could belong.

I quote from Davies and Leftow (eds.), *Questions on God*, p. 37.

[18] Davies and Leftow (eds.), *Questions on God*, p. 38.
[19] Ibid., p. 68.

Yet, in I 3.3 Aquinas is defending the idea that God is a subsisting pure form and not something exemplifying a form or participating in one. This, of course, means that in I 3.3 Aquinas is trying seriously to distinguish between God and those objects of which we can claim knowledge concerning what they are essentially. He takes the latter to be objects of sensory experience, which allows us to pick them out as individuals and to ascribe natures to them, this implying a distinction in them of individuality and nature. He takes God to be a single and undivided noncorporeal and subsisting nature. He thinks of God as something whose individuality is its nature, something that does not *have* a nature but *is* a subsisting nature that is individuated as such and that is, therefore, all that can be ascribed as "belonging" to it by nature. In the above quotation from I 3.3, this is the force of the words "God is ... identical with his own divinity, his own life, and with whatever else is ... predicated of him." Aquinas means that, say, God's goodness is not something different from God's power, and that neither of these is different from God.

In short, Aquinas thinks that the logic of our language fails us when we try to talk or think about God. Typically, we pick out individuals and note what properties or attributes they have. We say, for example, "John is brave," or "Mary is intelligent." For Aquinas, however, God does not *have* properties. Aquinas agrees that God is living, knowing, good, and powerful. Yet he does not think of God's life, knowledge, goodness, and power as attributes that God happens to have as we have various attributes. Nor does he think of them as being really distinct in God, as they are in us. And he does not think of them as distinct from the "individual" that God is. His view is that terms like "God" and "the power of God" both refer to one and the same reality. For this reason, it should be clear how crucial the thinking in I 3.3 is for Aquinas when it comes to his claim that we do not know what God is. For how can we claim to understand the nature of something that is not material, not one of a kind, and lacking properties or attributes distinct from itself?

One might say that there is nothing here to understand since Aquinas is talking nonsense while claiming that God is simple. Yet, and as Peter Geach has noted, there is a comparison to hand which might give us pause when consigning I 3.3 to the flames as obviously incoherent. What Geach says is worth quoting in full. He writes:

> The difficulty here is to exclude from one's mind the Platonism that Aquinas combats – the "barbarous" misconstruction of "the wisdom of God" as "wisdom," which belongs to, is a property of, God; if we do think along these lines, Aquinas will appear to be saying that wisdom and power are different,

but God possesses both, and in him they are not different but identical – which is sheer self-contradiction. The analogy of mathematical functions … proves valuable here … "The square of ___" and "the double of ___" signify two quite different functions, but for the argument 2 these two both take the number 4 as their value. Similarly, "the wisdom of ___" and "the power of ___" signify different forms, but the individualizations of these forms in God's case are not distinct from one another; nor is either distinct from God, just as the number 1 is in no way distinct from its own square.[20]

Even if we reject the comparison to which Geach refers, Aquinas's claim that God is all that God has (that there is no distinction in God of *suppositum* and nature) is not manifestly absurd since it is not offered as a *description* of God. In I 13.4 Aquinas accepts that "the many terms we predicate of God" are not synonymous. So, he does not think that, say, "good" and "wise" in "God is good" and "God is wise" are equivalent in meaning to each other. In I 3.3, however, Aquinas is concerned to *deny* something of God, not to paint a portrait of God. What he wants to say is that God is *not* to be thought of as being like those things the nature of which can be distinguished from the individuals that they are, that God is *not* one of a kind, that God is *not* something having distinct properties as, say, my property of having short hair is distinct from my property of having green eyes. You may think that in I question 3 Aquinas is describing God in positive terms. But he is actually noting what *cannot* be thought when it comes to God. That is because he is merely trying to flag ways in which God does *not* exist on the understanding that to say that God is not X, Y, or Z is not to be committed to any account of what God positively is. A zoologist might be able to tell me what my cat positively is. But Aquinas does not think that we can arrive at some comparable account of what God is.

3.3

So much, then, for I 3.3 and its contribution from Aquinas on our ignorance of what God is. In I 3.4, however, Aquinas introduces another thought that runs through the *Summa Theologiae*. This is that God is non-composite since in God there is no distinction of essence and existence, a notion that, as he dwells on what it might mean to speak of God as the Creator of all things, leads Aquinas to suggest that our knowledge of God is even more limited than we might take it to be even if we concede that there is no composition of *suppositum* and nature in God. Here

---

[20] Anscombe and Geach, *Three Philosophers*, p. 122.

Aquinas is drawing on his claim that God is the first cause of all creatures *from nothing* (*ex nihilo*). In Aquinas's view, this conclusion means that the act of existence (*esse*) of everything other than God directly, and without intermediaries or any preexisting subjects other than God, derives from God, whose nature cannot be something caused to exist by anything and can therefore be spoken of as "subsisting existence" lacking any conceivable potentiality. So, says Aquinas, God is not just his own essence. God "is also his own existence."[21] Hence, and drawing on the reasoning of I 3.4, Aquinas can say in I 13.11 that the "most appropriate name for God" is "He who Is" (*Qui Est*). "Since the existence of God is his essence," argues Aquinas, "and since this is true of nothing else ... It is clear that this name is especially fitting for God, for we name everything by its form."[22] He continues:

> All other names are either less general or, if not, they at least add some nuance of meaning which restricts and determines the original sense. In this life our minds cannot grasp what God is in himself; whatever way we have of thinking of him is a way of failing to understand him as he really is. So, the less determinate our names are, and the more general and simple they are, the more appropriately do we apply them to God. That is why Damascene says "The first of all names used of God is 'The One who Is,' for he comprehends all in himself, he has his existence as an ocean of being, infinite and unlimited." Any other name selects some particular aspect of the being of the thing, but "The One who Is" fixes on no aspect of being but stands open to all and refers to God as to an infinite ocean of being.[23]

The philosophical value of this way of talking has been challenged by authors anxious to insist that "being" or "existence" cannot be attributed to individuals but is what is expressed by the existential quantifier. According to this claim, "X exists" tells us something about concepts, not objects, and is equivalent to sentences of the form "Something or other is F" where F is equivalent to expressions such as "is canine" or "is hungry," which describe what something might be.[24] Yet Aquinas wants to speak of God as "existence itself," and his putting that wish into practice in the *Summa Theologiae* contributes to its consistent teaching that we do not know what God is. Note, however, that Aquinas does not think that

[21] Davies and Leftow (eds.), *Questions on God*, p. 35.
[22] Ibid., p. 163.
[23] Ibid., p. 163.
[24] For a trenchant defense of this position drawing on Gottlob Frege (1848–1925), see Williams, *What is Existence?* Williams applies this position while explicitly targeting Aquinas for criticism in Chapter 27 of Quinn and Taliaferro (eds.), *A Companion to Philosophy of Religion*.

"exists" can enter into a real definition of something that expresses what we know it to be. When speaking of God as "Being itself," Aquinas is not trying to define God. He is saying that, since God accounts for the existence of everything other than God, God is not something derived from anything and exists of necessity. In short, he is saying that God is not created.

At this point I should pay some attention to what Aquinas means when he speaks in the *Summa Theologiae* about God being the Creator, for this is something that does not just lead Aquinas to say that we do not know what God is. It is part and parcel of his teaching to that effect.

3.4

As we have seen, I 2 argues causally for the truth of "God exists" and claims that God accounts for there being change, numerous series of efficient causes, and things which exist but do not themselves account for their actually existing. We might put all this by saying that I 2 argues that God exists since the world or universe is created or made to exist by what is distinct from it. The words "creator" and "create" do not occur in I 2 (or, indeed, in I 3). But they are very much in evidence in I 44–6, which Aquinas presents as devoted to "the procession of creatures from God" (*de processione creaturum a Deo*). In this part of the *Summa Theologiae*, Aquinas draws on what he has been saying in I 2 so as to bring out its significance for the belief that God is Creator of all things. In doing so, of course, he is thinking of what we read in Genesis 1:1, according to which "In the beginning" God "created the heavens and the earth."[25]

The belief that God is the Creator of all things is often taken to mean only that God got the universe to begin to exist some time ago. So, some who believe that God exists think it critical to reject any theory that seems to suggest that the universe had no beginning. Aquinas is not of their mind, however. That is because he thinks that for God to create is for God to make something to exist for as long as it exists and whether or not it had a beginning of existence. As it happens, Aquinas believes that the world did begin to exist, but he does not think that this fact can be established philosophically.[26] For Aquinas, that the universe had a beginning is what he calls "an article of faith" derived from Genesis 1:1. Yet Aquinas does not think that we should reject belief in God as Creator

[25] I quote from the New Revised Standard Version of the Bible.
[26] Aquinas's most detailed defense of this conclusion comes in his *De Aeternitate Mundi* (*On the Eternity of the World*). In the *Summa Theologiae* he touches on the conclusion in I 46.2.

should we happen to conclude that the universe had no beginning. For, he holds, to speak of God as Creator is to speak of God as accounting for the sheer existence of things for as long as they exist.

In other words, Aquinas's view is that God is the Creator of everything since God accounts for there being *something* rather than *nothing at all* and *at any time*. So, in I 45.1 he says:

> It is not enough to consider how some particular being issues from some particular cause, for we should also attend to the issuing of the whole of being from the universal cause, which is God; it is this springing forth that we designate by the term "creation" … If we consider the coming forth of the whole of all being from its first origins we cannot presuppose to it any being. But no-being and nothing are synonymous. As therefore the begetting of a human being is out of that non-being which is non-human being, so creation, the introduction of being entirely, is out of the non-being which is nothing at all.[27]

This is not an argument for "God exists" that depends on the idea that for God to create is just for God to make something to begin to exist, which is why Aquinas can concede in I 46.2 "that the world has not always existed cannot be demonstratively proved but is held by faith alone."[28] In Aquinas's view, God is the efficient or agent cause of things that have being but do not exist by nature regardless of whether or not they began to exist. So, in I 46.1 he can say "The world exists just as long as God wills it to, since its existence depends on his will as on its cause."[29] What we need to realize is that "___ is *being created* by God" is, in Aquinas's thinking, truly to be affirmed of any creature. At the same time, however, we also need to note the extent to which Aquinas takes "creates" in "God creates" to take us beyond causality as he thinks that we understand it. In speaking of God as Creator, Aquinas is focusing on God as an efficient or agent cause. On the other hand, he also thinks that God cannot be an efficient or agent cause in what we might call "the usual sense."

Following Aristotle, Aquinas thinks that talk about efficient or agent causes has its roots in our recognition of change in the world and our looking, so to speak, for culprits in it. I start running a temperature. So, I ask, "What is responsible for this?" I return to my apartment to find it robbed and overturned. So, I ask, "Who did this?" I feel a tap on my

---

[27] I quote from Volume 8 of the Blackfriars edition of the *Summa Theologiae*, p. 27.
[28] Ibid., p. 79.
[29] Ibid., pp. 69 and 71.

shoulder. So, I instinctively turn around to confront the tapper. Unlike David Hume (1711–76), however, Aristotle and Aquinas have no inclination to construe talk about efficient causation as deriving from our experience of "constant conjunction." They think that causal explanation aims at understanding why this or that thing is producing a result of a certain kind regardless of how often it seems to us to do so. Also, and regardless of our experiences of what tends to follow what, they think of efficient causes as agents active in their effects, and they conclude that an efficient cause and its effect are, in a sense, one thing. As Aquinas puts it, "what the agent does is what the patient undergoes" so that "action and passion are not two changes but one and the same change, called action in so far as it is caused by an agent, and passion in so far as it takes place in a patient."[30] If I cause the drapes on my window to be drawn, that is because they *are being drawn* because of me, because my act of causing the drapes to be drawn amounts to the drapes being drawn by me. With all that said, however, this account of causation is an account of it as it occurs in the universe, and it diverges from what Aquinas thinks when it comes to God making the difference between there being something and nothing since Aquinas does not think of God's creating as making any difference to anything and, therefore, as bringing about a change in something.

In short, though Aquinas takes God's creating to be a form of making, he also takes it to be making that is not to be understood as we understand making in general. It is making that brings about something from *nothing*, not making that results in a transformation of some kind. It is making that does not *modify* anything but makes things to be what they are. It is the making performed by something that is not a thing as objects in the universe are things. It is making that is thoroughly mysterious to us.

One might, of course, say that if that is what "creating" as ascribed to God is, then "making" has undergone what Professor Antony Flew once referred to as "the death by a thousand qualifications," and that Aquinas is being incoherent in what he says about God.[31] Flew's point is that those who make assertions about God typically allow nothing to count against them and end up saying nothing of significance since the words they use when talking about God lose their original meaning. Unlike Flew, however, Aquinas welcomes this death by a thousand qualifications

---

[30] This is what Aquinas argues in his commentary on Aristotle's *Physics*. I quote from McDermott (ed.), *Selected Philosophical Writings*, pp. 83 and 84.
[31] For Flew, see Flew, "Theology and Falsification," p. 97.

when it comes to talk about God since he takes it to be a positive consequence of rightly seeking to account for there being something rather
than nothing, since he takes it as implied by his basic reason for supposing God to exist in the first place.

As I have said, in the *Summa Theologiae* Aquinas does not start from
an understanding of what God is when trying to say why we should
think that "God exists" is true. He starts from questions that arise when
it comes to what is in the universe, questions that lead him to a question about the very existence of the universe. Wittgenstein says: "It is not
how things are in the world that is mystical, but *that* it exists."[32] Aquinas
seems to agree with Wittgenstein here. However, while Wittgenstein
goes on to say that when wondering why the world exists we should
resort to silence, Aquinas, in the *Summa Theologiae*, tries to keep talking,
albeit that he recognizes the vertiginous result of doing so, albeit that
he is aware that he is using language that stretches to breaking point, to
the point where he is trying to say more than he can mean, to the point
where he ends up seriously asserting that we do not know what God is
and are better informed when it comes to what God is not.[33] To some
extent, thinks Aquinas, we know what created things in the universe are
and have devised ways in which to talk about them. Yet he also holds that
God is not a created thing having the gift of existence and is, therefore,
not a knowable thing at all. Why not? Because God is not one among
the beings in the universe that exist as created. In his Commentary on
Aristotle's *Peri Hermeneias*, Aquinas says that "God's will is to be thought
of as existing outside the realm of existents, as a cause from which pours
forth everything that exists in all its variant forms."[34] That is a conclusion
that emerges with a vengeance in the *Summa Theologiae*.

3.5

Yet is Aquinas not well known for holding that some of the words we use
when talking about creatures can be applied to God in a literal and non-
figurative sense? And is this not a position that he defends in the *Summa
Theologiae*? The answer to both of these questions is, indeed, "Yes." In

---

[32] Wittgenstein, *Tractatus Logico-Philosophicus*, 6.44.
[33] This point is developed by Herbert McCabe in Chapter 2 of *God Still Matters*.
[34] The Latin text here reads: *Voluntas divina est intelligenda ut extra ordinem entium existens, velut
causa quaedam profundens totum ens et omnes eius differentias.* I quote from McDermott (ed.),
Selected Philosophical Writings, pp. 282–3.

I 13 Aquinas argues that some words can be used both of God and creatures *analogically*, and he takes analogical predication to be a literal mode of discourse. Be that as it may, however, I 13 is not a text in which Aquinas goes back on anything that I have been reporting above. On the contrary, it amounts to a summary of it.

Readers of I 13 sometimes seem to regard it as breaking new ground. And, in a sense, it does since it raises questions not explicitly raised before in the *Summa Theologiae* and since, unlike I 1–12, it hones in on linguistic matters in keeping with its title, *De Nominibus Dei* (*On the Names of God*). I 13 is not so much concerned with what God is as with the words we use when talking about God. Its concern, we may say, is God-talk in general. So, it asks whether any words can refer to God, whether we can talk about God literally and not just metaphorically, whether words used of God are synonymous, and so on.

But I 13 has a distinctly retrospective character and in this sense resembles the annual State of the Union address given by the President of the USA. In part, this address reports and reflects on what has recently happened in the USA. In a similar way, I 13 reflects on what Aquinas thinks that he has established in previous questions of the *Summa Theologiae*. In this sense, he breaks little new ground in I 13. Instead, he brings together much that he has previously been saying.

At this point, we should, perhaps, be clear what that amounts to as a whole since in this chapter I have reported only some of it. Let me, therefore, note now that in I 1–14 Aquinas, to summarize him *very* briefly, makes the following points:

1 We need God to reveal truths about himself to us since our reason falls short of grasping what God is and what God is doing for us. We can reflect on this revelation since it can be expressed propositionally and defended in certain ways even though it cannot be demonstrated to be true (I 1).

2 We can know that God exists because of what we can take to be effects brought about by God, given certain nominal definitions of "God" (I 2).

3 God is not changeable, not an individual, and not created (I 3).

4 God is perfect in that God cannot be thought of as something that can be improved in some way since there is no potentiality in God and since the perfections of creatures exist "in a higher way" in God because they derive from God (I 4). A perfect thing is something "in which

nothing required by its particular mode of perfection fails to exist."[35] So, for God to exist at all is for God to be perfect.

5   "Good" means "desirable" or "attractive," and God is good since God is supremely desirable or attractive. That is because all creaturely goodness derives from God and must, therefore, reflect him somehow, and because all creatures aiming at their good aim at what is somehow in God as their maker before it is in them, on the principle that one cannot give what one does not somehow have (I 5–6).

6   God is unlimited since God is "existence itself" unrestricted by matter or the possession of a created form (I 7).

7   God, and only God, exists in all things and in all places as making things to exist and the places that they occupy (I 8).

8   God is unchangeable and eternal – meaning that God has no before and after, meaning that God has no lifetime that can be broken into sections lived at particular times (I 9–10).

9   God is One in the sense that there being two Gods makes no sense (I 11).

10 By the grace of God, people, after they have died, can come to have an understanding of what God is by means not derived from their natural faculty of knowing as things existing in the world. Yet people can never reach a comprehensive knowledge of what God is, even while enjoying "the beatific vision" (I 12).

Notice that in all of this Aquinas clearly takes himself to be arguing that certain affirmative statements about God can be known to be literally true for quite precise reasons. By implication, therefore, I 1–12 holds that when talking of God we are not always engaging in pure equivocation since this spoils arguments.[36] The text is also saying that God is not composite, so it is by implication also asserting that when we say that God is such and such (e.g., good) we are not speaking of God and of things in the world univocally – since things in the world can be distinguished

---

[35] Davies and Leftow (eds.), *Questions on God*, p. 45 (I 4.1). Note that we have a double negation here, one negating a lack of perfection. Cf. *Summa Contra Gentiles*, I 28.

[36] In I 13.2 Aquinas rejects the view that all positive-sounding statements about God are to be construed as denials. Perhaps wrongly, he attributes this view to Maimonides (1135–1204) while understanding it to amount to the claim that sentences like "God is F" should be understood as always denying something of God, that, e.g., "God is good" means "God is not bad," or that "God is living" means "God is not inanimate." Aquinas rejects this view, though without giving up on his claim that we do not understand what God is. For what seems to be a different reading of Aquinas here, see Stump, "God's Simplicity."

from the properties or attributes that they have while God cannot be so distinguished. Yet this is precisely the drift of I 13.

In I 13 Aquinas is looking back on I 1–12 and noting what has been going on there. He is spelling out what I just referred to as the implications for talk about God present in I 1–12. So, in I 13 he explicitly says that F in "This creature is F" and "God is F" cannot be construed univocally or purely equivocally though its use in both cases can *sometimes* be justified with reference to causal reasoning from creatures to God. This is where Aquinas's notion of analogical predication comes in. When it comes to some words signifying perfections, says Aquinas, we can "name" God from creatures without speaking metaphorically since God accounts for the existence of perfections in creatures who can, therefore, be said to resemble God to some extent (on the principle that you cannot give what you do not have).[37] In spelling out these points in I 13, however, Aquinas is not going back on the "we do not know what God is" emphasis in his thinking to which I have been drawing attention. Indeed, in I 13,1 he reiterates it while saying:

> We cannot see God's essence in this life. We know him only from crea-
> tures. We think of him as their source, and then as surpassing them all and
> as lacking anything that is merely creaturely. So, we can designate God
> from creatures, though the words we use do not express the divine essence
> as it is in itself ... Since we come to know God from creatures, and since
> this is how we come to refer to him, the expressions we use to name him
> signify in a way that is appropriate to the material creatures we ordinarily
> know ... God is both simple, like a form, and subsistent, like something
> concrete. So, we sometimes refer to him by abstract nouns (to indicate
> his simplicity) while at other times we refer to him by concrete nouns (to
> indicate his subsistence and completeness) – though neither way of speak-
> ing measures up to his way of being, for in this life we do not know him as
> he is in himself.[38]

---

[37] Aquinas thinks that *omne agens agit sibi simile* (which we might translate as "every agent cause acts so as to produce what reflects what it is"). He does not mean that, e.g., when I poach an egg I have to look like a poached egg. He means that poached eggs produced by me can, once we have made the right causal connection, be thought of as reflecting what I am as a potential poacher of eggs. He means that, typically, a cause (an agent or efficient cause) is something exerting *itself*, something that has an influence and imposes its character in some way, albeit not always in a way that results in a look-alike of itself (as, say babies, literally look like their parents by being human). For a short but reliable account of Aquinas on causality, see Appendix 2 to Volume 3 of the Blackfriars edition of the *Summa Theologiae*.

[38] Davies and Leftow (eds.), *Questions on God*, pp. 139–40.

And concluding I 13 on the note it struck at its outset, Aquinas observes:

> The difference between subject and predicate represents two ways of looking at a thing, while the fact that they are put together affirmatively indicates that it is one thing that is being looked at. Now, God, considered in himself, is altogether one and simple, yet we think of him through a number of different concepts because we cannot see him as he is in himself. But although we think of him in these different ways we also know that to each corresponds a single simplicity that is one and the same for all ... Our minds cannot understand subsisting simple forms as they are in themselves. We understand them in the way that we understand composite things, in which there is the subject of a form and something that exists in that subject. And so we apprehend a simple form as if it were a subject, and we attribute something to it.[39]

As we have seen, Aquinas thinks that attribution such as this always fails to represent God adequately. When we talk about God affirmatively, thinks Aquinas, we are always "signifying imperfectly." His notion of analogical predication concerning God does nothing to take away the emphasis that he wants to place on this fact. We may, he thinks, speak literally and positively about God while ascribing certain perfections to him. Indeed, in I 13,3 he says: "as far as the perfections signified are concerned, we use the words literally of God, and in fact more appropriately than we use them of creatures, for these perfections belong primarily to God and only secondarily to other things." Yet, Aquinas immediately adds: "But so far as the way of signifying these perfections is concerned, we use the words inappropriately, for they have a way of signifying that is appropriate to creatures."[40]

3.6

As Herbert McCabe says, it is the purpose of I 13 "to show in what way theological language must differ from ordinary usage."[41] As McCabe goes on to say, this is because Aquinas is deeply struck by our ignorance concerning what God is, ignorance that leaves Aquinas effectively saying that we do not know what "God" means. Or, as McCabe puts it:

> St Thomas thought that things in some way pointed beyond themselves to something which is not a thing, which is altogether outside the universe of things and cannot be included in any classification with them. Given this idea it is not too difficult to understand his notion that words can point

---

[39] Ibid., pp. 165–6.
[40] Ibid., p. 144.
[41] Volume 3 of the Blackfriars edition of the *Summa Theologiae*, p. 104.

beyond their ordinary meanings, and this he thought is what happens when we talk about God. We can use words to mean more than we can understand.[42]

If McCabe is right here, we should conclude that when Aquinas talks about God he is doing something seriously different from what people who think that God is a such and such (a "person," for example). Were he alive today, Aquinas would be appealing to the *Summa Theologiae* as a text that, if cogent in the details of its reasoning, ought to lead those who talk about God as one of an understandable kind to think again. An appeal like this from someone of the theological stature and reputation of Aquinas ought, perhaps, to be taken very seriously. Aquinas's treatment of God's unknowability in the *Summa Theologiae* might be full of mistakes. It might be thoroughly confused or to be rejected for some philosophical or theological reason. But it is surely something that should be borne in mind by anyone who wants to understand what the *Summa Theologiae*'s teaching on God amounts to.[43]

For many people it seems natural to think of God as the biggest thing around, the Top Person, and so on. Aquinas, however, definitely does not. As Victor White once said, Aquinas is very much an agnostic because while "modern agnosticism says simply 'We do not know and the universe is a mysterious riddle,'" Aquinas says:

> we do not know what the answer is, but we do know that there is a mystery behind it all which we do not know, and if there were not, there would not even be a riddle. This Unknown we call *God*. And if there were no God, there would be no universe to be mysterious, and nobody to be mystified.[44]

---

[42] Ibid.

[43] The *Summa Theologiae*'s teaching on God amounts to much more than I have reported in this chapter since, in spite of what I have been saying and because it is the work of a teacher of *sacra doctrina* ("holy teaching" or teaching concerning what Aquinas took to be divine revelation), it is grounded in belief in the doctrine of the Trinity. So, for Aquinas, God is not just the incomprehensible creator but is also and from eternity Father, Son, and Spirit. See *Summa Theologiae*, I 33–43. As Aquinas develops his account of the Trinity, the differences between him and those who think of God as a relatively understandable person simply leap off the pages that he writes, though I have no space to dwell on them here.

[44] White, *God the Unknown*, pp. 18–19. For a magisterial account of Aquinas and what we can know God to be, one which ranges over many of Aquinas's writings, see Chapter XIII of Wippel, *Metaphysical Thought*. For comments on earlier versions of the present chapter, or parts of it, I am, with the usual disclaimer, grateful to Christopher Arroyo, Jeffrey Hause, Gyula Klima, Paul Kucharski, Turner Nevitt, and John Wippel.

CHAPTER 4

The Trinity

JT Paasch

Aquinas's trinitarian theology has been studied since he penned it. Many of the commentators are household names (if your household has a theologian living in it). Cajetan comes immediately to mind, whose commentary on the *Summa Theologiae* comes packaged with the Leonine edition. Modern scholarship goes right back to de Régnon, but others like Bernard Lonergan and Karl Rahner made well-known contributions too.[1] Much of the technical literature from the past century focuses on the evolution of Aquinas's thinking about the production of the Son and Spirit. On this, Aquinas changed his mind over the course of his career. In the *Summa*, his views are mature, and his presentation is concise and self-contained.

This chapter discusses Aquinas's account of the Trinity in the *Summa* through four sections: the nature of divine production (Section 4.1), the ontology and consistency of it (Section 4.2), the nature of the divine persons (Section 4.3), and knowing about them through arguments (Section 4.4).

4.1 Production

By the time of the *Summa*, Aquinas had come to believe that minds are productive: They produce concepts.[2] He explains:

> Whoever understands, just from this – that they understand – there comes forth something inside them, which is a conception of the thing

---

[1] Oft-cited studies are, e.g., de Régnon, *Études de Théologie*, volume 2: pp. 133–232; Stohr, "Die Hauptrichtungen"; Schmaus, *Der Liber Propugnatorius*; Paissac, *Théologie du Verbe*; Vanier, *Théologie Trinitaire*; Malet, *Personne et Amour*; Lonergan, *Verbum*; Gelber, *Logic and the Trinity*, pp. 15–25; Luna, "Essenza divina e relazioni"; Schmidbaur, *Personarum Trinitas*; Emery, *Trinity in Aquinas*; and, of course, Rahner, *The Trinity*.

[2] Williams, "Augustine, Thomas Aquinas, Henry of Ghent, and John Duns Scotus," pp. 44–7; Pini, "Henry of Ghent's Doctrine of *Verbum*"; Boland, *Ideas in God*, pp. 235–48; Pasnau, *Theories of Cognition*, pp. 254–71. On the development of this in Aquinas's writings: Paissac, *Théologie du Verbe*; Meissner, "Some Aspects of the Verbum"; Chênevert, "Le verbum dans le Commentaire sur les Sentences"; Gunten, "In principio erat verbum"; Panaccio, "From Mental Word to Mental Language."

understood, issuing from their intellectual power and proceeding from their knowledge ... it is called a "word of the heart."[3]

The idea is simple enough. If you conceive of something (and assuming nothing blocks or halts your conceiving), you produce a concept of it. To put this into a formula:

1   For any thinker *x*, if *x* initiates an act of conceiving of something *F*, *x* produces a concept *y* of *F*.

In the Godhead, though, conceiving of the divine essence results in not just a concept, but another divine person.[4]

2   For any divine person *x*, if *x* initiates an act of conceiving of the divine essence, *x* produces another divine person *y*.

For Aquinas, this is how the Father produces the Son. The Father thinks about the divine essence, and that results in the Son.[5]

Another aspect of intelligent beings is their capacity to love, and Aquinas believes loving is productive too. But whereas thinking produces concepts, loving produces a certain impression of the thing loved.

> Just as from this – that someone understands something – there comes forth a certain intellectual conception of the thing understood ... so also from this – that someone loves something – there comes forth a certain impression, so to speak, of the thing loved.[6]

Aquinas thinks there are no proper names to describe this type of love-production.[7] For convenience, I will pick some labels. I will call it loving, and I will say that the activity of loving produces an affection.[8] To put it into a formula:

3   For any lover *x*, if *x* initiates an act of loving something *F*, *x* produces an affection *y* for *F*.

---

[3] ST I 27.1c: *Quicumque enim intelligit, ex hoc ipso quod intelligit, procedit aliquid intra ipsum, quod est conceptio rei intellectae, ex vi intellectiva proveniens, et ex eius notitia procedens ... et dicitur verbum cordis.*

[4] ST I 34.2c: *in nobis non est idem esse et intelligere ... Sed esse Dei est ipsum eius intelligere: unde Verbum Dei non est aliquod accidens in ipso, vel aliquis effectus eius; sed pertinet ad ipsam naturam eius. Et ideo oportet quod sit aliquid subsistens.*

[5] ST I 27.2c: *processio verbi in divinis dicitur generatio, et ipsum verbum procedens dicitur Filius.*

[6] ST I 37.1c: *Sicut enim ex hoc quod aliquis rem aliquam intelligit, provenit quaedam intellectualis conceptio rei intellectae ... ita ex hoc quod aliquis rem aliquam amat, provenit quaedam impressio, ut ita loquar, rei amatae.*

[7] ST I 36.1c: *cum sint duae processiones in divinis, altera earum, quae est per modum amoris, non habet proprium nomen ... Unde et relationes quae secundum huiusmodi processionem accipiuntur, innominatae sunt ... Propter quod et nomen personae hoc modo procedentis, eadem ratione, non habet proprium nomen.*

[8] Alternatives Aquinas uses: loving produces an impulse, an inclination, or a love for the object of love. E.g., ST I 37.1c: *aliquis rem aliquam amat, provenit quaedam impressio, ut ita loquar, rei*

Like conceiving of the divine essence, loving the divine essence also results in another person.

4 For any divine person *x*, if *x* initiates an act of loving the divine essence, *x* produces another divine person *y*.

This is how the Spirit is produced. The Father (and the Son) love(s) the divine essence, and that results in the Spirit.[9]

4.1.1 Production Is Necessary

Is it possible that these productive mental activities in God might not have happened? Aquinas says no, because in God, conceiving of and loving the divine essence are natural activities.[10]

The thing about natural activities is that they are done automatically. Agents do them whenever they can (provided the circumstances are right and nothing blocks them). We might put it like this:

5 For any agent *x* and any natural activity *A* that *x* can initiate, if *x* has the opportunity to initiate *A*, *x* initiates *A*.

In the Godhead, this is true for conceiving of and loving the divine essence. The persons do these activities whenever they can.

6 For any divine person *x*, if *x* has the opportunity to initiate an act of conceiving of (or loving) the divine essence, *x* initiates an act of conceiving of (or loving) the divine essence.

Of course, the Father has the opportunity to conceive of the divine essence, so he naturally does so (which causes the Son to spring forth).

---

amatae in affectu amantis; ibid., *Ex parte autem voluntatis ... non sunt aliqua vocabula imposita, quae important habitudinem ipsius impressionis vel affectionis rei amatae ... ad suum principium ... Et ideo, propter vocabulorum inopiam, huiusmodi habitudines significamus vocabulis amoris et dilectionis; sicut si Verbum nominaremus intelligentiam conceptam;* I 27.4c: *voluntas autem fit in actu ... ex hoc quod voluntas habet quandam inclinationem in rem volitam ... Processio autem quae attenditur secundum rationem voluntatis ... consideratur ... secundum rationem impellentis et moventis in aliquid."*

[9] ST I 27.3c: *Processio autem verbi attenditur secundum actionem intelligibilem. Secundum autem operationem voluntatis invenitur in nobis quaedam alia processio, scilicet processio amoris, secundum quam amatum est in amante ... Unde et praeter processionem verbi ponitur alia processio in divinis, quae est processio amoris* [*viz. Spiritus Sancti*].

[10] In fact, Aquinas makes a more general claim: Everything internal to God is natural because it can only turn out one way. There is no place for multiple possibilities there. ST I 41.2c: *Eorum igitur voluntas principium est, quae possunt sic vel aliter esse. Eorum autem quae non possunt nisi sic esse, principium natura est. Quod autem potest sic vel aliter esse, longe est a natura divina, sed hoc pertinet ad rationem creaturae: quia Deus est per se necesse esse.*

And similarly, the Father and Son have the opportunity to love the divine essence, so they naturally do so (which causes the Spirit to spring forth).

> God naturally understands himself, and on account of this, the conception of the divine Word is natural.[11]
> God naturally desires and loves himself ... The Holy Spirit comes forth as love, as God loves himself. Whence the Spirit comes forth naturally.[12]

This means that, since there is no possibility it could have been otherwise, the Son and Spirit are produced necessarily. As Aquinas puts it, the Son cannot not get produced (and by extension, the same holds for the Spirit):

> That which cannot not be is said to be inherently necessary. That is the way God's existence is necessary, and in this way the Father necessarily generates the Son.[13]

4.1.2 Repeat Productions?

What about repeat productions? After the Father conceives of the divine essence and produces the Son, can the Son (for instance) turn around and conceive of the essence again, thereby producing yet another person? Aquinas says no, because in God everything is understood in one act.

> In us, acts of understanding can be multiplied forever. By one act a man understands a stone, by another act he understands that he understands the stone, by another act he understands that he understands that other act, and so on ... But this has no place in God, since God understands everything by one act.[14]

Similarly, there cannot be repeat lovings. At one point Aquinas considers the following objection: If the Father produces the Spirit out of his infinite goodness, why doesn't the Spirit turn around and produce another person too? After all, the Spirit also has infinite goodness.[15]

---

[11] ST I 41.2 ad 4: *Deus autem naturaliter intelligit seipsum. Et secundum hoc, conceptio Verbi divini est naturalis.*

[12] ST I 41.2 ad 3: *Deus naturaliter vult et amat seipsum ... Spiritus autem Sanctus procedit ut Amor, inquantum Deus amat seipsum. Unde naturaliter procedit.*

[13] ST I 41.2 ad 5: *Per se autem dicitur aliquid necessarium, quod non potest non esse. Et sic Deum esse est necessarium. Et hoc modo Patrem generare Filium est necessarium.*

[14] ST I 28.4 ad 2: *quod in nobis relationes intelligibiles in infinitum multiplicantur, quia alio actu intelligit homo lapidem, et alio actu intelligit se intelligere lapidem, et alio etiam intelligit hoc intelligere: et sic in infinitum ... Sed hoc in Deo non habet locum, quia uno actu tantum omnia intelligit.*

[15] ST I 30.2 obj. 4: *ex infinita bonitate Patris est, quod infinite seipsum communicet, producendo personam divinam. Sed etiam in Spiritu Sancto est infinita bonitas. Ergo Spiritus Sanctus producit divinam personam, et illa aliam, et sic in infinitum.*

Aquinas responds by pointing out that this would follow only if the
Spirit had a different portion of goodness than the Father, which is not
the case.

> That objection would go through if the Holy Spirit had a goodness that is
> numerically distinct from the Father's goodness. For then it would follow
> that just as the Father produces a divine person through his goodness, the
> Holy Spirit would too. But the goodness in the Father and Holy Spirit is
> one and the same.[16]

This implies that when it comes to conceiving of or loving the divine
essence, in God it is total and complete. Once it has been done, so to
speak, it cannot be done again. Or better:

7   For any divine persons x and y and any act A of conceiving of (or lov-
    ing) the divine essence, if x initiates A and y does not initiate A, y can-
    not initiate another A.

Since the Father conceives of the divine essence, neither the Son nor the
Spirit can initiate any further conceptions. Similarly, since the Father and
Son love the divine essence, the Spirit cannot initiate any further lovings.

Consequently, only one person can be produced through conceiving of
the divine essence, and only one person can be produced through loving
the divine essence.

> God understands all things by one simple act, and similarly he loves all
> things [by another simple act]. Whence, in him there cannot proceed
> Word from Word, nor Love from Love, but there is in him only one com-
> plete Word, and one complete Love.[17]

4.1.3   How Many Kinds of Productions?

Aquinas thinks concept-production and love-production are different in
kind. The former produces a representation of its object, while the latter
produces an inclination or affection for its object.[18]

---

[16] ST I 30.2 ad 4: *ratio illa procederet, si Spiritus Sanctus haberet aliam numero bonitatem a bonitate
Patris: oporteret enim quod, sicut Pater per suam bonitatem producit personam divinam, ita et Spiritus
Sanctus. Sed una et eadem bonitas Patris est et Spiritus Sancti.*

[17] ST I 27.5 ad 3: *Deus uno simplici actu omnia intelligit, et similiter omnia vult. Unde in eo non potest
esse processio verbi ex verbo, neque amoris ex amore: sed est in eo solum unum verbum perfectum, et
unus amor perfectus.* Also I 37.1 ad 4 and 41.6c.

[18] ST I 27.4c: *haec est differentia inter intellectum et voluntatem, quod intellectus fit in actu per hoc quod
res intellecta est in intellectu secundum suam similitudinem: voluntas autem fit in actu, non per hoc
quod aliqua similitudo voliti sit in voluntate, sed ex hoc quod voluntas habet quandam inclinationem
in rem volitam.*

8 For any act A that produces a concept and any act B that produces an affection, A and B are different in kind.

Can there be other kinds of mental activities in God? And might those activities result in more persons? The Father produces the Son by producing a concept, while the Father and Son together produce the Spirit by producing love. Could the Father, Son, and Spirit all together perform some third kind of mental activity, which results in a fourth person? And then could those four perform a further kind of mental activity to produce a fifth?

Aquinas says no. As he sees it, there are no other kinds of mental production beyond concept-production and love-production.

> There is no need to go on forever with productions in the Godhead. For when it comes to things with an intellectual nature, internal production ends with procession from the will [namely, love].[19]

Whether it be a human mind or a divine mind, there are two, and only two, kinds of mental productions.[20]

9 For any intelligent being x, if x initiates a mental act A that produces something y in x, y is either a concept or an affection.

4.1.4 Shared Production

Aquinas claims the persons cannot be distinguished except insofar as they stand in opposing relationships.

> It is not possible to say the divine persons are distinct in some absolute sense, for then there would not be a single essence among the three ... That leaves only that they are distinguished from each other through relations. But they cannot be distinguished by relations unless they are opposed relations.[21]

Another way to put this: The persons have (or share) all the same features, except for ones that are opposed to each other.

---

[19] ST I 27.3 ad 1: *non est necessarium procedere in divinis processionibus in infinitum. Processio enim quae est ad intra in intellectuali natura, terminatur in processione voluntatis.*

[20] ST I 27.3c: *in divinis sunt duae processiones, scilicet processio verbi, et quaedam alia. Ad cuius evidentiam, considerandum est quod in divinis non est processio nisi secundum actionem quae non tendit in aliquid extrinsecum, sed manet in ipso agente. Huiusmodi autem actio in intellectuali natura est actio intellectus et actio voluntatis.* Also I 27.5c.

[21] ST I 36.2c: *Non enim est possibile dicere quod secundum aliquid absolutum divinae personae ab invicem distinguantur: quia sequeretur quod non esset trium una essentia ... Relinquitur ergo, quod solum relationibus divinae personae ab invicem distinguantur. Relationes autem personas distinguere non possunt, nisi secundum quod sunt oppositae.*

10 For any divine person x and for any F and G in the Godhead, x has F and G unless F and G are opposed to each other.

Note that there must be two things to stand in opposing relationships. For example, parent and child or double and half are opposing relationships, and indeed, there must be two people to be parent and child, or two quantities to be double and half.

So also in the Godhead. If we are talking about opposite relationships, we are talking about two persons.

> The only real distinction among divine relations is due to relative opposition. Two opposing relations must belong to two persons. If they are not opposed, they must belong to the same person.[22]

The only relationships in God that are opposed like this arise from production. To be the producer of a product is the opposite of being the product of that producer.

> The only real relations that can be accepted in God are those of actions, which in God's case, are internal productions (not external productions) ... But any production implies opposed relations, one for proceeding from the source, and the other for being the source.[23]

In other words:

11 For any F and G in the Godhead, F and G are opposed to each other only if F and G are opposed as producer and product.

What this means for production is that divine persons cannot share their productive activity with the person they are producing through that activity. But they can share it with any other available divine person, whom they are not producing through that activity.[24]

The Father alone produces the Son because there is no one around yet, so to speak, to share that activity with. But as the Father produces the Spirit, the Father can (and does) share his productive activity with the Son.

---

[22] ST I 30.2c: *Realis autem distinctio inter relationes divinas non est nisi in ratione oppositionis relativae. Ergo oportet duas relationes oppositas ad duas personas pertinere: si quae autem relationes oppositae non sunt, ad eandem personam necesse est eas pertinere.*

[23] ST I 28.4c: *relationes reales in Deo non possunt accipi, nisi secundum actiones secundum quas est processio in Deo, non extra, sed intra ... Secundum quamlibet autem processionem oportet duas accipere relationes oppositas, quarum una sit procedentis a principio, et alia ipsius principii.*

[24] ST I 32.3 ad 3: *cum sola oppositio relativa faciat pluralitatem realem in divinis, plures proprietates unius personae, cum non opponantur ad invicem relative, non differunt realiter.*

4.1.5 The Filioque

Aquinas uses the foregoing to argue for the *filioque*. Why not think the Father alone produces the Spirit? Aquinas says: If the Son did not participate in producing the Spirit, the Son and Spirit would not be distinct.[25]

We might formulate the argument as follows. Suppose (10) and (11) are correct. Then any two divine persons are distinct only if one produces the other.

12   For any divine persons x and y, if either x does not produce y or y does not produce x, x and y are not distinct persons.

Now suppose that, *ex hypothesi*:

13   The Son does not produce the Spirit.

If that were right, it would follow that:

14   The Son and Spirit are not distinct persons.

And that must be false, because it contradicts a claim all orthodox Christians accept, namely:

15   The Son and Spirit are distinct persons.

Since (12) and (13) lead to a false conclusion, one of them must be wrong. And Aquinas rejects (13), while he wholeheartedly affirms (12).

This was not particularly popular move. Many scholastics rejected (12), insisting instead that the Son and Spirit are distinct merely because they are produced in different ways.[26] For advocates of this alternative view:

16   For any divine persons x and y, x and y are distinct persons if x and y are produced by different kinds of productions.

But Aquinas rejects (16). He agrees that the Son and Spirit are produced in different ways (from [8] above). But he denies that it is enough to make them distinct. For Aquinas, (12) describes the only way divine persons can be distinct, and that makes his argument controversial, since that is precisely what his opponents will not accept.

---

[25] ST I 36.2c: *necesse est dicere Spiritum Sanctum a Filio esse. Si enim non esset ab eo, nullo modo posset ab eo personaliter distingui.* Emery, "La procession du Saint-Esprit"; Friedman, *Intellectual Traditions*, pp. 173–80; Pelikan, "The Doctrine of Filioque."

[26] Friedman, *Intellectual Traditions*, 85, note 80; ibid., "Relations, Emanations, and Henry of Ghent's Use of the *Verbum Mentis*," p. 144, note 14.

Aquinas has another argument for the Filioque that is not based on (12). Instead, it is based on this: The Father shares everything with the Son, unless it entails a contradiction.

17 For any divine persons x and y, if x has something F, x shares F with y unless it entails a contradiction.

Everyone agrees: that the Father produces the Spirit.

18 The Father produces the Spirit.

And there is nothing contradictory about the Son doing it too.

19 There is no contradiction if the Son produces the Spirit.

So the Father must share his production of the Spirit with the Son:

20 The Son produces the Spirit.

As Aquinas sees it, the persons share everything they can, so of course the Father shares all the productive activity he can with the Son.[27]

4.2 Ontology and Consistency

Aquinas maintains that the persons stand in opposing production relationships ([10] and [11] above). These relations are not opposed to each other just in our minds. Aquinas insists they are really opposed, outside our minds.

> Since the relation is real [i.e., extra-mental] in God, as was said, there must be real [i.e., extra-mental] opposition there.[28]

And with real opposition comes real distinction. The opposed relations are distinct from each other, extra-mentally.

> Relative opposition includes in its nature real [i.e., extra-mental] distinction, so there must be real [i.e., extra-mental] distinction in God.[29]

---

[27] ST I 36.2 ad 6: *quod Spiritus Sanctus perfecte procedit a Patre, non solum non superfluum est dicere quod Spiritus Sanctus procedat a Filio; sed omnino necessarium. Quia una virtus est Patris, et Filii; et quidquid est a Patre, necesse est esse a Filio, nisi proprietati filiationis repugnet. Non enim Filius est a seipso, licet sit a Patre.*

[28] ST I 28.3c: *Cum igitur in Deo realiter sit relatio, ut dictum est, oportet quod realiter sit ibi oppositio.* I 28.1c: *Aliquando vero respectus significatus per ea quae dicuntur ad aliquid, est tantum in ipsa apprehensione rationis conferentis unum alteri: et tunc est relatio rationis tantum ... Cum autem aliquid procedit a principio eiusdem naturae, necesse est quod ambo, scilicet procedens et id a quo procedit, in eodem ordine conveniant: et sic oportet, quod habeant reales respectus ad invicem.*

[29] ST I 28.3c: *Relativa autem oppositio in sui ratione includit distinctionem. Unde oportet quod in Deo sit realis distinctio.*

That is:

21 For any relations *F* and *G* in God, if *F* and *G* are extra-mentally opposed to each other, *F* and *G* are extra-mentally distinct from each other.

Consequently, the persons are extra-mentally distinct from each other too, since they stand in extra-mentally opposed relationships.

4.2.1 Applying Attributes to God

How are the persons not three Gods then? According to Aquinas, attributes are not stuck onto God, so to speak, as accidents in a subject. Rather, they just are the divine essence.

> Whatever has accidental being in creatures has substantial being when it is transferred to God, for nothing exists in God as an accident in a subject. Whatever is in God is God's essence.[30]

To put it another way: We might talk about attributes in God as if they were distinct extra-mental things, and we might think of them as if they were distinct too, but outside our minds, the extra-mental entity we are speaking of is just the divine essence.

22 For any attribute *F* in God, the extra-mental entity of *F* is the divine essence.

This goes for relations too:

> Although in creatures, a relation has accidental being in a subject, a relation that really exists in God has the being of the divine essence, existing entirely the same as it ... So it is clear that in God, the relation is not one thing, and the [divine] essence another. They are one and same.[31]

For Aquinas then, the relations are distinct only with respect to each other. In terms of their extra-mental entity, they are all one and the same thing (the divine essence).

This is puzzling though. One might think that things cannot be distinct if they overlap completely in extra-mental entity.

23 For any *F* and *G*, if *F* and *G* completely overlap in extra-mental entity, *F* and *G* are not extra-mentally distinct from each other.

---

[30] ST I 28.2c: *Quidquid autem in rebus creatis habet esse accidentale, secundum quod transfertur in Deum, habet esse substantiale: nihil enim est in Deo ut accidens in subiecto, sed quidquid est in Deo, est eius essentia.* Also I 28.2 ad 1.

[31] ST I 28.2c: *Sic igitur ex ea parte qua relatio in rebus creatis habet esse accidentale in subiecto, relatio realiter existens in Deo habet esse essentiae divinae, idem omnino ei existens ... Patet ergo quod in Deo non est aliud esse relationis et esse essentiae, sed unum et idem.*

But for Aquinas, the extra-mental entities of the relations do overlap, because they are just the divine essence (from [22]):

24   For any extra-mentally opposed relations F and G in God, F and G completely overlap in extra-mental entity.

But (23) and (24) entail that the relations cannot be extra-mentally distinct:

25   For any extra-mentally opposed relations F and G in God, F and G are not extra-mentally distinct from each other.

And that contradicts (21). It is hard to see how Aquinas could coherently maintain both (21) and (22). If he is serious about (22), then the relations would seem to be too thin to do any real distinguishing; for there would be just no extra-mental entity to them apart from the divine essence.

4.2.2   Transitivity and Contradiction

Even apart from a thin ontology, it might seem Aquinas is open to another contradiction. Each divine person is the same as the divine essence. For example:

26   The Father is the same as the divine essence.
27   The Son is the same as the divine essence.

However, sameness seems to be transitive:

28   For any x, y, and z, if x is the same as y and y is the same as z, then x is the same as z.

If that is right, then:

29   The Father is the same as the Son.

And that contradicts a claim held by all Christian scholastics:

30   The Father is not the same as the Son.

Aquinas rehearses this argument several times himself.[32] Each time he rejects it, by denying (28).[33]

---

[32] ST I 28.3 obj. 1: *relationes, quae sunt in Deo, realiter ab invicem non distinguantur. Quaecumque enim uni et eidem sunt eadem, sibi invicem sunt eadem. Sed omnis relatio in Deo existens est idem secundum rem cum divina essentia. Ergo relationes secundum rem ab invicem non distinguuntur.* I 39.1 obj. 2: *affirmatio et negatio simul et semel non verificantur de eodem. Sed affirmatio et negatio verificantur de essentia et persona: nam persona est distincta, essentia vero non est distincta. Ergo persona et essentia non sunt idem.*

[33] ST I 39.1c: *Relatio autem, ad essentiam comparata, non differt re, sed ratione tantum: comparata autem ad oppositam relationem, habet, virtute oppositionis, realem distinctionem. Et sic remanet una*

The problem with (28) is that "the same" is ambiguous. There are many ways to be the same, not all of which are transitive. Aquinas agrees that complete identity (i.e., classical identity) is transitive. He writes:

> That argument – that whatever things are one and the same as another thing are the same as each other – holds for those things which are the same in reality [i.e., extra-mentally] and in definition or account, like a tunic and a garment.[34]

So Aquinas would affirm this:

31 For any *x*, *y*, and *z*, if *x* is completely identical with *y* and *y* is completely identical with *z*, then *x* is completely identical with *z*.

But Aquinas thinks the kind of sameness that occurs in the Trinity is not transitive. As he puts it:

> That argument does not hold ... for things that differ in definition or account ... And so, although fatherhood is the same as the divine essence in reality [i.e., extra-mentally], and the same goes for sonship, nevertheless, these two are opposed to each other in their proper definition or account, so they are distinguished from each other.[35]

Whatever "the same as" means in (26) and (27), it is not transitive, so Aquinas does not fall prey to the proposed contradiction.[36]

4.2.3 Classical Identity

Still, what could "the same as" mean in (26) and (27)? Christopher Hughes argues it is just classical identity, rather than some weaker kind of identity.[37] For support, he discusses a number of passages where (on Hughes's reading) Aquinas seems to think sameness is identity.

But of course, classical identity is transitive. So how could Aquinas deny such an obvious feature of identity? According to Hughes, it is to avoid Sabellianism. Because Aquinas does not want to say that the Father, Son, and Spirit are really just one person, he denies that identity

---

essentia, et tres Personae. I 39.1 ad 2: *inquantum essentia et persona in divinis differunt secundum intelligentiae rationem, sequitur quod aliquid possit affirmari de uno, quod negatur de altero: et per consequens quod, supposito uno, non supponatur alterum.*

[34] ST I 28.3 ad 1: *argumentum illud tenet, quod quaecumque uni et eidem sunt eadem, sibi invicem sunt eadem, in his quae sunt idem re et ratione, sicut tunica et indumentum.*

[35] ST I 28.3 ad 1: *argumentum illud tenet ... non autem in his quae differunt ratione ... Et similiter, licet paternitas sit idem secundum rem cum essentia divina, et similiter filiatio, tamen haec duo in suis propriis rationibus important oppositos respectus. Unde distinguuntur ab invicem.*

[36] Even critics of Aquinas are sensitive to this point. E.g., Lamont, "Aquinas on Subsistent Relation," p. 268.

[37] Hughes, *On a Complex Theory*, Chapter 6.

is transitive. And that, thinks Hughes, is not viable. Identity obviously is transitive, so it makes no sense for Aquinas to deny that it is.

I am not sure how to verify Hughes's claims. An alternative account could be, say, that Aquinas is thinking of unity relations. Two things bound together very tightly could stand in for all the cases Hughes thinks require identity, but without being transitive.

4.2.4 Relative Identity

Another proposal comes from Peter Geach, who suggested that Aquinas holds a theory of relative identity. There are various kinds of relative identity, but Geach's illustrates the point well enough.

According to Geach, statements of the form "x is the same as y" are incomplete. Are x and y the same dog? The same color? The same height? We need to specify the particular way that x and y are the same – we need to say "x is the same F as y," and fill in F.

Once all identity statements are fleshed out and all the Fs are filled in, it might turn out that there are cases where x and y are the same F, but not the same G. In the Godhead, for example, the Father and Son are the same God, but not the same person.[38]

As with Hughes, I am not sure how to verify if Geach is right. But even if he were, I am not sure what it would clarify. What F should we fill in for (26) and (27)? Given (22), it seems Aquinas is saying the persons and the divine essence are the same extra-mental entity:

32 The Father is the same extra-mental entity as the divine essence.

33 The Son is the same extra-mental entity as the divine essence.

And being the same extra-mental entity does seem to be transitive:

34 For any x, y, and z, if x is the same extra-mental entity as y and y is the same extra-mental entity as z, then x is the same extra-mental entity as z.

4.3 Persons

Regarding the definition of persons, Aquinas follows Boethius, who says persons are the sorts of things that have rational natures.[39]

---

[38] Geach, "Identity"; also note Geach and Anscombe, *Three Philosophers*, pp. 118–19.
[39] Wald, "*Rationalis naturae individua substantia.*"

Every hypostasis with a rational nature is a person, which is clear from the definition of Boethius that says "a person is an individual substance with a rational nature."[40]

So, persons have mental capacities. Objects with no mental capacities cannot be persons.

35   For any person *x*, *x* has mental capacities.

Further, Aquinas says persons are the sorts of things that are in control of their actions.

A still more special and more complete kind of particularity and individuality is found in rational substances, who have dominion over their actions. They are not only acted upon, like other things, but they act by themselves.[41]

Persons are not just pushed and pulled about by external agents. They can act on their own.

36   For any person *x*, *x* is in control of its actions.

I take it this means not just any mental capacities will suffice. Objects that are in control of their actions at a minimum have both an intellect and a will so they can process information and make decisions.

4.3.1   Individuals

Boethius's definition picks out not just mental capacities. It picks out singular individuals with mental capacities.[42] Human kind is not a person. It is individual humans who are persons.

The term "substance" is placed in the definition of person not so as to signify an essence, but to signify a hypostasis. This is clear from the fact that the term "individual" is added to it.[43]

The principle is somewhat general here. For Aquinas, the singular individual in a kind is whatever is distinct in that kind.

[40] ST I 40.3c: *omnis hypostasis naturae rationalis est persona, ut patet per definitionem Boetii, dicentis quod persona est rationalis naturae individua substantia.*
[41] ST I 29.1c: *Sed adhuc quodam speciali et perfectiori modo invenitur particulare et individuum in substantiis rationalibus, quae habent dominium sui actus, et non solum aguntur, sicut alia, sed per se agunt.*
[42] ST I 29.1c: *Et ideo in praedicta definitione personae ponitur substantia individua, inquantum significat singulare in genere substantiae.* Also I 29.1 ad 3: *Et sic hoc nomen individuum ponitur in definitione personae, ad designandum modum subsistendi qui competit substantiis particularibus.*
[43] ST I 30.1 ad 1: *substantia non ponitur in definitione personae secundum quod significat essentiam, sed secundum quod significat suppositum: quod patet ex hoc quod additur individua.*

The term "person" generally signifies an individual substance with a rational nature, as was said. But the "individual" is that which is itself undivided, but yet distinct from others. So "person," in whatever kind [persons occur], signifies what is distinct in that kind.[44]

Put simply, persons are (as Aquinas also puts it) "distinct and unsharable" units[45]:

37   For any person x, x is an unsharable individual.

Aquinas believes the parts of primary substances are not substances themselves. Consequently, no part of a person can be a person, even if it is very person-like.

38   For any part x of a person y, x is not a person.

For example, the human mind is very person-like, but it is a part of a larger whole (a human being). I am a person, but my mind is not, any more than my hand is. This is why Aquinas thinks disembodied human minds – souls after death that have no bodies – are not persons.

> The soul is a part of the human species, and so, although it may be separated ... it cannot be called an individual substance (which is a hypostasis) or a primary substance, just as neither can a hand or any other part of a human. Thus, neither the definition nor the name "person" applies to it.[46]

Angels, by contrast, are persons, because they are not parts of a larger whole. They are just free-floating minds.

Another important case is the Incarnation. For Aquinas, Christ comprises a divine person (the Son), who assumed a human nature (Jesus of Nazareth). Jesus is very person-like, but as part of a larger whole, Jesus is not a separate person.

4.3.2   Who is the Person or Persons?

Given all that, who or what counts as a person in the Godhead? Obviously, Aquinas wants to say:

39   The Father, Son, and Spirit are each a person.

---

[44] ST I 29.4c: *Persona enim in communi significat substantiam individuam rationalis naturae, ut dictum est. Individuum autem est quod est in se indistinctum, ab aliis vero distinctum. Persona igitur, in quacumque natura, significat id quod est distinctum in natura illa.*

[45] ST I 29.4 ad 3: *in intellectu substantiae individuae, idest distinctae vel incommunicabilis. I 29.3 ad 4: Individuum autem Deo competere non potest quantum ad hoc quod individuationis principium est materia: sed solum secundum quod importat incommunicabilitatem.*

[46] ST I 29.1 ad 5: *anima est pars humanae speciei: et ideo, licet sit separata ... non potest dici substantia individua quae est hypostasis vel substantia prima; sicut nec manus, nec quaecumque alia partium hominis. Et sic non competit ei neque definitio personae, neque nomen.*

By contrast, the divine essence is not a person. It is shared by the Father, Son, and Spirit, and so it cannot satisfy (37).

40 The divine essence is not a person.

What about God as a whole? Is the triune God a person? Aquinas would not want to admit that, but it is hard to see how it would not follow. The triune God is an unsharable unit (there is only one triune God), it is not a part of a larger whole, and there is a sense in which God is intelligent. As Aquinas himself puts it:

> God could be said to have a rational nature, not if that implies discursive thought, but more generally an intelligent nature.[47]

It would seem that Aquinas's claims about personhood should lead him to affirm that God as a whole counts as a person:

41 The triune God is a person.

Aquinas presents an independent argument that seems to lead to this conclusion as well. He claims it is appropriate to describe God as a "person" because to be a person is a perfection, and all suitable perfections apply to God.

> The term "person" signifies that which is most perfect in the whole nature, namely subsisting with a rational nature. Whence, since everything of perfection should be attributed to God, for God's essence contains every perfection, it is appropriate that the term "person" be applied to God.[48]

The argument is structured along these lines:

42 For any term T, if T signifies a perfection, God is T.
43 The term "person" signifies a perfection.
44 Therefore, God is a person.

4.3.3 *Richard or Boethius?*

Richard of St. Victor offered an alternative definition: A (divine) person is an unsharable existent of the divine nature.[49] It might be tempting to

---

[47] ST I 29.3 ad 4: *Deus potest dici rationalis naturae, secundum quod ratio non importat discursum, sed communiter intellectualem naturam.*

[48] ST I 29.3c: *persona significat id quod est perfectissimum in tota natura, scilicet subsistens in rationali natura. Unde, cum omne illud quod est perfectionis, Deo sit attribuendum, eo quod eius essentia continet in se omnem perfectionem; conveniens est ut hoc nomen persona de Deo dicatur.*

[49] See Den Bok, *Communicating the Most High*, Chapters 5–6.

think Richard's definition fares better than Boethius's, since it seems to pick out only the three hypostases.

But in this respect, Richard's definition is equivalent to Aquinas's. Whatever Richard picks out with "unsharable existents," Aquinas picks out with (37). As Aquinas reads it, Boethius's definition identifies the same things Richard's does.

In addition, Boethius's definition highlights the mental characteristics of persons. For Aquinas, persons are thinkers and lovers, and at least as a tagline, Richard's definition does not capture that.

4.3.4 The Mental Lives of the Persons

Do the persons have mental lives? If so, what are they like? And how many are there?

On Aquinas's account, the persons do perform different mental activities. The Father performs one activity the Son and Spirit do not: He conceives of the divine essence in such a way that he produces a concept. Similarly, the Father and Son perform an activity the Spirit does not: They love the divine essence in such a way that they produce an affection.

Does this mean they have distinct mental lives? That is unclear, and the answer will depend in part on the answers to further questions.

For example, does Aquinas think there is something it is like to be a divine person? Do the persons each have a first-person perspective? Or are the persons more analogous to non-selved machines, i.e., entities that are in control of their actions, but process everything mechanically and have no first-person perspective of a self? These are questions that can only be answered by future research, if they can be answered at all.[50]

4.4 Knowing about the Trinity

Can humans know about the Trinity without any help from revelation? Aquinas says no. Humans can figure out a variety of things about God as a unified being, but they cannot figure out that there are three persons in God.

> It is impossible to come to knowledge of the Trinity of divine persons through natural reason ... Through natural reason we can know things

[50] There are some studies on the notional acts in Aquinas, but the questions are far from answered. Vanier, *Théologie Trinitaire*; Perrier, *La Fécondité en Dieu*; Boyle, "St. Thomas and the Analogy of *Potentia Generandi*"; Williams, "Augustine, Thomas Aquinas, Henry of Ghent, and John Duns Scotus," pp. 70–3.

about God that pertain to the unity of God's essence, but not those things that pertain to the distinction of persons.[51]

As Aquinas sees it, this is because humans can only reason about God as the cause of creatures, and the divine persons act toward creation in an entirely unified manner.

> Through natural reason one can know of God only what necessarily belongs to God insofar as God is the source of all beings ... But the creative power of God is common to the whole Trinity, so it pertains to the unity of God's essence, not to the distinction of persons.[52]

For Aquinas:

45 Without revelation, it cannot be known that God is triune.

4.4.1 *Proofs for the Existence of the Trinity*

Some scholastics constructed arguments aimed to show that God must be triune, without making any appeal to revelation. For example, Richard of St. Victor argues as follows[53]: God is infinitely good, and part of being good involves sharing that goodness.

46 For any x, if x is infinitely good, x shares its infinite goodness.
47 God is infinitely good.
48 Therefore, God shares God's infinite goodness.

Since God's goodness is infinite, there is a lot to share, so to speak. Only an equal could share it.

49 For any infinitely good x, if x shares its infinite goodness, x shares it with an equal.
50 God shares God's infinite goodness.
51 Therefore, God shares God's infinite goodness with an equal.

Further, two parties share goodness best if they partner up to share with a third.

---

[51] ST I 32.1c: *impossibile est per rationem naturalem ad cognitionem Trinitatis divinarum Personarum pervenire ... Per rationem igitur naturalem cognosci possunt de Deo ea quae pertinent ad unitatem essentiae, non autem ea quae pertinent ad distinctionem Personarum.*

[52] ST I 32.1c: *Hoc igitur solum ratione naturali de Deo cognosci potest, quod competere ei necesse est secundum quod est omnium entium principium ... Virtus autem creativa Dei est communis toti Trinitati: unde pertinet ad unitatem essentiae, non ad distinctionem personarum.*

[53] Den Bok, *Communicating the Most High*, Chapter 7. For a modern version, Swinburne, *The Christian God*, Chapter 8.

52 For any infinitely good x and an equal y, if x and y share infinite goodness, x and y share their infinite goodness with a third party.

53 God shares God's infinite goodness with an equal.

54 Therefore, God and an equal share their infinite goodness with a third party.

But again, in order to receive all that goodness, the third party must be an equal too.

55 For any infinitely good x and an equal y, if x and y share their infinite goodness with a third party, they share it with a third equal z.

56 God and an equal share their infinite goodness with a third party.

57 Therefore, God and an equal share their infinite goodness with a third equal.

So, there must be three equals in the Godhead, and those are the three divine persons.

In response, Aquinas rejects (49). As he sees it, God shared God's goodness appropriately by creating the world. There need not be an equal.

> The infinite goodness of God is expressed even in the production of creatures, since it is an act of infinite power to produce from nothing. For if God shares himself by his infinite goodness, it is not necessary that something infinite come forth from God, but only that something receive divine goodness in the way appropriate to it.[54]

4.4.2   Aquinas's Argument for the Trinity?

Despite his aversion to arguments for the Trinity, commentators have noticed that in the *Summa*, Aquinas provides all the pieces to construct his own argument that God must be triune.[55] Recall that, for Aquinas, conceiving of the divine essence is natural: It is done automatically by

---

[54] ST I 32.1 ad 2: *Bonitas enim infinita Dei manifestatur etiam in productione creaturarum: quia infinitae virtutis est ex nihilo producere. Non enim oportet, si infinita bonitate se communicat, quod aliquid infinitum a Deo procedat: sed secundum modum suum recipiat divinam bonitatem.* See also ibid., *Similiter etiam quod dicitur, quod sine consortio non potest esse iucunda possessio alicuius boni, locum habet quando in una persona non invenitur perfecta bonitas; unde indiget, ad plenum iucunditatis bonitatem, bono alicuius alterius consociati sibi.*

[55] Vagaggini, "La hantise"; Richard, *The Problem of an Apologetical Perspective*; even Milbank and Pickstock, *Truth in Aquinas*, pp. 52–3.

any divine person who has the opportunity. And the Father has the opportunity, so the Father conceives of the divine essence.

58 For any divine person x, if x has the opportunity to initiate an act of conceiving of the divine essence, x initiates an act of conceiving of the divine essence (from [6] above).

59 The Father has the opportunity to initiate an act of conceiving of the divine essence.

60 Therefore, the Father initiates an act of conceiving of the divine essence.

In the Godhead, though, conceiving of the divine essence results in another divine person. So, the Father produces the Son through conceiving of the divine essence.

61 For any divine person x, if x initiates an act of conceiving of the divine essence, x produces another divine person y (from [2] above).

62 The Father initiates an act of conceiving of the divine essence.

63 Therefore, the Father produces another divine person, the Son.

So, there must be at least two divine persons in the Godhead: the Father and the Son. We could continue like this, constructing further steps to show that, by Aquinas's own reasoning, there must also be a third person (the Spirit), who arises from love, that these persons are distinct, and that no other persons are produced in the Godhead.

It seems then, that Aquinas's own claims in the *Summa* build up to form an argument for the necessary existence of the Trinity. And hence, it seems that Aquinas should affirm this:

64 Without revelation, it can be known that God is triune.

And that contradicts (45). If Aquinas really believes (45), then he must think at least one of the premises I just listed does not qualify as a necessary reason. But which one? It is hard to see how he could say any of them are not necessary.

4.5 Conclusion

As I noted at the outset, Aquinas's account of the Trinity in the *Summa* is mature, concise, and self-contained. Earlier writings do not have the same content, succinct character, or proof-like structure that we find here. For the Aquinas of the *Summa*, divine thinking and loving are naturally occurring activities in God, which produce a Trinity of persons.

CHAPTER 5

Aquinas on the Soul: Some Intriguing Conundrums

Marilyn McCord Adams

In the First Part of his Treatise on Human Nature (I 75–89), Aquinas lays out his account of soul and soul–body relationship in considerable detail. His core idea involves the unlikely marriage of two theses: that the intellectual soul is incorporeal and subsisting (I 75.2) and that the intellectual soul is the form of the body (I 76.1). These claims can easily appear contradictory. Moreover, Aquinas's arguments for the one make assumptions that seem to be at odds with premises invoked to defend the other. In what follows, I will first show how his case for each is rooted in his fundamental philosophical commitments. Then I will examine four problems that provoke Aquinas to adapt and develop Aristotelian ideas in ingenious ways. I will close by setting Aquinas's conclusions up against those of the prominent positions against which he argues, the better to appreciate his theoretical choices.

5.1 Preliminaries

In treating the soul, Aquinas proceeds scientifically and aims for a high degree of systematic integration.

5.1.1 The Data of Experience

Unsurprisingly, for Aquinas, there are phenomena to be saved, givens of experience that are not to be explained away (the way Cartesian and contemporary physics explain away colors). Common sense takes for granted that

(E1) human beings are living and embodied; and
(E2) human beings are subjects of vital functions: vegetative, sensory, and intellectual.

In working out details, Aquinas maintains further that

(E3) we experience that *we* abstract from sense images; and

(E4) we experience that – when we think abstract thoughts –we turn to sense images.

Aquinas declares that the soul is the first principle of life, that by which living things engage in vital functions (I 75.1c). His task – as he sees it – is to probe its essence or ontological status, its powers (*virtutes* or *potentiae*), and its functions (*operationes*) (I 75 intro).

5.1.2 Theoretical Desiderata

Aquinas brings to his reasoning about the human soul distinctive assumptions about what any adequate theory should underwrite. These include the theses that:

(D1) the intellectual soul is incorporeal and subsistent (i.e., it does not cease to exist when separated from the body);

(D2) the intellectual soul and human body are related in such a way as to form a per se unity; and

(D3) each human being has its own intellectual soul.

(D1) and (D2) are philosophically driven claims. (D3) is a common-sense default. (D1) and (D3) together uphold the Christian commitment to individual post-mortem survival, while the trio – (D1), (D2), and (D3) – join other premises to lend support to Christian belief in bodily resurrection.

5.1.3 Aristotelian Scientific Method

Although Aquinas's introduction and the order of the questions suggest that first he will investigate the soul's essence (first in relation to itself [I 75], next in relation to the human body [I 76]), then its powers (I 77–83), and finally its functions (I 84–9), Aristotelian scientific method implies that the order of discovery is the reverse. In Aristotelian science, investigation starts with acts and functional patterns. Always-or-for-the-most-part functional regularities require explanation by some formal functional principle. The Aristotelian default is to locate such formal functional principles in the functioning thing (I 76.1 obj. 4 and c). Moreover, congeries of functions (and – by inference – functional powers) always-or-for-the-most-part travel together, and this in turn requires explanation in terms of a substantial form in which such powers are rooted and from which they "emanate" or "flow" (I 77.6c, ad 1, and ad 3).

Thus, Aquinas recognizes within Aristotelian substances a certain teleological structure. For Aquinas, the best nature is identical with its functioning. God as pure act is always actually functioning. God's essence is identical with God's *esse* (I 3.4c), which is also identical with God's *intelligere* (I 14.3c) and *velle* (I 19.1c). But everything other than God is a composite of act and potency (of essence and *esse*, of substance and accident). For each species there are characteristic perfecting forms and functional states. The powers and bodily structures (if any) are for the sake of the functions. Thus, in human being, the senses are for the sake of intellectual functions, and bodily organs are for the sake of the sensory and ultimately for the intellectual functions (I 76.5c; I 84.4c; I 89.1c).

For Aquinas as for Aristotle, powers and their root substantial form are in the thing to which the function is attributed, and functions are attributed to what possesses the powers, to that in which the powers and their formal root are found (I 76.1 obj. 4 and c). The form by which something primarily functions is the form of the thing to which the function belongs (I 76.1c; cf. I 75.4c). Put precisely,

(P1) a thing X is the subject of functional activity F *if and only if* the formal functional principle for F-ing is in X.

5.1.4   Distinctive Metaphysical Assumptions

Certainly, Aquinas's conclusions about the soul rely on distinctive metaphysical assumptions. First, God is pure act. Therefore God's essence is identical with God's *esse* (I 3.4c). But creatable essences receive any actuality they have from God. Accordingly, creatable essences are not identical with their *esse*, but in potentiality with respect to receiving their *esse*. Because what is received is received after the manner of the receiver, creatable essences are potency limiting act (limiting *esse* to *esse hominem* or *esse bovem*). For Aquinas, it is essence–*esse* composition that marks the fundamental divide between Creator and creature (*De Ente et Essentia*, Chapters 4–5).[1]

Second, if God is utterly simple (I 3.7c), Aquinas recognizes that what is distinctive about Aristotelian substances is their essential unity: They are one per se. Because material substances are generable and corruptible,

---

[1] Roland-Gosselin edition.

and because Aristotelian change presupposes that there is something that persists through the change, material substances are composites of what persists through substantial change (namely, prime matter) and what does not (namely, substantial form). But how can *a composite* have essential unity? Aquinas explains that it is because substantial form is that through which a substance gets its actuality *(esse)* and is constituted as the very thing that it is. Prime matter is pure potentiality and receives any actuality it has through the constituting substantial form. For Aquinas, the per se unity of material substances would be spoiled if there were more than one constituent through which it received actuality – if there were more than one constituent that had an actuality of its own. Once the substantial form has constituted the substance in actuality as the very thing it is, any further forms to be added would be accidents. Aquinas draws the corollary conclusion that there can be at most one substantial form per substance thing (I 76.3c; I 76.4c).

For Aquinas, prime matter in itself is pure potentiality and so is of itself indivisible. It receives its divisibility into parts and its extension (so that it has "part outside part") from the quantity that inheres in it. Material substances are extended; and while matter has part outside part, that does not mean that substantial form united to it is extended. On the contrary, Aquinas reasons that since the substantial form is the source of the *esse* and constitution of the whole composite, the substantial form perfects not only the whole composite but each and every one of its parts. Hand and heart, liver and brain are alike human, so long as they are unsevered from the whole. This is the philosophical reason why not only the intellectual soul but any substantial form is whole in the whole composite and whole in each of its parts (I 76.8c).

5.1.5 Apt Cognitive Psychology

If powers and essence are inferred from always-or-for-the-most-part functional regularities, Aquinas's principal strategies for securing (D1) and (D2) rely on his analysis of Aristotelian cognitive psychology, according to which cradle-to-grave human cognition begins with sensation, which is required to make intelligible contents relevantly present to the soul's intellectual power. Aquinas takes over the idea that

(P2) ante-mortem human cognition involves literal in-formation.

As Aristotle says, sensory cognition involves the reception of sensible form without the sensible matter. Sensible forms have natural (characterizing)

existence in material substances. But sensible forms cannot act directly
on sense organs, because there is no action at a distance. Instead, they act
directly on spatially proximate media (e.g., air, water) to propagate sensible species (either the same form [SCG II 50.7] or a likeness of it [I 85.4c;
I 88.1 ad 2]) through the medium to the sense organ, in such a way that
sensible forms have intentional (non-characterizing) existence first in the
medium and then in the sense organ. Sensation gives rise to sense images
or phantasms stored in the imagination and sorted by the common sense.
But Aquinas takes it to be axiomatic that

(P3) forms in a material subject are not actually intelligible (I 79.3c;
SCG II 50.2–3; *De Ente et Essentia*, Chapter 4, p. 31).

Because phantasms exist in modifications of a corporeal organ and so,
by (P2), are not actually intelligible, they cannot by themselves actualize the intellect's potentiality for understanding. Following Aristotle,
Aquinas posits the agent intellect to be power to illumine the phantasms,
to abstract the intelligible content from its material conditions, and to
impress an intelligible species on the possible intellect. In understanding
the universal (e.g., what it is to be human, what it is to be a cow), it is
necessary for the intellect to turn to the phantasms to see the universal
nature existing in the particulars (I 84.7c; I 85.1c and ad 3–5).

Thus, phantasms are that in the presence of which the intelligible content is abstracted, and that to which the intellect turns to understand the
nature in the particular. The agent intellect is the formal active principle
to abstract and impress the intelligible content on the possible intellect,
while the possible intellect is the formal passive principle which receives
the intelligible species and thereby forms a concept. Aquinas emphasizes:
The abstracted intelligible species is *not the object* of understanding, but
that by which the material quiddity is understood (I 85.2c).

5.2   The Soul Is Incorporeal and Subsisting

For Aristotle, to be is either to do or to be able to do. What cannot function
alone, cannot exist alone. Of course, both Aristotle and Aquinas often say
that the *proper* subject of functional activity is the whole per-se-unified substance (I 75.2 ad 2). When the soul is separated from the human body
at death, the whole human being (temporarily) ceases to be. Happily,
it is possible to distinguish between *proximate* and *remote* subjects. For
example, one might say that the surface of a body (which is an accident
in the category of quantity) is the proximate subject of color, while the

individual corporeal substance is the remote and proper subject of color. Although Aquinas does not explicitly deploy these distinctions here, they help us to make his point precise. What is at stake is whether or not there is any functional activity of which the soul alone is the proximate subject. For an Aristotelian, there being such is a necessary condition of the soul's subsistence. Organic functions such as digestion and sensations are non-starters because they have the living organ itself as their proximate subject. Aquinas concludes that non-human animal souls are not subsistent, because they are first principles only of organic functions and so are forms "immersed" in matter (I 75.3c). Aquinas's argument that the human intellectual soul is incorporeal and subsisting turns on his contention that intellectual cognition is essentially inorganic and so is "an activity that the body does not share" (I 75.2c).

Aquinas takes this conclusion – that intellectual cognition is essentially inorganic – to be firmly underwritten by his cognitive psychology. Thus, Aquinas argues that angels cannot be matter–form composites because understanding is – for them – an essential function, and no matter–form composite can be the proximate subject of understanding (*De Ente*, Chapter 4, pp. 30–2 and SCG II 50.2). His reasons are that (P2) understanding is by in-formation, and (P3) no form inhering in matter is actually intelligible, because matter is potency limiting act. Certainly, Averroës had argued and Aquinas agreed that the proper objects of understanding include universal quiddities. If the proximate subject of understanding were a matter–form composite, any form received into it would be re-individuated. It would not be universal and so could not be a principle by which a universal is cognized (I 75.5c; SCG II 50.2 and 5; II 59.2).

The argument Aquinas actually gives in *Summa Theologiae* I 75.2c seems weaker. In it, he appeals to a more particular cognitive-psychological principle that

(P4) the proximate subject that cognizes items of a genus G cannot itself be naturally characterized by features falling under genus G.

Aquinas motivates (P4) with the example of taste: When we are ill, the tongue is infected with bitter humors, and the bitterness of the humors interferes with our perception of sweet taste in the food. His argument also relies on the assumption that the natural object of ante-mortem human understanding is the quiddities of material things. Thus, he reasons by analogy: If the proximate subject of human understanding were corporeal, the subject's own corporeal nature would interfere with its grasping the material quiddities of other things. One difficulty is that the example of taste muddies the waters, because Aquinas does think that the organ of taste is naturally characterized by flavors, even though it perceives flavors (I 78.3c).

Having argued that the human soul has an activity that the body does not share, Aquinas contends that this is not only necessary but sufficient for subsistence, because

(P5) nothing can function per se that does not subsist per se.

Once again, Aquinas attempts to persuade by way of illustration. When we put a kettle on the stove, we do not say that the heat heats, but rather that what is hot (namely, the fire) heats. Because heat is a quality that does not subsist per se but rather depends for its existence on the substance in which it inheres (namely, fire), heat does not function per se either (I 75.2c). Per se subsistence is a *necessary* condition of functional independence.

But do Aquinas's arguments from cognitive psychology that the intellectual soul is the proximate subject of understanding establish that the soul is functionally independent enough to imply per se subsistence? Objectors contend that other aspects of Aquinas's own cognitive psychology support a negative answer. For he maintains that ante-mortem the human intellect acquires intelligible content only by abstraction from phantasms (I 75.6 ad 3; I 89.1c and ad 3; I 89.2 ad 1). If the soul were separated from the body, it would not be able to receive intelligible species this way (I 75.1 obj. 2). Doesn't Aristotelian method lay it down that "nature does not fall short"? Doesn't that mean that the subject of a function should include everything required to carry out the function?

Aquinas's ingenious reply calls on readers to distinguish between what is required for being the kind of thing that can be a subject of cognition, and what is required for object-access. To qualify as a subject of a certain kind of cognition, a thing must be such that it would be able to cognize its object were that object relevantly present to it. The cognitive power does not and need not itself include power to make the object always to be relevantly present. Vision is power to see colors, but it does not include power always to make colors actually present or actually visible. Vision is vision even if it sees no colors in the dark. Ante-mortem phantasms function to present the object. Senses and imagination are *object-presenters* – the cognitive-psychological mechanisms required to make the object relevantly present. But neither senses, nor the imagination constitutes part of the *subject* of understanding (I 75.1 ad 2).

Aquinas has established that the intellectual soul meets the necessary condition for per se subsistence: namely, that it is the proximate subject of intellectual functions. His arguments for incorruptibility seem to presuppose that this is sufficient for per se subsistence, however. Thus, he argues that corruption per se belongs to composites and involves the separation of their matter and form(s) (I 75.6c; SCG II 55.2). Accidental forms and substantial forms "immersed" in matter are corruptible per accidens, because they exist in a subject and depend on that subject for their existence. They are corrupted per accidens when their subject or the composite of which they are a part is corrupted. But if the human intellectual soul subsists per se, its existence is not thus dependent on any subject it informs or composite of which it is a part. Aquinas maintains that it cannot be corrupted per se either, because as subsistent its actuality *(esse)* pertains to it per se, and it cannot be separated from itself (I 75.6c).

5.3   The Per Se Unity of Human Being

It is one thing to establish (as Aquinas thinks he has) that the human intellectual soul is incorporeal, per se subsistent, and incorruptible. It is another to show what this subsistent intellectual principle has to do with human beings and human bodies. In *Summa Theologiae* (I 76), Aquinas argues that the intellectual soul is the one and only substantial form of the human composite.

Aquinas's strategy is straightforward. He begins with experience, with the fact that we experience in ourselves that (E2) the same human being senses as understands. In *Summa Theologiae* I 76.1, Aquinas could be more fully explicit. But his reasoning there assumes not only the experienced fact (E2) that human beings sense and understand, but a philosophical interpretation of that fact: namely, that where human beings are concerned, both sensation and intellectual cognition are *essential* functions. Common sense tells us that there is no sensation without the right sort of body. Aquinas's Aristotelian cognitive psychology gives us a distinctive philosophical explanation: namely, that living sense organs are the proximate subjects of sensation. If sensation is an essential function of human beings, we already have the conclusion that what human beings are includes a hylomorphic composite (I 75.4c, I 76.1c).

Yet, Aristotle's definition – human beings are rational animals – implies that intellectual cognition is essential to human beings; indeed, that it is the function that differentiates human beings from other animals. And Aquinas has just argued in I 75.2c, that the intellectual soul is incorporeal and subsisting. Hylomorphic composites are generable and corruptible per se, but the intellectual soul is immune to generation and corruption. Where human beings are concerned, what can the proximate subject of sensation (a living sense organ) and the hylomorphic compos-ite of which it is a part, have to do with the proximate subject of intel-lectual functioning? If each were a *hoc aliquid*, if each were a complete substance in its own right, how could the per se unity of a human being be secured?

Once again, for Aquinas, it is cognitive psychology that comes to the rescue. For he maintains that the above-sketched scenario involving abstraction from and turning toward the phantasms is not only the *actual* way human beings come to understand the quiddities of material things; it is the *natural* way, the way that pertains to human being *essentially* (I 75.6 ad 3; I 89.1c and ad 3; I 89.2 ad 1). The Aristotelian slogan "nature does not fall short" is usually taken to mean that nature builds into a substance-kind all of the equipment needed for it to be able to per-form its natural functions. It is natural to angels to understand by means of intelligible species infused into them by God at their creation (I 55.2c and ad 1). They do not need sensation to deliver up images from which intelligible species can be abstracted. In themselves, therefore, angelic substances can be utterly incorporeal. But as intellects go, human intel-lects are "bottom of the line." In this present state it is natural for human intellects to begin as *tabulae rasae* and have to acquire content by abstrac-tion from sense experience. Aquinas's conclusion is that an organic body with sensory powers and functions must be built into the individual sub-stance to which the human intellect itself belongs. Aquinas thinks that the only way for this to happen metaphysically is for the intellectual soul to be the substantial form of the human body. Moreover, because – for Aquinas – per se unified Aristotelian substances have one and only one substantial form, he concludes that the intellectual soul is the one and only substantial form of the human composite (I 76.3c; I 76.4c).

5.4   Functional Dependence or Functional Independence: Which Is It?

The first problem with Aquinas's arguments sits right on the surface. How can Aquinas consistently reason from functional independence of the body to subsistence in *Summa Theologiae* I 75.2 and from functional dependence on the body to form of the body in I 76.1? Aquinas has an answer to this question, although he does not confront it with optimal directness. In I 75.2, Aquinas is arguing that the intellectual soul is functionally independent in the sense that it can and must be the subject of understanding all by itself; understanding is an inorganic activity. In I 76.1, Aquinas is relying on his claim that the intellectual soul depends on the organic body and the senses for object-presentation. Aquinas is not saying that the latter are built into the proximate subject of cognition, but rather into the per se unified substance whole that is the proper subject of understanding.

Moreover, for Aquinas, there is a difference between sensory and intellectual functioning in this regard. Sensible qualities actually have mind-independent existence. Where they actually exist and circumstances are such as to make them actually sensible (as colors are when illuminated), the only remaining question is whether they are relevantly proximate to the sense organs. Neither Aquinas nor Aristotle believes that powers to insure relevant proximity have to be built into the animal substance that is the proper subject of sensation. But Aquinas thinks that universals do not have mind-independent existence. Rather material quiddities have mind-independent existence only in particulars, where – by (P3) – they are not actually intelligible. Thus, the mere existence and presence of material substances is not enough to make material quiddities relevantly present to the intellect. Any cognitive inputs such material substances make will first be to the senses, and these will have to be processed to make them actually intelligible. Aquinas is maintaining that since it is natural to ante-mortem humans to understand material quiddities (I 12.4 ad 4; I 84.8c; I 85.1c), the equipment necessary for receiving and processing such inputs will have to be built into what a human being is. In general, animal-natures do not have to build in powers to make sure the objects of cognition actually make inputs into the animal's cognitive apparatus. But if such inputs from the objects have to be processed in order to be digestible by the animal's cognitive powers, the animal-nature has to include processing-powers and any bodily apparatus required.

5.5   The Form of Some Matter?

There is a second difficulty. If the intellectual soul is the form of the body, then it is the form of some matter. But if – according to Aquinas's cognitive psychology, in particular, (P2) and (P3) – no matter-form composite can be the proximate subject of understanding, then won't being the form of some matter be just as bad? If the intellectual soul unites with prime matter signed by quantity to form an individual human being, won't any form that is received into the intellectual soul likewise be received into matter, be rendered only potentially intelligible?

Aquinas's daring answer to these questions is "no." Metaphysically, for Aquinas, the substantial form is the internal root of all of the dynamic and static structures of the substance. Porphyry divides predicables into genus, species, differentia, propria, and accidents. Because those structures are not the substance but are proper to the substance in that they are conditions of the possibility of functioning characteristic of that substance-kind, they count as "propria" in Porphyry's scheme. Because they are not the substance but are proper to the substance, they count as accidents in Aristotle's categorial scheme (I 77.1 ad 5). Aquinas holds that these structuring elements emanate from the substantial form which is somehow their active cause (I 77.6c and ad 3; I 77.7c and ad 1). Moreover, the many emanate from the one substantial form in a certain order (I 77.4c): in material substances, quantity which shapes up the matter into body, and then qualities which give the body an appropriate "complexion" to receive vital powers (which are qualities of the second species). Nevertheless, because Aristotelian substances come into existence at an instant, this ordering is not a temporal ordering. Rather, the sequence of structures is naturally consequent upon or a natural resultant of the substantial form (I 77.7 ad 1).

When Aquinas frequently declares that the intellectual soul is "the form of the body," he is not assuming that the body is already a substance or *hoc aliquid* to which the soul is added as a form. Rather, he understands that the human body is naturally consequent upon the union of the intellectual soul with its matter. The human body is part of a composite substance metaphysically constituted by the intellectual soul and its matter. Since a thing cannot exist without its essential metaphysical constituents, the human body cannot exist separated from the soul. Aquinas does think that the intellectual soul is a *hoc aliquid*, if that means only that it is subsistent. But usually *hoc aliquid* refers to a *complete* individual of a substance nature (I 75.2 ad 1). The intellectual soul is subsistent, but – because it is the substantial form of the body – it is not a complete substance individual but rather the principal constituent of the composite substance individual. Because hylomorphism keeps the body from being a substance independent of the intellectual soul and prevents the intellectual soul from being a complete substance individual, Aquinas thinks he is in a position to say that a human being is not two things, but one.

Because the intellectual soul is a *substantial* form, Aquinas insists that it is whole in the whole composite and whole in its parts (I 76.8c).

But the same is not true of all of the powers emanating from the soul. Aquinas maintains (P1) that the proximate subject of the power is the proximate subject of the acts. Since organic functions (e.g., digestion, sensation) belong to the living organs, organic powers have the living organs as their proximate subjects, too (I 77.5c). When Aquinas says that the intellectual soul is the form of the body, he is also expressing his conviction that the body's vital powers are emanated into it by its constituting substantial form, the intellectual soul. Sensible species are received into material subjects. But the subject of intellectual cognitions is the soul alone; so active and passive intellectual powers belong to the soul alone and not to the composite. Aquinas is insisting that just because the intellectual soul unites with matter and emanates static and dynamic structures into it, this does not keep the intellectual soul from having activities and powers that the body does not share. Aquinas is claiming that the same substantial form can be the root principle of both organic and inorganic acts (I 76.1 ad 1–4).

5.6   Numerically Many Human Intellectual Souls?

Because Aquinas takes matter signed by quantity to be the principle of individuation (*De Ente*, Chapter 2, pp. 10–11; I 76.2 ad 1), he concludes that incorporeal substances such as angels cannot be numerically multiplied within the same species. If Gabriel and Michael are two archangels, they are angels of distinct specific kinds (I 50.4c and ad 1). If the human intellectual soul were not the form of some matter, there could be only one intellectual soul – or, as Averroës thought, one agent intellect and one possible intellect – for the whole human race. Aquinas claims it as an advantage of his hylomorphic hypothesis – that the intellectual soul is the form of some matter – that it can accommodate his third desideratum. The substantial form of cow is numerically multiplied in distinct hunks of matter, so that the bovine soul of Beulah the cow is numerically distinct from the bovine soul of Ferdinand the bull. Likewise, it is their relation to matter that individuates the intellectual souls of Plato and Socrates.

Problems both of clarity and consistency arise, however.

5.6.1   *Which Relation?*

Aquinas is coy about just what this relation to matter is. In his early work *De Ente et Essentia*, Aquinas speaks of intellectual souls being individuated "on the occasion" of their union with matter (*De Ente*, Chapter 5, p. 39), which makes it sound as if the souls' actual union with matter does not play any explanatory role. In *Summa Theologiae* I 76.2 ad 1, he says that the intellectual soul does not have matter from which *(ex qua)* but it is the form *of* some matter (genitive case). This may be an allusion to Aquinas's contention that the intellectual soul as subsistent is not naturally generable or corruptible but is created *ex nihilo* directly by God (I 90.2c; I 90.3c). He adds that intellectual souls are numerically multiplied "*according to* the division of matter" (I 76.2 ad 1), which might be contrasted with "*because of* the division of matter." In any event, the required relation cannot be *actual* union with this hunk of matter as opposed to that, because the soul's individuation needs to persist not only through its existence in different hunks of matter over time (as when the human being grows from infancy to adult stature) but also through its separation from any and all hunks of matter at death (I 76.2 obj. 2).

Perhaps the most charitable hypothesis is that Aquinas thinks human intellectual souls are individuated by their contrasting aptitudes to unite over time with one series of hunks of matter as opposed to another series. The aptitude would first be expressed by the intellectual soul actually inhering in the relevant hunk, but then – after death and before resurrection – it would revert to a mere aptitude. Moreover, the aptitude would pertain to the intellectual soul even if, contrary to nature and by divine power, it existed without ever being united to matter. The reader would be left to wonder where these aptitudes come from and what their ontological status is. What is clear is this: Aquinas thinks that the *esse* belongs primarily and permanently to the intellectual soul and is only temporarily shared with relevant hunks of matter (I 76.2 ad 3).

5.6.2   Individuated Subjects, Universal Objects?

The individuation of human souls also raises cognitive-psychological difficulties. Given (P2), the proximate subject of understanding must not be a matter–form composite lest the form received be re-materialized so that it is neither – by (P3) – actually intelligible nor universal. But even if the individuation of the intellectual soul does not involve a relation to matter that would make the proximate subject of thought material, it would still seem to keep received forms from being universal. If Plato's intellectual soul is numerically distinct from that of Socrates, then – even when they are both thinking about what it is to be a cow – the intelligible species received into Plato's intellectual soul is numerically distinct from the intelligible species received into the soul of Socrates. Each intelligible species would be individual, so that neither would be universal. How then could the received form enable either Plato or Socrates to think about universals? How could it be true that they are both thinking the same thought (I 76.2 obj. 3)?

Aquinas's reply relies on a distinction between the ontological status of intelligible species from their representative capacities. The form that Plato receives may be numerically distinct from the form that Socrates receives, but the two intelligible species are exactly alike and so equivalent in representative capacities. Although the received forms are themselves particulars, what they represent is universal (I 76.2 ad 4 and ad 5). This response seems to undercut (P2), however. If particulars can represent universals, why insist on the immateriality of the intellectual soul?

In any case, Aquinas insists, the individuation of human intellectual souls has cognitive-psychological advantages, because it explains how – at a given time – Socrates could think a thought that was the contradictory opposite of the thought Plato was thinking, as well as how one man could know something of which the other was ignorant.

5.7 Expanded Cognitive Modalities

To be is to do or at least to be able to do. How then can the intellectual soul subsist in such a way as to survive separation from the body (as Aquinas claims in I 75.2c), when its natural way of understanding involves dependence on the body for the sense images from which it abstracts the intelligible species by which it thinks, the sense images to which it turns when it understands (I 75.6 obj. and ad 3; I 89.1c)? *Postmortem*, how would the intellectual soul even be *able* to do anything? In SCG II 97.2, Aquinas suggests something stronger: that actually to be is actually to do. He declares that for every living substance, there is some vital function that – by its nature – always actually pertains to it. Separate souls would no longer be party to nutrition or sensation. Understanding would be the only vital function left to them. Cut off from natural access to intelligible species, how could they continue to *be* at all?

5.7.1 Separate Souls

This time, Aquinas' solution is to complicate his cognitive psychology. There are different modes of understanding for different modes of being. In this present cradle-to-grave state, the natural mode of understanding is by abstraction from and turning to the phantasms. But separated from the body between death and resurrection, the intellectual soul will understand the way the angels do, through intelligible species infused by God (I 89.1 c and ad 3; I 89.2 ad 1; I 75.6 ad 3).

In his *Quaestio Disputata de Anima*, Aquinas expands on this idea, using two models. According to the first, understanding involves cognitive power and intelligible species that carry the intellectual content. Where God is concerned, God's essence is identical with God's *esse*, which is identical with God's *intelligere*. The divine essence virtually contains all beings insofar as creatable natures are at bottom ways of imperfectly imitating the divine essence. The divine essence *is* the intelligible species through which God understands all things. In the order of explanation, God first understands the divine essence in itself. Next, God understands the divine essence as many ways imitable, so that the divine ideas are secondary objects of God's thought through which God comprehends not only creatable natures but also creatable individuals (I 14.5c; I 14.6c; I 15.2c). Created intellects, whose *esse* is not identical with their functioning (*operari*), are in potency with respect to understanding. For each creatable separate substance, there is an essential quantity of intellectual power. In order for separate substances to understand clearly, their potency must be actualized by intelligible species that are proportioned to their power.

According to the second model, intelligible content is contained in the intellectual light.[2] God is pure light which distinctly contains and understands all intelligible contents. Creatable separate intellects are participated lights which contain intelligible contents diffusely. For them to have a distinct and determinate thought, intelligible species are required. Depending on how bright the light or dim the wit, creatable separate intellects require fewer or more intelligible species to have determinate thoughts of intelligible contents (DA 18c; *In IV Sent.* d.49 2.6 ad 3; I 89.1c).

Either way, optimal functioning for creatable intellects requires intelligible species that are proportioned to their intellectual power. Aquinas explains:

> if a lower intellectual substance had forms as universal as the higher, its knowledge would remain incomplete, because it does not have as much intellectual power. It would understand only in a general way and would not be able to move from those fewer [and more universal] species it had to particulars. (DA 15c; see also *In IV Sent.* d.49 2.1 ad 2)

---

[2] For an examination of these two models, see Smit, "Aquinas's Abstractionism."

What opens the way for Aquinas to solve the "separate souls" problem, is that it is metaphysically possible for a lower intellectual substance to receive intelligible species proportioned to a higher power. The species proportioned to human intellectual power are those acquired by abstraction from and applied by turning to sense images. They are what give humans clear, determinate thoughts. And this is why, Aquinas insists, the soul's union with the body is not merely per accidens (I 89.1c; *In IV Sent.* d.50 1.1c). After death, we retain the intelligible species we acquired that way (I 89.6c and ad 1), but we are also infused with a supply of intelligible species that are proportioned to brighter separate substances. Our dimmer wits will not be able to get as much out of them as angels would. Consequently, our new information will allow us only imperfect – confused and general – knowledge of substance kinds. Separate souls have knowledge only of those individuals for whom they have a particular attachment (e.g., through previous knowledge or affection, through some natural disposition or divine ordinance) (I 89.3c; I 89.4c and ad 2–3).

Is this alternative mode of understanding *natural?* Systematically, would it not be advantageous to say that both modes pertain to the intellectual soul by nature – that when embodied, it naturally understands by using phantasms; when separate, it naturally understands by means of infused species? If natural, the infused species would be "owed" to the separate soul in the same way they are "owed" to the angels. Its receiving them would be secured by general divine policy that (always or for the most part) endows things with what their natural functioning requires. If natural, why not take a further step and allow for infused intelligible species that are proportioned to our weaker intellectual powers? Systematically, there is a drawback to these proposals: If understanding by (proportioned) infused species were natural to us, why would the soul be united to the body at all?

Turning to the texts, we find Aquinas equivocating on this issue. On the one hand, he declares that "the nature of the soul is not changed by the death of the body" but remains the same in different states, just as much as the nature of a light body remains the same whether it is in its natural place up high or violently thrust lower down. If abstraction from and turning to phantasms is natural, then understanding through infused species is "outside our nature" *(praeter naturam)*. It is a superior way of understanding absolutely speaking, but it is not better for us (I 89.1c).

On the other hand, in *Quaestio Disputata de Anima*, Aquinas announces that the separate soul's "essence pertains to the genus of separate intelligible substances and has the same mode of subsistence,

although it is least in this genus" (DA 18c), which seems to contradict his contention that the intellectual soul is the substantial form of
the human body and so the principal constituent of a substance in the
genus body and so itself in the genus body by reduction. And in *Summa
Theologiae* I 89.1–2, he speaks of cognition through infused species as the
mode "natural" to separate souls (I 89.1 ad 3; I 89.2c). He also remarks
that the separate soul's cognition will be somehow "freer" because the
purity of its understanding will no longer be obstructed by bodily dis-
tractions (I 89.2 ad 1). In this present state, we are able to abstract only
those intelligible contents that are common to material things. But,
Aquinas holds, material and immaterial things have nothing real in common. However many times we abstract from the contents presented in
the phantasms, however abstract the concept, we will never get to a concept univocally common to both material and immaterial things. Rather,
in this present state, we conceive of immaterial things only by analogy
(I 13.5c and ad 1; I 88.2 ad 1; I 88.3c). When the soul is separated from
the body, it will be freed from such restrictions. Receiving infused species of immaterial substances themselves, the separate soul will be able
to conceive of them non-analogically although not so clearly as the more
powerful angelic intellects do (I 89.2 ad 2). Aquinas affirms that the separate soul will be able to understand by turning not to the phantasms but
to things that are intelligible in themselves (because they are immaterial)
(I 89.1c), and so will be able – among other things – to understand itself
through itself (I 89.2c).

5.7.2   *Supernatural Cognition*

Embodied or separate, both modes of intellectual cognition have created intellects understanding through received intelligible species. This
much is natural to created intellects. But our supernatural end is beatific
vision of the divine essence. Aquinas concludes that for this, yet another
mode of cognition, a supernatural one without intelligible species, will be
required. Intelligible species can serve as media only where they are proportionate to the thing understood. Because God is infinite, nothing that
inheres in a created subject could mediate a proper cognition of God.
Happily, because God is pure act, utterly subsistent and actually intelligible, the divine essence itself can be the form by which it is understood (*In
IV Sent.* d.49 2.1c, ad 3 and ad 6). What is required for understanding is
not (P2) inherence, but cognitive contact, a union of "cognitive presence"
of the knowable to the knower (*In IV Sent.* d.49 2.6c).

If the size-gap between finite and infinite is the problem, Aquinas's worries are not over, for he has insisted that the form by which an intellect understands must be properly proportioned, not only to the object, but to the cognitive power. Will the size-gap not rule out any and all created intellects as subjects of such cognition? Aquinas concedes that for humans and angels to enjoy the beatific vision, an upgrade in cognitive power will be required. Created intellects will receive the *lumen gloriae*, a supernatural disposition that exceeds any and every natural faculty (*In IV Sent.* d.49 2.6c; 2.7c). But this is an incomplete response. For whatever is infused is itself a creature. However the *lumen gloriae* compares with created intellects and their natural powers, it will still not be proportionate to the divine essence, which is the form by which it is to understand. Perhaps Aquinas's best response would be that proper proportion is required for perfect understanding. Perfect understanding of the divine essence belongs only to God (I 14.3c), while beatific vision falls short of comprehension.

5.8   Charting the Options

Aquinas works hard to make his conclusions about the soul cohere with his own foundational commitments. At the same time, he develops his positive position over and against those of distinguished predecessors. One curious feature of Aquinas's *Summa Theologiae* discussion is that he not only surveys an array of opposing views; he keeps bringing them up even after he has firmly rejected one or more of their central theses. However much Aquinas may want readers to agree with him, his reviews of Plato, Aristotle, Avicenna, and Averroës show them paying different prices to win contrasting advantages. Despite his trenchant criticisms, Aquinas allows us to see their theories as worthy competitors that achieve systematic coherence in their own right.

To weigh what Aquinas was affirming, it helps to reconsider what he was rejecting. For present purposes, it is enough to compare and contrast the opposing theories along five parameters: the nature of human being, the location of intelligible content, the housing of active and passive intellectual principles, the relation of intellectual principles to sensory principles, and the cognitive psychology of human understanding.

5.8.1   Aquinas

For Aquinas adapting Aristotle, a human being is a rational animal. The intelligible content human intellects are after ante-mortem is the quiddities of material things, which really exist only in particulars of those substance kinds, where they are – by (P2) – only potentially intelligible. This gives rise to an epistemic-access problem, which Aquinas meets with an Aristotelian cognitive psychology according to which the agent intellect abstracts intelligible species from sense images and impresses them on the possible intellect that receives them and forms a concept. To understand that quiddity existing in a particular, the intellect turns back to the phantasms from which the intelligible species was abstracted. For Aquinas, both the agent intellect and the possible intellect are inorganic powers that emanate from and exist in the intellectual soul as in a proximate subject, while the intellectual soul is the form of the body (which satisfies [D2]) and as such is individuated and numerically multiplied in numerically distinct human beings (which accommodates [D3]). Because the proximate subject of understanding must be immaterial, the intellectual soul has an activity the body does not share and so is incorporeal and subsisting (hence, [D1]). By contrast, for Aquinas, the proximate subject of both sensation and imagination is the soul–body composite, in particular, a vital organ.

5.8.2   Plato

By contrast, for Plato, a human being is a soul using a body (I 75.4c); alternatively, a human being *is* his intellectual soul (I 76.2c). Given that there are many human beings, there must be many intellectual souls (I 76.2c) (hence [D3]). Plato locates the intelligible content in really existent "Platonic" Forms or Ideas, which are immaterial and hence actually intelligible. Both the power to understand and the power to sense find their proximate subject in the intellectual soul (I 75.3c; I 75.4c; I 77.5 ad 3), which relates to the body as a mover and to sense organs as external instruments (I 76.1–2 *passim*; SCG II 57.2). Indeed, it is not only the intellectual soul that relates to the body as a mover. Each human being has many souls related to its body as movers: the vegetative soul in the liver, the concupiscible soul in the heart, and cognitive soul in the brain (I 76.3c). As to cognitive psychology, Plato forwards his theory of recollection according to which intellectual souls preexist embodiment and acquire concepts of the natures of things by direct cognitive contact with the actually intelligible Platonic Forms. If the shock of incarnation causes the soul to forget what it already knows, sensible things excite the soul to sense, and sensation stirs the soul to recollect the Ideas of which sensible things are imperfect likenesses (I 84.3c; I 84.6c).

Aquinas counters that Platonic Ideas cannot be the essences of things here below for the Aristotelian reason (P1) that the essence of a thing must be in the thing whose essence it is. In Aquinas's language, they must share the same *esse* (I 84.1c; I 84.4c). Aquinas dismisses Plato's theory of recollection as perverse: Embodiment benefits the soul by providing sensory reminders of thoughts the soul would not have forgotten if it had not been embodied in the first place (I 84.3c)! Aquinas's most persistent complaint is that Plato cannot provide any positive account of why the soul should be embodied (I 89.1c). Plato can say that the same human being both senses and understands, but sensing is not essential to the soul's primary function of understanding. So the soul's relation to the body is at most per accidens (I 75.4c; I 76.1c). Since souls cannot be individuated by some merely accidental relation to some matter, Aquinas charges that Plato will not be able to accommodate (D3) either (I 75.7c). Nevertheless, every one of the points that Aquinas raises is philosophically contentious.

5.8.3   Averroës

Like Aquinas in *Summa Theologiae* I 75, Averroës begins with his conviction that understanding is an immaterial function. Like Aquinas in I 76, Averroës agrees with Aristotle: that the quiddities of material things really exist only in the individuals and as such (via [P2]) are not actually intelligible. Averroës concludes that it is necessary to posit an agent intellect to do the abstracting and a possible intellect to receive the abstracted intelligible species. Averroës reasons that for a universal intelligible species to stay universal, it must be received into a subject that is altogether immaterial. Not only can the possible intellect not be a matter–form composite; it cannot be the form of some matter either. Individuated soul forms would mean individuated intelligible species and spoil the universality of the content (I 76.1 obj. 3). Accordingly, Averroës holds that both agent and possible intellect are subsistent separate substances, and concludes that there can be only one of each for the whole human race (I 76.1c; I 76.2c; I 78.5c). The agent intellect will be able to cause the possible intellect actually to think of something, only if it has access to relevantly sorted phantasms. Happily, human beings are hylomorphic composites with high-grade sensory souls and top-of-the-line phantasm-sorters, the *vis cogitativa* (SCG II 60.1). These suit the human being for functional coupling with the separate possible intellect. When the agent intellect abstracts the intelligible species from Socrates's sorted phantasms, then numerically the same form exists in the possible intellect and Socrates's phantasms, and Socrates can be said to understand (I 76.1c).

Aquinas protests that Averroës's cognitive psychology turns Socrates into a mere object-presenter rather than a subject of understanding (I 76.1c). Although the motion of the batter can be passed on to the bat, understanding is an activity that remains within its proximate subject and is not sharable with instruments of its action (which is all Socrates would turn out to be) (I 76.1c). In Aquinas's reading, Averroës accommodates (D1), but forfeits both (D2) and (D3). Averroës might counter, however, that what is essential to humans is to sort phantasms in a way that triggers functional coupling with the separate possible intellect. This is an activity that lower animals with their inferior phantasm-sorters cannot share.

5.8.4 Avicenna

The feature of Avicenna's theory that interests Aquinas is his choice of housing for the intelligible objects. They exist in reality, separately from sublunary particulars and from human souls, not as Platonic Forms but in the separate agent intellect which is thought identical with the intelligible objects that it thinks. Avicenna's separate agent intellect is the "giver of the forms" to appropriately configured matter to produce a cow and to human souls with appropriately sorted phantasms to yield a thought of what it is to be a cow (I 76.4c; I 84.4 obj. 1–3 and c). Like Aquinas and Averroës, Avicenna takes human beings to be hylomorphic composites. Unlike Averroës but like Aquinas, Avicenna takes each human being to have a possible intellect of its own. In Avicenna's cognitive psychology, human sensation and phantasm-sorting do not serve to make content available to the agent intellect for abstraction. Rather such activities dispose the soul to receive the intelligible species that are eternally actually intelligible in and actually understood by the separate agent intellect itself.

In response, Aquinas first appeals to experience. Not only do we experience within ourselves (E2) that we sense and understand (I 76.1c), so that the possible intellect must exist in us as the proximate receiving subject of our act of understanding; we also experience (E3) within ourselves that *we* abstract from sense images. Since by (P1) the action and the power belong to the same subject, the agent intellect must be in us as well (I 79.4c).

Aquinas also raises a philosophical difficulty. Aristotelian science makes it a methodological default that sublunary phenomena have sublunary causes to explain them. To be sure, there will be no generation and corruption here below, without the circulation of the heavens. But the sun is a universal cause of generation and corruption. To explain what happens when Beulah and Ferdinand beget Elsie, one also needs to posit particular causes – namely, active and passive generative causes in Beulah and Ferdinand. Likewise, Aquinas reasons, even if some separate intellect were a universal cause of human understanding, particular causal principles in the intellectual soul would still be needed to explain how we come to understand what it is to be a cow (I 79.4c).

Yet, Aquinas himself treats this Aristotelian default as defeasible. In the generation of human beings, sublunary causes are involved in fetal development. But sublunary causes cannot produce the intellectual soul, because it is subsistent. Rather, when the fetus is sufficiently developed, the intellectual soul is created immediately by God (I 90.2c; I 90.3c). Avicenna simply generalizes that no substantial form is produced by sublunary causes; rather, when sublunary causes produce the right disposing conditions, the "giver of forms" infuses the substantial form. Nor was Avicenna's position lacking in Aristotelian motivation. Aristotelian substances act through qualities. But the Causal Nobility Principle stipulates that causes cannot be less noble than their effects. How could accidents produce substances? Aquinas might reply that it is not the quality (e.g., heat) that acts but the substance by means of the quality (e.g., the fire by means of the heat) in an essentially ordered causal chain. That dictum would not bring the debate to an end. There is no action at a distance. Aristotelians could not figure out how any excellent enough substantial form could be carried along by seminal stuff!

5.8.5 *Theoretical Trade-Offs*

Plato, Avicenna, and Averroës all think that human intellectual functioning involves something that transcends the sublunary sphere. To be sure, Aquinas believes that God and the heavens are universal causes of what transpires here below. But Plato and Avicenna go further to locate intelligible *objects* in transcendent realities (the Platonic Idea or the separate agent intellect). Averroës reasons that because intelligible objects must be universal, and human beings are material, the proximate and primary *subject* of understanding must be a separate intellect. Plato, Avicenna, and Aquinas locate the proximate subjects of understanding in the individual human souls – for Avicenna and Aquinas, in the individual possible intellects.

Neither Plato nor Avicenna needs an abstracting power, because they hold that the quiddities of things really exist as actually intelligible eternally, whether as Platonic ideas or thoughts identical with the separate agent intellect or giver of forms.

By contrast, Averroës and Aquinas agree that material quiddities really exist only in individuals, and that sensation and phantasm-sorting are the natural beginnings for human understanding. Following Aristotle, both see the need to posit an agent intellect with power to abstract intelligible species from phantasms. Aquinas is driven by the data of experience – (E2) *we* experience in ourselves that *we* sense and understand, (E3) *we* abstract intelligible contents from sense images, (E4) *we* turn to the phantasms to understand the quiddities existing in particular things – to locate both the proximate and the proper subjects of understanding in particular human beings here below. Aquinas follows the Aristotelian default that the functional power is in the thing that functions, and so concludes that the agent intellect is a soul-power, numerically multiplied in numerically distinct human souls.

Averroës forsakes Aristotelian defaults, when he insists that both agent and possible intellects are separate substances. Human beings, their sensation and phantasm-sorting, become essential instruments. Human understanding will not actually occur without them any more than vision can actually happen without color made actually visible by light. But there is no problem in their remaining *external* instruments. Because of the eternity of the species, such content-processing instruments are eternally available to be coupled with, in acts of actual understanding.

CHAPTER 6

Emotion and Desire in the Summa Theologiae

Nicholas E. Lombardo, O.P.

If the *Summa Theologiae* were an opera, its length would put Wagner to shame, but unlike one of Wagner's operas it would not be performed in darkness. It would be performed in daylight and the open air. Creation itself would provide the scenery. The orchestra would be huge, the chorus would be a cloud of witnesses from every age and religion, the soloists would be the prophets and evangelists, and the star tenor bringing everything to unity would be Christ.

As the opera progressed, we would notice the same theme coming up again and again: sometimes soft, sometimes loud. It would be in the orchestra, in the chorus, in the singing of the soloists, on the lips of Christ himself. It would be of a piece with everything else, sharing in everything that marked the opera of its time and place, yet it would also stand out as presciently modern, like a piece of medieval sculpture whose bright paint and primitive exuberance could pass for contemporary expressionism. For a while, we would wonder what it was and why it kept coming back, and why it seemed to play such a pivotal role. Then it would hit us. The theme was *appetitus*: desire.

The *Summa* may not be opera, but it does have movement, and it does have a plot. It begins with God and tells how creation flows from God and then returns to him through Christ.[1] Aquinas spoils the story right at the start:

> Since, as should be clear from what has already been said, the principal object of sacred teaching is to hand on knowledge of God – and not only knowledge of God as he is in himself, but also knowledge of God as the origin and end of all things, and especially of rational creatures – our

---

[1] Marie-Dominique Chenu was the first to propose this *exitus-reditus* model for the structure of the *Summa*. See his "Le plan de la Somme théologique de saint Thomas," and *Towards Understanding St. Thomas*. His proposal has been widely but not universally accepted by scholars of Aquinas. For a critique and an alternative proposal, see Te Velde, *Aquinas on God: The 'Divine Science' of the Summa Theologiae*. In my view, Chenu's analysis is well supported by Aquinas's own words.

exposition of this teaching will treat: first, of God; second, of the movement of rational creatures toward God; third, of Christ who, through his humanity, is our way of attaining to God.[2]

Aquinas does not mention desire in his overview of the *Summa*'s plot, but desire is its unspoken engine. It makes the story's movement possible. From beginning to end, the theme of desire courses through the *Summa* and gives it shape. There are many other themes in the *Summa*, but only this one can claim to supply its architectonic structure. In the First Part, Aquinas tells how God brought the world into being through his will, or intellectual appetite, and how God guides created things toward their proper end by the appetites he implants within them. In the Second Part, Aquinas outlines how we bring our desires to fruition, or fail to, through our free actions, and discusses the role of emotion, virtue, and grace in bringing us to human and spiritual maturity. Finally, in the Third Part, he tells how, through the harmonious exercise of Christ's divine and human appetites, Christ's humanity became a bridge between heaven and earth, for our humanities. Aquinas died before completing the Third Part, but if he had lived long enough to finish it, he would almost certainly have brought the story to completion with a treatment of glorified humanity and created appetite's fulfillment in heaven (as his Dominican confreres did for him posthumously in their supplement to the *Summa*, written within the timespan of his living memory).

Given the centrality of desire to the *Summa*'s structure and, as we shall see, to Aquinas's theological project more generally, it would be impossible for a brief essay to touch on its every manifestation. This chapter will instead content itself with a broad overview of the following select topics: appetite and desire; the passions and affections and their relation to the contemporary category of emotion; passion, reason, and virtue; and the place of emotion in human flourishing.[3]

---

[2] ST I 2 prologue.
[3] For a more detailed discussion of most topics covered in this essay, see Lombardo, *The Logic of Desire: Aquinas on Emotion*. Other recent works that are especially recommended include: Gondreau, *The Passions of Christ's Soul in the Theology of St. Thomas Aquinas*; Miner, *Thomas Aquinas on the Passions: A Study of Summa Theologiae 1a2ae 22–48*; Cates, *Aquinas on the Emotions: A Religious-Ethical Inquiry*; and Pinckaers, *Passions & Virtue*.

6.1   Appetite, Desire, and God

For Aquinas, intrinsic and essential to every type of being is an inclination toward what perfects and completes it. He calls this perfective inclination "appetite." It is what orients a being toward its proper end. It does more than simply point being in the right direction, however. Once triggered by a stimulus, appetite propels a being toward that being's proper perfection and completion.

Following Aristotle, Aquinas describes appetite as a "passive power."[4] As such, appetite is a capacity for movement. It lies dormant until an external object acts upon it and moves it from potency to act. Aquinas identifies three kinds of appetite according to the kinds of objects to which they respond. These objects are in turn defined according to the kind of cognition, or lack thereof, that they involve. He explains:

> Some things are inclined toward the good only by natural disposition, without cognition, such as plants and inanimate objects. And this sort of inclination toward the good is called natural appetite. Other things are inclined toward the good with some amount of cognition, but not like those things that know the good as good. They know only some particular good, as when the senses apprehend the sweet and the white and other such things. The inclination that follows this sort of cognition is called the sensory appetite. Still other things are inclined toward the good with the cognition that knows the good as good; this sort of cognition is proper to the intellect. And these things are most perfectly inclined toward the good … And this inclination is called the will.[5]

All physical beings have natural appetites; animals and humans have sensory appetites; and humans, angels, and God have wills, or intellectual appetites (also called rational appetites). When an object triggers an appetite, the kind of movement that results varies according to the kind of appetite. Natural appetite leads to physical movement; sensory appetite lead to passion, a kind of psychological movement; and intellectual appetite leads to intellectual affection, another kind of psychological movement.

---

[4] ST I 80.2. After 1270, when the Bishop of Paris condemned a number of theological propositions, Aquinas avoids referring to the will as a passive power, because it could be seen to run afoul of the bishop's condemnations, but he nonetheless seems to continue thinking of it as such. See Sherwin, *By Knowledge and By Love: Charity and Knowledge in the Moral Theology of Thomas Aquinas.*
[5] ST I 59.1. See also ST I 80.1–2.

While appetite is found also in God, divine appetite is different from created appetite in some important respects. First, in God, there is no passivity, so appetite in God is never dormant; it is always in act.[6] Moreover, created appetite sometimes strives for an end not yet attained, and sometimes it rests in an end already attained. God, however, does not lack for anything. So while God's appetite aims at what is perfective and completing – which, ultimately, is nothing other than God's own being, since nothing else can satisfy desire for infinite good – it never strives toward it as though it were an end not yet attained.[7] Finally, since the divine being is a perfect unity lacking any division, he is supremely simple. God does not merely possess an intellectual appetite. God is his own appetite, just as he is his own intellect, his own act of loving, and his own act of knowing.[8] From our perspective, they may seem different, but in God there is no real distinction. It is like standing on the equator looking from one degree of longitude to another. At the equator, the degrees of longitude are at different places, but beyond the horizon, at either pole, they meet at the same place. Consequently, for Aquinas, the claim that God is love is not poetry; it is a technical claim about God's identity. God is identical with a movement of the intellectual appetite: the intellectual affection of love.[9]

Aquinas's account of appetite and its relationship to cognition features prominently in how he explains the distinction of Persons in the Trinity. Following a longstanding Christian tradition of reading scriptural references to God's Word and God's Wisdom as prophetic types of Christ, Aquinas relates the Son's procession to the act of knowing. He holds that the divine act of knowing is proper to the divine essence and thus common to all three Persons, but he also maintains that the act of forming a mental word – which, according to Aquinas, is intrinsic to the act of knowing, and yet capable of being distinguished from it – corresponds, somehow, to the procession of the Word from the Father.[10] Aquinas makes a similar move in his explanation of the procession of the Spirit. While holding that the divine act of loving is common to all

---

[6] ST I 9.1, 25.1. Aquinas's attribution of appetite to God in ST I 19.1 stands in a certain amount of tension with his description of appetite as a passive power in ST I 80.2. If there is no passivity or potential in God, how can there be passive power in God? Aquinas's solution is to say that God himself moves God's appetite, and that appetite is in God only in the sense of resting in a good already attained: namely, himself. See ST 19.1 ad 2–3.

[7] ST I 19.1 ad 2.

[8] ST I 14.4, 19.1, 20.1.

[9] See ST I 20.1.

[10] ST I 27.2, 34.1–2, 36.2.

three Persons, he explains that "when anyone loves something, a certain impression, so to speak, of the loved thing originates in the affection of the lover," and the Spirit's procession corresponds, somehow, to the forming of this impression in the affection.[11] This approach to the Spirit's procession allows him to explain why the Spirit proceeds from the Son as well as the Father. Since love follows and depends on what is known, and since the Spirit proceeds by way of the will while the Son proceeds by way of the intellect, it follows that the Spirit's procession follows and depends on the Son's procession.[12]

Aquinas's implicitly positive valuation of appetite becomes explicit in his account of goodness and evil. For Aquinas, goodness implies desirability.[13] If something is good – and anything that exists is necessarily good – then it is also appetible, or desirable: first and foremost, with respect to God's appetite, since God wills everything that exists, but also with respect to those created appetites that it somehow completes or perfects.[14] Conversely, Aquinas describes evil (both physical and moral) as the effect of something being prevented from attaining to "its natural and due disposition."[15] Following patristic tradition, he defines evil as the privation of being,[16] but by describing evil with respect to something's natural disposition, he is suggesting that the privation proper to evil consists in the frustration of appetite. Aquinas's account of goodness and evil is elegantly simple and applies to all realms of being: If something is good, it is desirable and perfecting, and if something is evil, it thwarts appetite and leads to disintegration.

6.2 Passions, Affections, and Emotions

Emotion is a relatively recent psychological category, dating to the early nineteenth century,[17] and etymologically it lacks a direct parallel in the Latin vocabulary of the thirteenth century.[18] Consequently, to say what in Aquinas's writings corresponds to the contemporary category of emotion requires a good amount of interpretation. For reasons that cannot

---

[11] ST I 37.1.
[12] ST I 36.2.
[13] ST I 5.1.
[14] See ST I 5.1, 5.2, 16.1, 19.1–2, 20.1–2.
[15] ST I 49.1. See also DM 1.1–3.
[16] ST I 48.1.
[17] Dixon, *From Passions to Emotions: The Creation of a Secular Psychological Category.*
[18] The closest etymological parallel to "emotion" in Latin is *motus*. See Dixon, *From Passions to Emotions*, pp. 39–40.

be explored here,[19] there are strong grounds for seeing Aquinas's category of affection (in Latin, *affectio* or *affectus*) as roughly equivalent to the contemporary category of emotion.

For Aquinas, there are two kinds of affection. There are affections of the sensory appetite, which he usually calls passions of the soul (*passiones animae*) or movements of the sensory appetite.[20] They are experienced by animals and humans, and they directly involve both body and soul. Then there are what Aquinas variously calls intellectual affections, simple affections, or passionless affections: movements of the intellectual appetite that could be called (though Aquinas does not) affections of the will (to parallel his description of the passions as affections of the sensory appetite).[21] Intellectual affections are experienced by humans, angels, and God, and they directly involve only the will, though in the case of humans they can spill over to the body. Affections are intentional, that is, they are oriented toward objects. The passions respond to objects known through sense cognition; intellectual affections respond to objects known through intellectual cognition (Figure 6.1).

Confusingly, but importantly, some passions do not correspond to our contemporary category of emotion. In addition to passions of the soul, Aquinas also talks about passions of the body (*passiones corporales*) (Figure 6.1). Whereas passions of the soul include such things as love, anger, and fear, passions of the body include such things as aches, pains, and physical pleasure. According to Aquinas, both kinds of passions involve both body and soul, but passions of the body begin in the body and end in the soul, as when we stub our toe and our bodily suffering then affects us in our soul, while passions of the soul begin in the soul and end in the body, as when we hear a loud noise and become fearful and this interior disturbance triggers the release of adrenaline and affects us in our body.[22] We could also say that passions of the body are not intentional – they are not "about" anything, they are just there, generally in a particular part of the body – whereas passions of the soul are always "about" some object or another.

---

[19] For the reasons for this judgment, see Lombardo, *Logic of Desire*, pp. 15–19, 224–9.

[20] Although he often speaks about affections in a way that implies or includes the passions, ST III 15.4 is the only place in the *Summa* where he explicitly identifies the passions as affections of the sensory appetite.

[21] For some of the more important places in the *Summa* where he speaks about this category of affection, see ST I 19.11, 20.1, 21.3, 59.4, 60.1, 82.5 ad 1; ST I-II 22.3 ad 3, 31.4 ad 2, 59.5 ad 3; ST II-II 162.3. See also SCG I 89.1–2. For his description of the passions as affections of the sensory appetite, see ST III 15.4.

[22] DV 26.2, 26.3 ad 9.

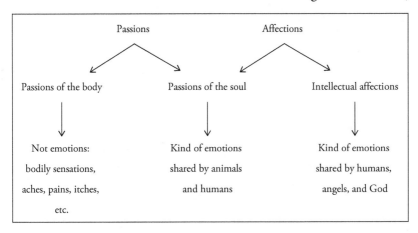

Figure 6.1   Passions, affections, and emotions

As movements of appetite, passions of the soul and intellectual affections are intrinsically ordered to human flourishing. Just as appetites are ordered to what is perfective and completing, so too are their movements. There is a difference, however. Appetites are defined exclusively by what is perfective and completing, but the same is not true of appetitive movements. According to Aquinas, every appetitive movement is defined by its immediate object, and its immediate object can be a good or an evil. Some movements such as love and joy are indeed defined by what is good and desirable, but other movements such as sadness and fear are instead defined by what is evil and harmful. Even movements defined by evil objects, though, are ultimately oriented toward the good. We feel fear, for example, so that we can avoid threats to our well-being.

This orientation toward the good permeates the structure of appetitive movements. According to Aquinas, the first movement of every appetite is love, that is, a configuring of appetite toward a particular object that somehow corresponds to its *telos*. The first movement then sets off a chain of other appetitive movements. Some movements propel the subject toward the attainment of the loved object; other movements help it overcome or avoid obstacles to that attainment. Eventually, hopefully, the loved object is attained and the subject rests in its possession. In this way, appetitive movements are ordered to rest, which, paradoxically, is itself a kind of movement, insofar as the resting implies that the loved object is moving the appetite from potency to act.

In his Treatise on the Passions (I-II 22–48), Aquinas identifies 11 distinct passions. He groups them into two categories: the concupiscible

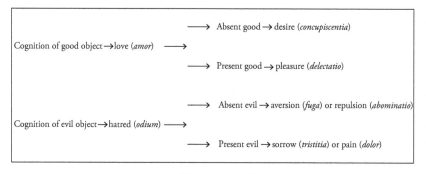

Figure 6.2 The concupiscible passions

passions and the irascible passions. The six concupiscible passions are first-order emotions. They respond to straightforward sense goods and sense evils. After the subject apprehends a sensory object, depending on whether the object is good or evil, the appetite is moved to either love (*amor*) or hate (*odium*). If the object is absent or not yet attained, the passion of desire (*concupiscentia*) or aversion (*fuga* or *abominatio*) also results; if the object is present or already attained, the appetite rests in the object and is moved to either pleasure (*delectatio*) or sadness (*tristitia* or *dolor*) (Figure 6.2).

The five irascible passions are more complicated. They are second-order emotions. They assist the first-order emotions, the concupiscible passions, to attain what they love and avoid what they hate. The irascible passions respond to sensory objects not for their own sake, but because they are somehow relevant to interests of the concupiscible passions. Furthermore, as they are needed only in situations when the concupiscible passions would have difficulty managing on their own, the irascible passions respond to *arduous* sensory objects, that is, sensory objects that are some-how difficult to obtain or avoid (Figure 6.3). When we apprehend an arduous sense good that seems possible to obtain, we experience hope (*spes*), which provides supplementary emotional resources to obtain that sense good; when the arduous sense good seems impossible to obtain, despair (*desperatio*) follows instead. Conversely, when we apprehend an arduous sense evil on the horizon, if we judge it possible to overcome, we are moved to daring (*audacia*), but if we do not think we can overcome it, and can only hope to avoid it, we instead experience fear (*timor*). Finally, if we are faced with a sense evil that is both difficult and present – that is, it is not just on the horizon but it has already happened – and if we think that we can overcome it, our sensory appetite is moved to anger (*ira*).

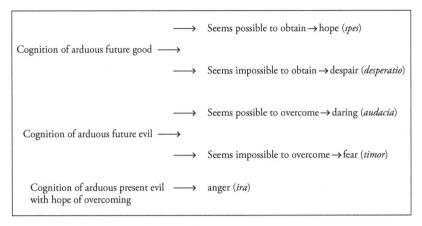

Figure 6.3   The irascible passions

Many aspects of his account of the passions are not original to Aquinas. He takes the distinction between the concupiscible and the irascible from Aristotle and the schema of eleven passions from John of La Rochelle, and much of his analysis of individual passions is likewise borrowed from other thinkers.[23] The synthetic quality of his account is both a strength and a weakness. Aquinas's dedication to engaging with his predecessors and drawing on their wisdom gives his Treatise on the Passions a breadth and a depth he could not have achieved on his own. The same synthetic impulse, however, leads to some unresolved tensions. His adoption of the eleven-passion schema, for example, sits uneasily with his metaphysical principles. He maintains that passions move toward goods and away from evils,[24] and that passions are distinguished from each other by their intentional objects,[25] but he has despair moving away from a good and daring moving toward an evil, and he does not adequately explain how love has a different intentional object from either desire or pleasure. A more internally coherent application of his own principles would arguably lead to a reduced schema of seven passions.[26]

Aquinas writes far less about the intellectual affections than he does about the passions, and what he does write tends to be in the context of

[23] On Aquinas's sources, see Gondreau, *Passions of Christ's Soul,* pp. 101–35, 211–18.

[24] ST I-II 22.1, 22.2.

[25] ST I-II 23.4.

[26] For an analysis of internal difficulties in Aquinas's taxonomy of the passions and possible solutions, see Lombardo, *Logic of Desire,* pp. 57–62, 68–74.

other topics. There is nothing like a Treatise on the Affections or even a single article on intellectual affection. Yet the category seems to have been clearly fixed in his mind, and he seems to have grown increasingly conscious of its significance as he progressed through the *Summa*.[27] By attending to scattered asides and his treatment of particular emotions that he seems to have considered intellectual affections (most notably, perhaps, his question on joy in the Second Part of the Second Part), we can piece together a tentative reconstruction of his thought.

The structure of intellectual affection parallels the structure of the concupiscible passions. The first movement of the intellectual appetite is love (*amor*). If the loved object is absent or not yet attained, love leads to desire (*desiderium*); if the loved object is present or attained, love leads to joy (*gaudium*). He gives less attention to intellectual affections concerned with negative objects, but especially in his discussion of spiritual beings and separated souls, he affirms that there is a kind of sadness (*tristitia*) that is not a passion but instead a movement of the will.[28] We can assume that he would also argue for similar parallels to the passions of hate and aversion among the intellectual affections.

Intellectual affections tend to overflow to the passions. When sufficiently intense, joy overflows into the passion of pleasure, and spiritual sorrow overflows into the passion of sadness.[29] This overflow is not the only way that the passions and intellectual affections influence each other. Aquinas gives a good deal of attention to what he calls non-natural passions: passions whose objects are determined not simply by our sensory inclinations, but are also influenced by intellectual cognition and the infinite desires of the will. Aquinas does not speculate about the percentage of our passions that are natural or non-natural. His principles, though, seem to imply that, after infancy, almost all of our passions are non-natural, and thus involve both the sensory appetite and the intellectual appetite.[30]

6.3   Passion, Reason, and Virtue

For Aquinas, there is no simplistic opposition between passion and reason. The passions are appetitive movements, not cognitive acts, but the

---

[27] See Lombardo, *Logic of Desire*, pp. 148–9.
[28] ST I 64.3, 77.9 ad 5; ST III 84.9 ad 2.
[29] See ST I-II 3.3 ad 3, 24.3 ad 1, 30.1 ad 1, 37.2, 38.4 ad 3, 77.6. On the mechanism of this overflow, see Lombardo, *Logic of Desire*, pp. 89–91.
[30] See Lombardo, *Logic of Desire*, 87–9.

sense appetite responds to reason, and so the passions manifest reason's guidance. Passion and reason are complementary. Each has a role to play in bringing the human person to perfection. The passions supply motivation and energy, and reason provides guidance. The passions operate according to their own principles, and so can from time to time oppose reason's judgment, but these occasional instances do not negate their general tendency to obey reason and move us toward our ultimate *telos*. Over time, reason's guidance can become embedded in the sensory appetite, so that the sensory appetite habitually responds to sensory objects according to reason's prior judgments. When that embedded guidance is just and true, the passions become virtuous; when it is false and corrupt, the passions become vicious.

Aquinas's account of passion and reason is subtle and complex. His key move is to distinguish between two kinds of reason: particular reason and universal reason. Aquinas locates particular reason, also called the cogitative power, in the body, and following Islamic physicians, more specifically in a bodily organ in the middle of the head.[31] Particular reason judges sensory objects according to their existential significance and forms what Aquinas calls intentions (*intentiones*): the mental objects to which the passions respond.[32] The sensory appetite does not respond to sensory objects directly; it responds to them as mediated through intentions. So, for example, if we are walking down a dark alley and hear a sudden loud noise, our particular reason might judge the noise to represent a threat and form an intention accordingly. In response to this intention, our sensory appetite is moved to act and we experience the passion of fear. Animals also evaluate sensory objects and form intentions, but in animals, this function is performed by the estimative power.[33] The estimative power judges sensory objects purely according to natural instinct. Particular reason, however, can be influenced by a higher cognitive power: namely, universal reason.[34]

Aquinas usually refers to universal reason without any adjective, as simply "reason." Reason moves from something known to something not yet known, and it abstracts universals from particulars.[35] Universal reason

---

[31] ST I 78.4; Gasson, "The Internal Senses – Functions or Powers? Part I," at 4.

[32] ST I 78.4; ST I-II 22.2.

[33] ST I 78.4, 81.3.

[34] ST I 81.3.

[35] Aquinas maintains that "reason" (*ratio*) and "intellect" (*intellectus*) refer to different aspects of one and the same cognitive power. "Reason" refers to that power when it is occupied with discursive reasoning, and "intellect" refers to that power when it is occupied with understanding. The

cannot influence the passions directly, but it can influence them through
the mediation of particular reason. By applying general considerations to
particular reason's judgments about sensory objects, it can reshape intentions – and thus change the way the sensory appetite responds to sensory
objects. Aquinas explains: "Anyone can experience this in himself: by
applying some universal considerations, anger, fear, and other such passions can be mitigated or instigated."[36] The will also has a role to play,
because it is the will that directs universal reason to influence particular
reason in how it forms intentions, and because the will, not the passions,
decides on a course of action.[37]

In view of the role that particular and universal reason play in forming intentions, Aquinas's claim that the passions naturally obey reason
becomes more comprehensible. Since the sensory appetite responds to
intentions, and since particular and universal reason form intentions, the
sensory appetite cannot but obey reason. Nevertheless, Aquinas acknowledges that the passions are not completely subject to reason, and that
they can and do resist reason from time to time. When explaining how
passion's occasional resistance does not diminish its essential inclination
to obey reason, Aquinas borrows a metaphor from Aristotle:

> Aristotle says in the *Politics* that "both despotic and political rule can be
> observed in living things: for the soul governs the body with despotic
> rule, but the intellect governs the appetite with political and regal rule."
> Rule is despotic when someone rules slaves, who cannot in any way resist
> their master's commands, because they have nothing of their own. Rule is
> political and regal, however, when someone rules the free, who, while sub-
> ject to the ruler's governance, nonetheless have something of their own, on
> account of which they can resist the ruler's commands. Accordingly, the
> soul is said to govern the body with despotic rule, because the members
> of the body cannot in any way resist the soul's commands: Hand and foot
> are moved immediately according to the soul's desire, as is any other bod-
> ily member naturally moved by the will. But intellect or reason is said to
> govern the irascible and concupiscible powers with political rule, because

---

relation between reasoning and understanding, according to Aquinas, "is that of moving to resting,
or of acquiring to having" (ST I 79.8).

[36] ST I 81.3. Aquinas does not explain every step of the process, but from what he does say and from
his general account of the sensory appetite, it is clear that universal reason's primary influence over
particular reason consists in the way it prompts particular reason to reform intentions. In many
ways, Aquinas's distinction between universal and particular reason maps well on the contemporary categories of the conscious and unconscious. See Lombardo, *Logic of Desire*, p. 240.

[37] ST I 81.3. In various places, Aquinas acknowledges that in special circumstances such as bodily
indispositions the passions can overpower the will. See ST I-II 9.2 ad 3, 17.7 ad 2, 77.1, 77.3,
77.6–7.

the sensory appetite has something of its own, and therefore can resist the commands of reason.[38]

Aquinas frequently adverts to this metaphor in the *Summa* when talking about passion and reason.[39] It is not difficult to imagine why: The metaphor captures many important features of his understanding of passion's relation to reason. On the one hand, it suggests that the passions are generally inclined to accept reason's guidance; on the other hand, it suggests that the passions have their own independent dynamism, and if reason asks more of the passions than it can legitimately demand, the passions, like oppressed subjects, may not cooperate.[40]

Intellectual affections relate to reason in a more straightforward way than the passions. As movements of intellectual appetite, they respond to intellectual objects, not sensory objects. Consequently, they are influenced directly by universal reason without mediation from particular reason. If an intellectual object appears good and desirable, or begins to appear so after a process of discursive reasoning, the intellectual appetite will be moved immediately to love and then, depending on whether the object has been attained, to desire or joy. Conversely, if an intellectual object appears evil and undesirable, it will immediately inspire intellectual affections of hate and then either aversion or sorrow.[41] Intellectual affections can involve the will to varying degrees. Some intellectual affections are a natural response of the will's inclination toward goodness as such to the cognition of a good; other intellectual affections are rationally chosen and fully ratified.[42]

Repeated action leads to the formation of character traits, which Aquinas calls *habitus*. These *habitus* are not routine habits performed in an unthinking way.[43] They are stable dispositions which only become

---

[38] ST I 81.3 ad 2. See Aristotle, *Pol.* I.5, 1254b5.

[39] Besides ST I 81.3 ad 2, see ST I-II 9.2 ad 3, 17.7, 56.4 ad 3, 58.2, 74.1.

[40] For more on the significance and implications of Aquinas's use of this metaphor, see McAleer, "The Politics of the Flesh: Rahner and Aquinas on *Concupiscentia*" and his book *Ecstatic Morality and Sexual Politics: A Catholic and Antitotalitarian Theory of the Body*. See also Lombardo, *Logic of Desire*, pp. 99–101.

[41] Aquinas's comments about the intellectual affections are scattered and unsystematic, as noted above, and he does not give as much attention to negative affections, that is, to affections concerned with evil objects, as he does to their positive counterparts. Consequently, though the summary given here constitutes an accurate representation of Aquinas's thought, it is based on inference as well as Aquinas's explicit words.

[42] In the *Summa*, Aquinas gives the most attention to the difference between movements of the will that are fully ratified by the will and those that are not in his discussion of Christ's prayer in the garden of Gethsemane. See ST III 18, 21.

[43] See Pinckaers, "Virtue Is Not a Habit."

active after free and creative action. Every *habitus* involves the intellect and will, and thus intellectual affection, and some *habitus* also involve the sensory appetite, and thus the passions. Over time, our free choices form our appetites so that our appetites begin to respond to objects in ways that anticipate our prior choices. If our choices are in accord with right reason, they form virtue, that is, *habitus* oriented toward our perfection and completion; if not, they form vice, that is, *habitus* oriented toward objects not in keeping with our *telos* and thus disintegration and self-destruction.

Aquinas holds that the sensory appetite and not just the intellectual appetite can be the subject, that is, the seat or location, of virtue.[44] Many of his contemporaries did not agree and thought that only rational powers could be the subject of virtue.[45] While acknowledging that *habitus* require rationality, he argues that because the sensory appetite responds to reason's guidance, it is rational by participation, and thus can also be the subject of virtue.[46] For Aquinas, virtue in the sensory appetite does not lead to the eradication of passion,[47] not even of passions such as sadness[48] or anger.[49] To the contrary, "virtue in the irascible and concupiscible powers is nothing other than a certain habitual conformity of these powers to reason,"[50] and virtuous passions assist the execution of reason's command.[51] Moreover, virtue actually increases ordinate passion, that is, passion inclined toward what is perfective of the human person. For example, speaking of moral virtue, Aquinas writes, "The more perfect the virtue, the more it causes passion."[52] Virtue harnesses the passions and guides them toward our best interests, so that we can better and more easily attain our *telos*.

6.4   Emotion and Human Flourishing

Among his contemporaries, Aquinas stands out for his position that the passions are movements, not qualities. The texts of Aristotle could

[44] ST I-II 56.4, 56.5 ad 1.
[45] See Chenu, "Les passions vertueuses: L'anthropologie de saint Thomas"; Gondreau, *Passions of Christ's Soul*, pp. 276–81.
[46] See ST I-II 50.3, 55.4 ad 3.
[47] ST I-II 59.2.
[48] ST I-II 59.3.
[49] ST II-II 158.1–2.
[50] ST I-II 56.4.
[51] ST I-II 59.2 ad 3.
[52] ST I-II 59.5.

support either view, but Aquinas opted for the minority position.[53] By now it should be clear that, for Aquinas, this categorization was not a mere technical precision. It lies at the heart of his understanding of emotion. Our appetites orient us toward our perfection and completion, and our emotions move us toward it. The passions have a receptive, passive dimension, as indicated by the word "passion," insofar as they are triggered by their subject's apprehension of intentional objects, but their active dimension is primary.[54] Without appetite, we would not be inclined toward our *telos*, and without movements of appetite, we would not actually advance toward it, let alone attain it. The emotions, therefore, are not simply relevant to human flourishing. As movements of appetite, they move us toward what completes our nature and then allow us to enjoy it to the extent that we attain it.

The connection between appetite, emotion, and human flourishing sheds light on one of the most distinctive features of Aquinas's ethics: his grounding of natural law in our natural inclinations.[55] Since our natural inclinations point us toward our ontological perfection, Aquinas reasons, they must also point us toward our moral perfection. His approach to ethics has startling implications for moral normativity in the realm of emotion. Since our natural inclinations are nothing other than the tendencies of our appetites, it follows that the emotional tendencies of human nature are morally normative.[56] What morally good affectivity looks like is determined by the structure of human affectivity itself. For Aquinas, when we judge the moral value of a particular emotion, the relevant question is whether that particular emotion respects, or does not respect, the structure of human affectivity. For example, Aquinas holds that acedia is a vice because it involves sadness about spiritual good, something that is obviously not a genuine evil, the proper object of sorrow.[57] But when sadness results from a genuine evil, Aquinas argues, it is good – not merely tolerable – to feel sad.[58]

In the Second Part of the Second Part, in his discussion of particular virtues or vices and their related emotions, Aquinas frequently refers back

---

[53] Knuuttila, *Emotions in Ancient and Medieval Philosophy*, pp. 248–55.
[54] This point is demonstrated most clearly by the fact that Aquinas excludes all forms of passion from the divine nature, and yet nonetheless attributes to God appetite and intellectual affections. For more on the primacy of the passions' active dimension, see Lombardo, *Logic of Desire*, pp. 38–40.
[55] ST I-II 94.2.
[56] For a developed argument for this reading of Aquinas, see Lombardo, *Logic of Desire*, pp. 111–17.
[57] ST II-II 35.1.
[58] ST I-II 39.1.

to the Treatise on the Passions.[59] (The frequency of his references suggests that he was very deliberate in his strategy of comparing specific instances of emotion to their essential structure, and it perhaps explains why the treatise is so long in the first place.[60]) If an emotion respects the structure of human affectivity, he judges it morally good; if not, he judges it morally defective.[61] For example, in the Treatise on the Passions, Aquinas defines anger as a passion that responds to a present evil and seeks redress.[62] If a specific instance of anger responds to a genuine evil and seeks just redress, and if its intensity is proportionate to that evil, then it is in keeping with the generic structure of anger and therefore morally good. But if a specific instance of anger does not respond to a genuine evil or seeks unjust redress, or if its intensity exceeds due proportion, then it violates the essential structure of anger and is therefore sinful and morally defective.[63]

While looking to the structure of human affectivity as morally normative, Aquinas is well aware that concrete instances of passion do not necessarily move us in the right direction. Our passions can draw us toward sense goods that do not serve our ultimate happiness, and they can also repel us from sense evils that we must engage. Yet despite the possibility of misdirection, in their essential structure, our passions serve an integral if paradoxical role in moving us toward our *telos*. The function of our passions is not to point us in a definitive direction; their function is to alert us to sense goods and sense evils and then present the data to our intellects and wills for analysis and decision. If we did not respond to objects through our passions, and if that response was not essentially oriented toward our flourishing, however misleading it might

---

[59] For instances where Aquinas refers back to the Treatise on the Passions in the Second Part of the Second Part, see ST II-II 2.10, 7.1, 17.1, 17.4, 17.8, 19.2, 23.3 ad 2, 23.4, 28.1, 28.3, 34.1, 34.3, 34.5 obj. 2, 36.1, obj. 3–4, 41.2, 47.1 ad 1, 47.9 ad 3, 54.2 ad 3, 58.9 obj. 1, 123.3, 123.8, 123.10, 123.11 ad 1, 125.1 obj. 1, 125.2, 127.1, 128.1 ad 6, 129.6 ad 2, 129.7, 141.3, 141.4 obj. 4, 141.7 obj. 3, 144.1–2, 147.8 obj. 2, 158.1–2, 158.5, 161.1, 168.2, 171.2 obj. 1, 180.1, 180.7.

[60] Lombardo, *Logic of Desire*, pp. 113–14.

[61] Which is not to say that he thinks everyone experiencing a morally good or morally defective emotion should automatically be praised or blamed. Significantly, Aquinas distinguishes between the moral value of emotions in themselves and our moral responsibility in particular instances. He distinguishes between what he calls antecedent and consequent passions and maintains that we are morally responsible for our emotions only to the degree that they result from previous voluntary acts. See Claudia Eisen Murphy, "Aquinas on Our Responsibility for Our Emotions"; Lombardo, *Logic of Desire*, 109–11.

[62] ST I-II 46.2.

[63] Aquinas does not put it in quite the same way, but this summary accurately represents the logic of how he distinguishes between morally good and morally defective anger. See ST II-II 158.1–2.

be in particular instances, we would never take the first step toward happiness.[64] The role of the passions in leading us to our proper end becomes even stronger when they are permeated with virtue and spontaneously anticipate the judgment of right reason in their response to sensory objects.

Still, for all the ways in which our emotions move us toward our perfection and completion, tension inevitably arises between emotions responding to what is good (or evil) from a limited perspective and emotions responding to what is good (or evil) from a holistic perspective. Christ himself experiences this tension, as evidenced by his agony in the garden and his hunger after fasting for forty days.[65] According to Aquinas, even before sin, the tension between our emotions is such that human nature requires God's grace to function properly.[66] After sin enters human history, our need for God's grace becomes greater. While sin does not destroy nature or nature's principles, it impedes nature from attaining its proper end,[67] and it wounds every faculty of the human person.[68] Our fallen condition and personal sins lead our emotions to become attuned to false goods and false evils, so that we habitually experience not merely emotions in tension with each other, but also disordered emotions. Significantly, Aquinas holds that these negative effects result from the privation of grace and original justice, not the injection of a positive inclination toward sin.[69] The vacuum created by the privation of grace and original justice deprives the various powers of the soul of coordination among themselves. As a result, we are pulled in different directions, and our ability to choose the good is weakened.[70]

---

[64] On the paradoxical role of the emotions in leading us toward happiness and our ultimate fulfillment, see Gondreau, "The Passions and the Moral Life: Appreciating the Originality of Aquinas," and Lombardo, *Logic of Desire*, pp. 40–3.

[65] Aquinas discusses these episodes and what they imply about Christ's affectivity in ST III 18, 21.2–4, 41. Aquinas will say that there was no conflict between Christ's appetites, by which he seems to mean that in Christ this interior tension was harmonious and balanced, not that he did not want one thing on the level of his intellectual appetite and another thing on the level of his sensory appetite. See ST III 18.6.

[66] Aquinas's position on nature's dependence on grace for its perfection and completion has been a subject of considerable controversy over the centuries. Texts such as ST I 95.1 and *In II Sent.* d.31 1.2 ad 3 suggest that nature requires grace to function properly, while texts such as ST I-II 109.8 suggest that fully intact nature could avoid all sin even without grace. In my view, the former texts should be given interpretive priority.

[67] ST I-II 85.1–2.

[68] ST I-II 85.3.

[69] ST I-II 82.1.

[70] ST I-II 82.2 ad 2.

Aquinas's diagnosis of our condition leads him to hold out hope for the healing and rehabilitation of human affectivity through virtue and grace. Through virtue, our natural powers acquire *habitus* and our passions and affections gradually become more conformed to our *telos*. Through grace, which Aquinas defines as a certain mode of divine presence, we are transformed not just spiritually but emotionally as we are elevated to share in God's life, healed from the wounds of sin, and filled with infused virtue.[71] Grace does not replace or override nature; it perfects human nature and human affectivity so that it can flourish on a higher level. Throughout the Second Part of the Second Part, Aquinas shows great interest again and again in how specific virtues and vices influence our passions and affections, whether for good or for ill.[72] He also discusses how the gifts of the Holy Spirit, in a way transcending normal human modes of acting, elevate and perfect human affectivity through a kind of *habitus* responsive to the Spirit rather than our reason, either to compensate for our shortcomings and limitations or to infuse emotions transcending normal human psychology.[73]

In his treatment of the theological virtues of faith, hope, and charity, Aquinas gives particular attention to their influence on human affectivity. For Aquinas, faith is primarily a virtue of the intellect, but it is not simply about intellectual assent to divinely revealed truth; it also involves the will and its affections. "The faith that is a gift of grace inclines us to believe by imparting affection for the good."[74] Hope and charity, meanwhile, are virtues of the will, and therefore appetite.[75] When they are brought to act, they produce intellectual affections: Through hope, we love God for the good things he gives us, and through charity, we love God for himself.[76] Beyond their immediate influence, faith, hope, and charity have ripple effects that shape our affections in other ways. Immediately after finishing the questions on charity, Aquinas turns to joy and peace, for example, and it is here – in the context of the theological virtue of charity – that he gives his most extended discussion of either. Aquinas explains that, since charity implies, through grace, the possession of the good toward which it strives, namely God himself, acts of charity

---

[71] ST I 43.3; ST I-II 109.2, 110.4.
[72] On his treatment of specific virtues and vices and their influence on human affectivity in the Second Part of the Second Part, see Lombardo, *Logic of Desire*, pp. 148–200.
[73] ST I-II 68. See also Bouchard, "Recovering the Gifts of the Holy Spirit in Moral Theology."
[74] ST II-II 5.2 ad 2.
[75] ST II-II 18.1, 24.1.
[76] ST II-II 17.2, 25.1.

necessarily attain the good that they seek and thus necessarily result in joy.[77] Charity also leads to peace, which Aquinas describes as "a union of the inclinations of the appetites."[78] By its shaping of the affections in these and other ways, charity unites our affections in our affection for God and brings them into harmony with God's affections.[79]

For Aquinas, Jesus is, of course, the ultimate model and exemplar of human affectivity. Despite a strong tendency in his theological milieu to distinguish sharply between Christ's sinless humanity and our wounded nature, Aquinas emphatically affirms the essential similarity between Christ's experience of being human and our own. Christ assumed a true human nature "with all its natural affections"[80] and "permitted all the powers of the soul to act in their own proper ways."[81] Aquinas does hold that "passions were in Christ in a way different than they are in us,"[82] but the reason for this dissimilarity is not that his passions somehow transcended normal human functioning. "Christ had absolutely no disordered desires,"[83] and since disordered passion is not natural to human nature,[84] his affectivity is more human than ours, not less.

6.5 Conclusion

When Aquinas finished his Treatise on the Passions in 1271, it was probably the longest sustained discussion of the passions ever written.[85] From this brief chapter, it should be evident that he had abundant reasons for giving the topic of the passions such unprecedented attention. But what put him on to the theological significance of emotion and desire in the first place? Many factors surely contributed, not the least of them being the influence of Aristotle. But more fundamentally, his attention to emotion and desire flows from two theological convictions. The first was a deep, thoroughgoing trust in the ineradicable goodness of creation – something intrinsic to the culture of the Dominican order in its early days, the order having been founded in response to those who doubted it – which made him more optimistic than many of his contemporaries

---

[77] ST II-II 28.1.
[78] ST II-II 29.3 ad 3.
[79] ST I-II 73.1 ad 3; ST II-II 26.9 obj. 3.
[80] ST III 21.2.
[81] ST III 18.5.
[82] ST III 15.4.
[83] ST III 7.2 ad 3.
[84] ST I-II 82.4 ad 1.
[85] See Gondreau, "The Passions and the Moral Life," p. 426; Lombardo, *Logic of Desire*, p. 1, n. 2.

about how much of that goodness could survive after sin, and about the extent to which God's original purpose in giving us emotions and desires was still relevant in our fallen condition. The second is a certain belief that creation reflects its Creator, that the goodness of creation points to the goodness of God, and that God is the guarantor of desire: both as the one who guarantees the fulfillment of the desires he put in us, and as the one who fulfills them.

CHAPTER 7

Aquinas on Moral Progress

Tobias Hoffmann

It is bad enough that, out of weakness, we often act contrary to our own better judgment. What is worse, sometimes we do not even care about doing what is right, and do evil deliberately. In neither case is there an easy solution. Moral instruction does not seem to help, because weak evildoers already know what is right but fail to act accordingly, while deliberate evildoers do not even want to listen to moral instruction – nor would they understand it if they did. Compulsion does not seem to help, because moral goodness implies not only doing what is good, but also doing it willingly. How, then, is moral progress possible?

This chapter studies Thomas Aquinas's theory of moral progress, especially in the First Part of the Second Part of the *Summa Theologiae*. While the text does not offer much explicit discussion of moral progress, the topic is present throughout the First Part of the Second Part, which contains his fundamental theory of morality. Study of the topic of moral progress thus has the added benefit of providing an overview of Aquinas's moral thought.

The chapter begins with Aquinas's view on happiness as the endpoint of moral progress (Section 7.1). For Aquinas, human happiness is two-fold: One is imperfect happiness, which is attainable by our own natural capacities by means of virtuous activity; the other is perfect happiness, which is supernatural happiness, bestowed on us gratuitously. Aquinas's theory of the progress toward natural, imperfect happiness makes up the central part of this chapter, which discusses Aquinas's theory of virtue acquisition, the different challenges faced by weak and deliberate sinners in progressing toward the virtues, the function of the civil law as an external motivator, a person's internal motivations, and the acquisition of prudence (Sections 7.2–7.6). The chapter ends with brief remarks

Previous versions were read at the University of St. Thomas in Minnesota and at the Hoger Instituut voor Wijsbegeerte in Leuven. I have greatly profited from comments from both audiences. I also thank Jeffrey Hause, Angela Knobel, and an anonymous reader for comments on previous drafts.

on Aquinas's specifically Christian perspective on moral progress. What orders us to supernatural happiness as our ultimate end are divinely infused virtues; this raises the question of what is the function of the naturally acquired virtues in view of our ultimate end, and how they relate to the infused virtues and in general to grace (Section 7.7).

7.1   Twofold Human Happiness

According to Aquinas, like all natural things, human beings by nature seek their end, that is, their perfection, the full realization of their potential. If we want to know how to reach the end, we must have a correct conception of the end, as Aquinas makes clear at the beginning of the First Part of the Second Part: "First we must ponder about the ultimate end of human life, and then about that by which human beings can attain this end or stray from it; for it is on the basis of the end that we must identify the characteristics of what promotes the end" (I-II 1.1 prol.).[1] Now this ultimate end is happiness (ibid.), which all people desire. But while we cannot fail to desire *something* as the ultimate end (I-II 1.1, 1.4), we can go right or wrong in identifying the end concretely (*DV* 22.7 lines 61–82). Indeed, not all people seek happiness in the same things; for example, some search for it in riches, and others in bodily pleasures (I-II 1.7).

So in order to seek happiness rightly we must know what happiness consists in. Aquinas's approach to this question is deeply Aristotelian, and yet his solution departs considerably from Aristotle's. Aquinas adopts Aristotle's view that happiness must be self-sufficient (that is, completely fulfilling human desire so that nothing is left to desire) and final (that is, not merely a means to some further end) (I-II 1.5–6). He furthermore infers from Aristotle's account of happiness that it must be everlasting (*In I Ethic.* 10 lines 155–65).[2] But according to these criteria, there can only be imperfect happiness in this life. Aquinas attributes this conclusion to Aristotle: Given the limitations of life, we can only be called happy "as humans" (I-II 3.2 ad 4, 5.4c).[3] Aquinas argues that perfect happiness does not consist in anything attainable in this life, but only in the next: It can consist only in the vision of the divine essence, because it alone

---

[1] All translations are my own.
[2] While the first two criteria are clearly pronounced by Aristotle, the third is not; see Müller, "*Duplex beatitudo,*" pp. 60–2, 65–8.
[3] Müller, "*Duplex beatitudo,*" p. 62; Aristotle, *Nicomachean Ethics* 1.10.1101a20–1.

appeases all human desire (I-II 3.8c, 5.4c), and it alone is everlasting (I-II 5.4c).[4]

The imperfect happiness attainable in this life consists in the activity of the speculative and practical intellect (I-II 3.5c, 4.6c). In other words, it consists in theoretical knowledge (*contemplatio*) – that is, in the activity of the speculative intellectual virtues of scientific knowledge, wisdom, and insight (*scientia, sapientia, intellectus*) – and in the practice of the moral virtues (I-II 3.6 ad 1, 5.4c, 5.5c). The moral virtues are stable dispositions (*habitus*) that perfect the appetitive powers – that is, the will and the sensitive appetite, which is the seat of the passions – and they order our actions and passions according to right reason (I-II 55.1–2, 59.4). In fact, for Aquinas what contributes to moral perfection is not only a good will and good actions, but also well-ordered passions (I-II 24.3c, 59.5).

The main focus of this chapter is not the attainment of happiness as such, but rather the progress toward the moral virtues, without which imperfect happiness cannot be had. For Aquinas, there are also virtues that order us toward supernatural happiness, as we will see at the end of the chapter. We now turn to Aquinas's basic account of virtue acquisition, in which we are not yet concerned with the existential circumstances that condition the path to virtue.

7.2 The Basic Account of Virtue Acquisition

Human life contains circular causal relations. Following Aristotle, Aquinas discusses two circular relations in virtue acquisition. One is this: The virtue of justice is acquired by performing just actions, and it would seem that in order to perform just actions, one must possess the virtue of justice; the same holds for temperance and so forth (NE 2.4). Another is this: Each moral virtue presupposes prudence, and prudence presupposes all the moral virtues (NE 6.12–13). Are these interdependences viciously circular? Then the acquisition of virtue would be impossible.

Aristotle had already shown that the interdependence between just actions and the virtue of justice, if rightly understood, does not involve a vicious circle. He argued that those who are not yet virtuous can indeed perform virtuous actions, although not *virtuously*, that is, not in the same way as a virtuous person would perform them. The non-virtuous can

---

[4] For a thorough study of Aquinas's account of imperfect and perfect happiness as the two human ends, see Bradley, *Aquinas on the Twofold Human Good.*

do just actions without doing them justly. In order to act *virtuously*, one must have knowledge of what one is doing, choose the act and choose it for its own sake, and act from a firm and unchangeable character (NE 2.4.1105a17–34). Aquinas makes Aristotle's solution his own, at times repeating Aristotle's formula of acting knowingly, willingly, and firmly (I-II 100.9c), at other times phrasing the conditions as acting promptly and with pleasure (e.g., I-II 107.4c; II-II 32.1 ad 1).

According to Aquinas, the basic capacity for doing virtuous acts (virtuously or otherwise) is grounded in the intellect and the will. On the side of the intellect, it is based upon the insight into what Aquinas calls "the first practical principles," which he considers to be self-evident, and which he calls the "seeds of the virtues" (I-II 51.1c, 63.1c, 63.2 ad 3). Examples of such self-evident practical principles are that "good is to be done and evil to be avoided" (I-II 94.2), that "God is to be obeyed," and that one must live according to reason (*DV* 16.1 ad 9). On the side of the will, the possibility for virtuous actions is grounded upon the will's natural desire for the good that conforms to reason (I-II 63.1c). Repeating virtuous acts generates virtue proper, by disposing the individual more and more not only to do virtuous acts, but also to do them *virtuously* – that is, promptly and with pleasure (DVC 9c, ad 13, ad 14). So the relation is indeed circular, but not viciously circular. Notice that sheer repetition of external acts does not generate any virtue. One acquires virtue by acts that conform to the rule of reason (I-II 63.2c, DVC 9c, ad 14). This presupposes that the acts be done for a good end (I-II 18.4–6). In fact, to abstain from an affair because to entertain a mistress would be too costly does not make one chaste (cf. II-II 23.7c). From the start, then, one must act knowingly and willingly, but only when virtue is attained can one also act firmly, promptly, and with pleasure.[5]

For Aquinas, the interdependence between the moral virtues and prudence is not viciously circular either. But before addressing this kind of circularity, we must see how Aquinas argues for this interdependence. Prudence presupposes the moral virtues, for they guarantee that prudential reasoning proceeds from the correct principles of action (*principia agibilium*). These principles of action may be either general or particular. General principles of action consist in the just-mentioned self-evident practical principles and in other principles that belong to general practical knowledge (*scientia practica*). These general principles of prudential

---

[5] For a more detailed analysis of Aquinas's solution, see Verbeke, "L'éducation morale et les arts chez Aristote et Thomas d'Aquin."

reasoning, which indicate the generic ends of the moral life (e.g., that one must live justly) do not presuppose the moral virtues. In fact, as we have seen, the self-evident practical principles are themselves the foundation for acquiring the moral virtues; they are the "seeds of virtue." But in addition, prudential reasoning requires correct particular principles of action, which are the particular ends of action (e.g., that now justice is to be done, or that now such and such pleasure is to be avoided). These particular ends must be good ends, and their goodness is a result of the moral virtues, for the virtues make it connatural to a person to judge correctly about the end. When a judgment about what is to be done becomes connatural, it is apprehended not only as good in the abstract, but it is felt as good "in the heart," that is, as good for me, here and now.[6] In addition to producing this connaturality of judgments, the moral virtues check the passions so that they do not interfere with the proper working of practical reason.[7] For example, it is thanks to the virtue of courage that the courageous intend to brave dangers rather than to run away from them and that they are not overly frightened.

Not only does prudence presuppose the moral virtues, but also the moral virtues themselves presuppose prudence, for it is prudence that allows us to make the right choices in view of virtuous ends (I-II 58.4c, 65.1c). Thanks to prudence, the courageous can decide in a particular situation how best to act courageously. One might think that each moral virtue has its own specific prudence, so that there are as many prudences as there are moral virtues.[8] Then each virtue could be acquired separately, together with its corresponding prudence. But Aquinas insists that there is a single virtue of prudence that directs our choices with regard to all the moral virtues, indeed with regard to all moral matters, that is, with regard to life as a whole. He argues that human passions and actions, which are the subjects of the different virtues, are all interconnected, and so they must all be directed by a single virtue of prudence (I-II 60.1 ad 1, 65.1 ad 3, 73.1c; cf. *In VI Ethic.* 11 lines 154–64). Prudence, then, connects all the acquired moral virtues together; one moral virtue cannot be

---

[6] I-II 58.5; see also I-II 57.4; DVCard. 2c; for more detailed discussion, see Hoffmann, "Prudence and Practical Principles," pp. 175–81.
[7] For the effect of strong passions on prudence, see I-II 34.1, II-II 47.16; for the effect of sexual pleasure on prudence, see II-II 53.6, 153.5 ad 1.
[8] This hypothesis had in fact some following, especially after Aquinas; see, e.g., Duns Scotus, *Ordinatio* III 36 n. 42, *Opera Omnia* vol. x, p. 239.

had without the others, since prudence presupposes the moral virtues, and each moral virtue presupposes prudence (I-II 65.1).[9]

How is this interdependence not viciously circular? The answer is that the moral virtues and prudence can only be attained together (I-II 65.1 ad 1, DVCard. 2 ad 9, ad 10). This response, as Duns Scotus would observe, seems to be vulnerable to the objection that a single act would then generate all the moral virtues and prudence by transforming the pre-virtuous dispositions all at once into virtuous dispositions.[10] To respond, two observations must be made. First, we have already seen that for Aquinas one attains the moral virtues by means of virtuous acts that are not yet done virtuously. In the context of the connection of the virtues, we find an explanation that accounts for the same psychological phenomenon in different terms. Before we attain the moral virtues, we have "imperfect virtues," which derive from one's individual particular bodily constitution or from habituation. The imperfect virtues can exist and increase separately from one another. Aquinas describes them as "conditions" (*dispositiones*), that is, as transitory qualities (II-II 141.1 ad 2, DVCard. 2 ad 12), or as *habitus*, that is, as stable qualities.[11] Imperfect virtues which are *habitus* are not yet virtues because they lack prudence (I-II 65.1 ad 1). They allow us to do good acts, albeit without doing them well. In contrast, "perfect virtues" incline us to do these acts well, that is, virtuously. Only the perfect virtues are connected (I-II 65.1c, DVCard. 2).[12] The second observation is this: Aquinas thinks that *habitus* in general and virtues in particular are indeed attained all at once and

---

[9] Aquinas develops this particular argument for the connection of the acquired virtues on the basis of Aristotle, NE 6.12–13. But he also argues for the connection of the virtues on other grounds that he takes from the Stoic-Patristic tradition; see I-II 65.1, *DVCard.* 2. Kent argues that according to Aquinas, prudence requires only the cardinal virtues of temperance, courage, and justice; see Kent, "Dispositions and Moral Fallibility," pp. 153–5.

[10] Duns Scotus, *Ordinatio* III 36 nn. 27–30, *Opera Omnia*, vol. x, pp. 230–3.

[11] Aquinas follows Aristotle, who distinguishes between two ways of being disposed or conditioned: *diathesis* and *hexis* (plural *diatheseis* and *hexeis*). The former changes more easily, while the latter is more lasting and harder to change. Aquinas comments on this distinction at some length in I-II 49.2 and 3. Aristotle's examples for *diatheseis* are heat/cold and health/sickness, while for *hexeis* his examples are knowledge and the virtues; see *Cat.* 8.8b26–9a13. The word *hexis* is not easily translated to English. Literally, it simply means a "having" of something. The Latins translated it as *habitus*. The English word "habit," however, is not a suitable translation because a habit results from habituation, which is true for the moral virtues but not for knowledge. A better translation is "disposition," but it has other disadvantages, including the fact that the Latins use *dispositio* to translate *diathesis*. For the difficulties of translation, see Kent, "Dispositions and Moral Fallibility," pp. 144–5. I will leave the word *habitus* in the Latin.

[12] For detailed discussions of the connection of the virtues, see Porter, "The Unity of the Virtues and the Ambiguity of Goodness" and Osborne, Jr., "Perfect and Imperfect Virtues in Aquinas."

not by increments; he writes: "Not every act accomplishes the generation of a virtue, but every act works toward it as disposing to virtue, and the last, which is more perfect because it acts in virtue of all the previous acts, reduces [the virtue] in act, just as it happens with many drops piercing a stone" (II-II 24.6 ad 2, cf. DVC 9 ad 11). It is indeed plausible that the attainment of perfect virtues may happen on one particular day in one's life, when doing a particular act that transforms one's practical intelligence into the virtue of prudence, which now informs all the aspects of one's moral life.

Once one has attained the virtues, together with prudence, one can continue to make moral progress. Yet for Aquinas the virtues themselves cannot grow, for each virtue consists essentially in a maximum. For example, temperance regards the mean in all pleasures of food, drink, and sex (II-II 141.4). So one does not become more temperate by extending one's temperance to more kinds of pleasures, but rather by participating in this virtue to a higher degree, that is, by being more disposed to its acts and thus to perform the acts more firmly and with greater delight and promptness. Growth of the virtues – in the sense of a greater participation – can happen either because of greater habituation, or by a more acute judgment of reason, or by a greater gift of grace (I-II 66.1, 52.1). The connectedness of the virtues is also reflected in the growth of the virtues, for they grow proportionally to one another, like the fingers of a growing hand (I-II 66.2).

Aquinas's explanation serves to show how virtue acquisition is possible in principle; but the more interesting question is how virtue acquisition is possible under the individual's concrete existential conditions. Moral progress toward the virtues presupposes that one sees the point of changing and hence wants to change, but people entrenched in a corrupt way of living are not easily convinced that they ought to change.

7.3   Weak and Deliberate Sinners

The problem of moral progress poses itself differently for those who struggle with their weakness than for those who are content with their depraved lifestyle. Aristotle famously distinguishes between two character types who err in the domain of food, drink, and sex: the incontinent and the intemperate. The incontinent err in these matters contrary to their better judgment because of momentary passion, and once the passion has calmed, they regret their evil actions. In contrast, Aristotle says that the intemperate err in these matters without regretting their actions, and without even being aware of their vice, by which he seems to intend that they fail to see that it is not worth living a life of self-indulgence. Aristotle therefore considers the incontinent to be curable and the intemperate to be incurable (NE 7.8.1150b29–36).

This Aristotelian distinction is in the background of Aquinas's distinction between those who sin "from weakness" (*ex infirmitate*) and those who sin from deliberate evildoing (*ex malitia*).[13] We may call the first "weak sinners" and the second "deliberate sinners."[14] Aquinas considers the fundamental difference between weak and deliberate sinners to be this: The will of weak sinners is ordered to a good end – weak sinners at least have the good resolution to abstain from sinning. In contrast, the will of deliberate sinners is fixed on an evil end, for they are intent on sinning.[15] Deliberate sinners are in a comparable situation to those who are in error about the first theoretical principles: The latter cannot be easily corrected because there are no prior principles by which they could be shown to be mistaken. Analogously, deliberate sinners err about practical principles, which are the ends they pursue (DM 3.13c lines 91–108). Apparently Aquinas intends to say this: If they merely pursued inadequate means to good ends, they could be corrected concerning the bad means by appealing to their interest in the good end; but as a matter of fact they pursue unfitting ends, so there is nothing in virtue of which one could appeal to motivate them to change.

Yet according to Aquinas, the mistake of deliberate sinners is not entirely beyond correction. In his view, one can be intent on evil ends, but one cannot be cognitively mistaken about the first, self-evident practical principles.[16] It is impossible to err about the principle that "good is to be done and evil is to be avoided," and so one cannot fail to understand that the pursuit of the good is the ultimate end of life. As we have seen above, one can err merely about what the good that is the ultimate

---

[13] I-II 77–78; DM 3.9–13. At first glance, Aquinas's weak and deliberate sinners are generalizations of Aristotle's incontinent and vicious persons: the first sin from whichever passion, the second from whichever vice. But for Aquinas, not all deliberate sinners sin from a *habitus*; see I-II 78.3, DM 3.14–15. See the helpful discussion in Kent and Dressel, "Weakness and Willful Wrongdoing in Aquinas's *De malo*." See also McCluskey, *Thomas Aquinas on Moral Wrongdoing*, Chapters 5–6.

[14] For Aquinas, the word "sin" belongs not only to moral theology but extends to moral philosophy as well; see I-II 71.6, especially ad 5.

[15] Yet for Aquinas, even deliberate sinners are not intent on sinning under the description in which it is a sin, but rather pursue evil under the guise of good; see I-II 78.1 ad 1, ad 2.

[16] He makes this clear in his discussions of *synderesis*, the fundamental moral compass which is the foundation for judgments of conscience. According to Aquinas, *synderesis* is the dispositional, indelible knowledge of the first practical principles; see DV 16.1–2; I 79.12.

end specifically consists in. For Aquinas, whatever state of moral corruption one may be in, the self-evident practical principles remain seeds of virtue. Accordingly, Aquinas is less pessimistic than Aristotle about the prospects of the intemperate for making moral progress. Aquinas believes that the intemperate, who are inclined to sin not by momentary passion but by a persistent disposition, *are* able to repent, although "not easily" (DM 3.13c lines 73–90).

A further reason why Aquinas is more optimistic than Aristotle about moral reform is that Aristotle and Aquinas have a fundamentally different conception of *habitus*. According to Aristotle, a *habitus* can fix a person's character irreversibly: Just as those who have repeatedly ignored the advice of their doctor can become incurably sick, and just as those who have thrown away a stone cannot have it back, so too "it was at the beginning possible for the unjust and the intemperate not to become unjust and intemperate, and so they are this way voluntarily; but once they have become that way, they can no longer be otherwise" (NE 3.5.1114a12–21). Appealing to the authority of Averroes, Aquinas argues on the contrary that *habitus* are in the control of the will. Thus one is always free to use or not to use one's *habitus*.[17] So even viciously inclined people can do virtuous acts by which over time they can overcome their vice. Accordingly, in his *Ethics* Commentary Aquinas softens Aristotle's claim about the irreversibility of vice. He says that evil *habitus* are not "fully" (*omnino*) in the will's control and that vicious *habitus* cannot be "immediately" (*statim*) abandoned (*In III Ethic.* 12 lines 109–10, line 131).[18]

But in another way Aquinas is more pessimistic than Aristotle: According to Aquinas, even the virtuous do not entirely overcome their disordered desires (DVC 10 ad 14), nor can they, without the assistance of divine grace, consistently avoid all evildoing for an extended period of time. This would in fact require constant attention, which because of the weakening of human nature due to original sin exceeds the human capacity (I-II 74.3 ad 2, 109.8). Aquinas's virtuous person thus resembles Aristotle's continent person more than his virtuous one.[19]

---

[17] See, e.g., I-II 50.3 ad 2; 50.5c; 71.4; 78.2c; DM 3.13 ad 4; cf. Averroes, *In De Anima* 3.18, ed. Crawford, p. 438. On Aquinas's theory of the will's control of *habitus*, see Kent, "Dispositions and Moral Fallibility," pp. 147–53.

[18] For the same reasons, Aristotle and Aquinas disagree about whether virtuous people can backslide; according to Aristotle they cannot, while according to Aquinas they can. See Kent, "Losable virtue: Aquinas on character and will."

[19] Cf. Kent, *Virtues of the Will*, p. 210.

We must now see how moral progress is possible, existentially speaking, for deliberate sinners. Aquinas thinks that they can be motivated to pursue virtue by the force of law. His solution depends largely on Aristotle's discussion of moral education, and yet in a key respect departs from it.

7.4   Moral Reform by Force

In discussing the moral reform of habitual evildoers, Aristotle stresses two functions of law in making people good (NE 10.9.1179a33–1180a24). First, it regulates the upbringing of the young so that they might develop a taste for the noble and a delight in acting virtuously (1179b23–6). Second, it forces by penalty of punishment those who do not act virtuously of their own accord, presumably because they either did not benefit from such upbringing or because it was unsuccessful. Such individuals cannot attain virtue proper, but at best only attain a share in virtue (1179b16–20).

Aquinas carefully analyzes this passage in his *Ethics* Commentary and integrates its main points into an article of the *Summa Theologiae* in which he discusses the usefulness of what he calls the "human law," and specifically civil law, that part of human law which has present relevance.[20] Here is the key passage of the article:

> Since some people are shameless and prone to vice, who cannot easily be moved by words, it was necessary that they be kept back from evil by force and fear, so that they may at least stop acting badly and let others have a peaceful life, and so that they, by being accustomed in this way, may eventually be brought to do willingly what before they performed out of fear, thus becoming virtuous. And this kind of education, which forces by the fear of punishment, is the education of the laws. (I-II 95.1c)

It is significant that Aquinas thinks that by fear of punishment, people of corrupt character might eventually be brought to do what is good *willingly*, that is, no longer from fear, and that they may thus attain virtue (see also I-II 92.2 ad 4). Again, Aquinas is more optimistic than Aristotle: While Aristotle promised merely a share in virtue, Aquinas promises

---

[20] For Aquinas, the human law splits into *ius gentium* and *ius civile*; see I-II 95.4. *Ius gentium* could be translated as "international law"; it contains principles of just commerce (I-II 95.4) and international relations, for example, that treaties are to be honored (*pacta sunt servanda*); see *In V Ethic.* 12 lines 71–2. – For Aquinas's theory of moral education by means of the civil law, see also George, *Making Men Moral*, Chapter 1.

virtue proper.²¹ So law enforcement and fear of punishment play an initial role in moral education by bringing a person to do repeatedly good actions. Virtue, however, is not attained by mere repetition, but only if in addition there is a change of mind, namely when what was previously done from fear is later done of the individual's own accord. Recall that virtues are acquired by repeated acts done for the right reason; repeatedly doing just acts merely from fear of punishment will not make a person virtuous.

But how far does the power of human laws extend in making people overcome their vices? Although in the above quotation Aquinas seems to grant to human law quite a strong role in making people better, what he writes shortly afterwards suggests that he considers its role to be rather limited. In fact, he holds that the task of human laws is not to prohibit all vices, but only the most severe and harmful ones:

> The human law is put down for the multitude of people, the majority of which is not perfected by virtue. And therefore the human law does not prohibit all the vices from which virtuous people abstain, but only the more serious ones, from which it is possible for the majority of the multitude to abstain, and it prohibits above all those that are harmful to others, without the prohibition of which human society cannot be preserved. What is prohibited by the human law is, for example, murder, theft, and the like. (I-II 96.2c)

This passage is in line with what Aquinas writes a little later: "The end of human law is the temporal tranquility of the state, which end the law attains by prohibiting exterior actions as to those evils that can upset the peaceful condition of the state" (I-II 98.1c). Specifically, the task of the human law is not to repress intemperance as such. In fact, elsewhere Aquinas states explicitly that the human law does not (and Aquinas intends to say: *rightly* does not) punish fornication, for there are too many who are unable to abstain from it (II-II 69.2 ad 1). Aquinas furthermore argues that the human law rightly tolerates some evils in order to prevent the elimination of greater goods, and he cites Augustine who says that prostitution should be tolerated in order to avoid greater evils (II-II 10.11c; cf. I-II 91.4c).²² How can human law pressure the

---

²¹ Aquinas seems unaware of this subtle but significant difference; see also his interpretation in *In X Ethic.* 14 lines 86–92. In part this is due to the Latin translation he uses, where μεταλάβοιμεν τῆς ἀρετῆς (10.9.1179b19–20) – "we may attain a share of virtue" – is translated with "accipiamus virtutem" – "we may attain virtue."

²² On Aquinas's view about the toleration of vices, see MacIntyre, "Natural Law as Subversive."

intemperate to abandon their vice if its scope is restricted in this way? In many cases, it cannot.

If not by the force of law, how can the intemperate be motivated to change? Aquinas thinks that the desire to change may come from the person's own initiative, albeit possibly triggered by an external event.

7.5   Moral Reform from Within

Aquinas suggests that deliberate sinners, such as the intemperate, might get disgusted by their vice, and at least in this regard, they might more easily change their way of living than those who are slack in doing good: "Sinners who consider their evil are sometimes stirred against it so intensely that it causes them to aspire to perfection; whereas those who do what is good, but laxly, do not have anything very abhorrent, and so they are more content with their situation and are not easily bettered" (DM 3.13 ad 3).

Another reason they might change could be that they become attracted to virtue. Aquinas does not develop this idea to address the possibility of moral reform, but he provides some interesting considerations from which we can construct a theory *ad mentem Thomae*. In Aquinas's view, there is something intrinsically attractive about the moral virtues, for they have an inner beauty, a "spiritual beauty." This spiritual beauty is what Aquinas understands to be indicated by the term *honestum*, by which Cicero translated the Greek word for beautiful, *kalon* (II-II 145.2c, ad 1).[23] In Aquinas's view, spiritual beauty applies in particular to temperance, because it repels disgraceful lusts (II-II 145.4). How can the intemperate perceive the beauty and hence the attraction of temperance? Aquinas is silent on this. For deliberately intemperate people, it is not attractive to act temperately; on the contrary: They are attracted to evil, which because of their corrupt *habitus* they experience as something consonant (*conveniens*) to them (I-II 78.3c). Nonetheless, it may well be attractive to them to be in the presence of temperate people, by whom they do not feel reduced to their potential value for sexual pleasure but instead feel treated in a disinterested way. And this may provoke the beginning of a change.[24] Analogous considerations can be made about

---

[23] For Aquinas's theory of spiritual beauty, see Ramos, "Moral Beauty and Affective Knowledge in Aquinas."

[24] I had made this suggestion in my "Aquinas on the Moral Progress of the Weak Willed," p. 243. For an example from literature, see Milosz, *Miguel Mañara*. The seducer don Miguel Mañara meets

cowards being attracted to courage by actions of courageous persons, and so forth.

Obviously, with the new desire to attain the virtues, one has not yet attained moral perfection. As we have seen, one does not become virtuous instantaneously. But according to Aquinas, the principal step toward moral progress consists in the change of mind by which a person is no longer fixed upon a bad end but rather starts to desire what is good. What consolidates this change of mind is the virtue of prudence, the acquisition of which we will consider next.

7.6 Acquiring Prudence

The need for consolidating a change of mind returns us to the question of the role of proper moral knowledge in moral progress. In one sense, this role is limited, because correct moral knowledge does not guarantee good willing and good action. One may well know what is best without doing it. The incontinent know that they should abstain from certain pleasures, but, as Aquinas says, they do not feel this "in their heart" (DM 3.9 ad 8; *In VII Ethic.* 3 lines 215–17). Moral knowledge becomes useful only if we make it fully our own, if we internalize it. Prudence, that is, "wisdom in human affairs" (II-II 47.2 ad 1), is the virtue of internalized moral knowledge. Prudence allows us to make good decisions that concern life as a whole.[25]

How do we acquire prudence? Aquinas does not discuss this question directly, but an indirect answer is found in two aspects of his conception of prudence. We have already considered the first aspect: Prudence requires the moral virtues, which guarantee that one pursues virtuous ends. Hence the more one advances in the acquisition of moral virtue, the more one disposes oneself to acquiring prudence. We will now look at the second aspect, which sheds light on how Aquinas seems to think prudence is acquired. According to Aquinas, various abilities and attitudes, which he calls the components (*partes integrales*) of virtue, "have to act together (*concurrere*) for a perfect act of that virtue" (II-II 48.1c). The virtues are not constituted of parts in a literal sense, for *habitus* are indivisible forms, and thus one *habitus* is not composed of other *habitus* (I-II

Girolama and is amazed by her purity. This makes him want to give up his dissolute life.

[25] As Aquinas expresses it in more technical language, prudence allows us to deliberate well, to draw a good conclusive judgment from our deliberation, and to apply this judgment in our action so as to act accordingly; see II-II 47.13c.

54.4c, ad 2). Accordingly Aquinas usually speaks of *quasi*-components (e.g., I-II 57.6 ad 3, II-II 53.2c).

Aquinas calls the components of prudence a prerequisite for prudence (I-II 56.5 ad 3; 57.6 ad 3). Yet he does not suggest that they are also a sufficient condition for prudence. Acquisition of all the components of prudence does not yet constitute prudence proper. Indeed, someone might possess them and abuse them, and hence lack genuine prudence (cf. II-II 53 intro, 55.1 ad 1).

Aquinas mentions eight components of prudence, some of which he finds in Macrobius, others in Cicero, and still others, albeit less explicitly, in Aristotle (II-II 48–9).[26] They are memory (*memoria*, knowledge of the past, by which one acquires experience), insight (*intellectus*, which as a part of prudence concerns the right appraisal of a particular end), docility (*docilitas*, the willingness to learn from others), quickness of mind (*solertia*, the ability easily and promptly to draw inferences), reason (*ratio*, the good use of reason in practical deliberation), foresight (*providentia*, the ability to see how present decisions affect things that lie at a distance so as to be able to order the actions to the end of human life as a whole), circumspection (*circumspectio*, paying attention to all the relevant factors in the present), and caution (*cautio*, by which one avoids evil that risks being mixed in with the good one aims to attain). All of these traits seem to include solicitude (*sollicitudo*), which Aquinas takes to be essential to prudence and which he characterizes by means of quotations from Aristotle and Augustine as careful deliberation and vigilance (II-II 47.9 s.c. and 47.9c). The contrary of due solicitude is negligence, a vice directly opposed to prudence (II-II 53 intr., 54.1–2). Solicitude involves not only taking into account everything relevant for a prudent decision, but also being willing to do so; in fact, Aquinas equates it with diligence (*diligentia*), "for in those things we love (*diligimus*), we employ a greater solicitude" (II-II 54.1 ad 1). Solicitude should be principally about spiritual matters; when it is too concerned about temporal goods, it is inordinate (II-II 55.6c). Aquinas brings the role of solicitude out with particular clarity in discussing two of these components: memory and docility.

Memory is crucial for prudence because it lays the foundation for gaining experience. Indeed, for Aquinas, and for Aristotle (whom he cites), experience comes only from repeated memories (II-II 49.1c; *Met.* 1.1.980b28–981a1). But memory is not generated by mere repetition; the acquisition of memory requires assiduity (*industria*), solicitude, and

---

[26] For further discussion, see Mulvaney, "Wisdom, Time, and Avarice in St. Thomas Aquinas's Treatise on Prudence."

the application of one's affection (*affectus*) to what one tries to remember (II-II 49.1 ad 2). And just as these traits are crucial for memory, and memory is crucial for experience, so too, in turn, experience is crucial for prudence, because prudence is concerned with actions, which are essentially contingent. To direct human actions, knowledge of what is simply and necessarily true is insufficient. What is needed is knowledge of what happens for the most part, and this knowledge is obtained by experience (II-II 49.1c).

But even someone who is rich in experience cannot always sufficiently take into account all the relevant factors for making good decisions. Therefore it belongs to prudence to ask advice from others and to welcome it when it is given. To be so disposed to other people's advice is docility. And such docility involves a person's solicitude and receptivity, as Aquinas explains in this passage:

> For the full attainment of docility, human effort is most important, that is, when one carefully [*sollicite*], frequently, and respectfully applies one's mind to the example of the more experienced [*maiorum*], not neglecting it because of laziness, nor despising it out of pride. (II-II 49.3 ad 2)

Aquinas expresses here clearly what he seems to think of all the attitudes and abilities necessary for prudence: Prudence requires solicitude and receptivity, that is, an attitude of mind that is cognitive and affective at the same time. Although a fully virtuous and prudent person lives in this attitude more easily than others, in principle this attitude seems possible at any stage of moral progress, because the capacity for solicitude and receptivity lies in the very nature of intellect and will.

7.7 Acquired and Infused Virtues, Nature and Grace

What we have considered so far concerns Aquinas's theory of moral progress toward the so-called "acquired virtues," which we can attain through our own efforts and which contribute to imperfect, natural happiness. The virtues that order us to perfect, supernatural happiness are the "theological virtues" of faith, hope, and charity; they are infused in us by God (I-II 62.1c). Furthermore, so that these theological virtues can come to full fruition in our lives, we need "infused moral virtues" by which we can live the various aspects of our lives as informed by charity (I-II 63.3–4).[27] The infused and acquired virtues have the same object, for example,

---

[27] Although the theological virtues of faith, hope, and charity, too, are infused by God, Aquinas normally appropriates the name "infused virtue" to the infused moral virtues.

infused and acquired temperance have pleasures and desires of touch and taste as their object, but they are not specifically the same *habitus*, as though God simply infused in us the *habitus* of an acquired virtue. God can do that (I-II 51.4c), but Aquinas hardly devotes any attention to such divinely generated "acquired virtues." In addition to their origin as either acquired or infused, these two kinds of virtues differ in two further respects: Acquired virtues concern human affairs while infused virtues concern the relation with God; acquired virtues follow the rule of reason, while infused virtues follow the rule of divine law. For example, while by acquired temperance a certain diet might be chosen in view of health, by infused temperance a different diet might be chosen in view of chastising our body (I-II 63.4).

Progress toward acquired virtues and reception of infused virtues – are these two separate stories or are they linked? Can a person progress toward the acquired moral virtues without divine assistance? Conversely, are the person's own efforts a presupposition for receiving the infused virtues? In short: How are nature and grace related in moral progress? In what follows I will provide a rough sketch of Aquinas's answers.

The infused virtues are given altogether gratuitously. But according to Aquinas, we also need grace to attain the acquired virtues. The problem is not that grace is required to prevent us from sinning, for occasional sins do not impede virtue acquisition, just as sporadic evil acts do not corrupt a virtuous *habitus* (I-II 63.2 ad 2). The problem is rather that under the conditions of our present life, marked by original sin, we need healing grace to enable us to do virtuous acts; only prior to original sin were virtuous acts attainable without grace (I-II 109.2c, 109.4c).[28] Furthermore, without the grace of divine guidance and protection we do not fully know what is expedient for us, making it impossible to always do good and avoid evil (I-II 109.9c).

While our efforts are futile without grace, grace can operate without our contribution. God can convert a sinner in an instant, with no preparation on the part of the sinner. This happened in the case of the Apostle Paul: "While he was still on his course of sin, all at once his heart was perfectly moved by God to listen, to learn, and to come, and thus he immediately received grace" (I-II 112.2 ad 2). Nonetheless, our own efforts are not in vain. According to Aquinas, the practice of good actions

---

[28] For a detailed study of the relation between nature and grace in Aquinas, see Torrell, "Nature et grâce chez Thomas d'Aquin," especially pp. 192–7 on the ability to accomplish moral actions without grace.

not only causes the acquired virtues, but also disposes us to the infused virtues and conserves and advances them (I-II 92.1 ad 1). Concerning charity in particular, Aquinas writes that we can dispose ourselves to receiving it and that it is up to us to use it when we have it (I-II 100.10c, DVC 11c).

Accordingly, despite his insistence on the infused virtues, Aquinas does not think they make acquired virtues obsolete.[29] The infused virtues are obtained instantaneously together with charity, but they do not instantaneously remove previous bad *habitus*. For example, formerly intemperate persons who receive infused temperance still struggle to act temperately. Thanks to infused temperance, they no longer have the vicious *habitus* of intemperance, but they still have a bad condition (*dispositio*) resulting from their previous intemperate actions, and this condition makes it more difficult for them to act temperately (I-II 65.3 ad 2, DVCard. 2 ad 2). Those already in possession of acquired temperance experience this struggle less because they are less troubled by passions inclining to evil. But whereas the acquired virtues are better than the infused virtues in calming such passions, the infused virtues are better in keeping us from succumbing to them. For as long as one possesses infused temperance, one will not give in to inordinate desires, whereas one who has acquired temperance might occasionally yield to them (DVC 10 ad 14, ad 16).[30]

The importance Aquinas attributes to the acquired virtues, even from a theological perspective, can be seen also in his discussion of the moral precepts of the Old Law (the law revealed to Moses). These moral precepts are intended to make us good so that we can have friendship with God; in order to make us good, they command the acts of the virtues (I-II 99.2c). Aquinas does not here seem to intend only acts of infused virtues, but also of the acquired virtues. In fact, the moral precepts of the

---

[29] Scholars widely disagree on how Aquinas views the relation between the acquired and the infused virtues. The main issue is whether acquired and infused virtues coexist side by side in the Christian who is in the state of grace or whether the infused virtues somehow integrate the acquired virtues to form a unity; for a discussion of these alternative interpretations of Aquinas, see Knobel, "Two Theories of Christian Virtue." For a recent, but in my view unconvincing argument that in the state of grace the Christian has only infused virtues and altogether lacks acquired virtues, see Mattison III, "Can Christians Possess the Acquired Cardinal Virtues?" I myself defend the coexistence theory. I do not think, however, that for Aquinas the acquired and the infused virtues are mutually dependent, as some scholars hold. For an argument against such an interpretation, see Knobel, "Relating Aquinas's Infused and Acquired Virtues."

[30] Concerning the respective advantages of acquired and infused virtues, see Hause, "Aquinas's Complex Web."

Old Law pertain to natural law (I-II 98.5c, 99.2 obj. 1, ad 1, 99.4c); what belongs to natural law is proportionate to human nature (I-II 91.4 ad 1); and it is the acquired virtues, not the infused virtues, that are proportionate to human nature (I-II 63.2c, 65.2c). The New Law (the evangelical law), too, contains moral precepts concerning the moral virtues; in addition it enjoins the reception of the sacraments (I-II 108.2c, 108.3 ad 3).

For Aquinas, without charity the infused virtues cannot exist at all and the acquired virtues are only virtues in some diminished sense (I-II 65.2–5, DVCard. 2c).[31] Though relatively speaking imperfect, it seems that for Aquinas the acquired virtues without charity are nonetheless genuine virtues.[32] But the acts of acquired virtues can be meritorious, that is, they can contribute to supernatural happiness, only thanks to charity and insofar as they are coupled with infused virtues which order them to supernatural happiness (DVC 10 ad 4; see also II-II 23.7).

7.8   Conclusion

For Aquinas, moral progress can mean quite different things depending on whether it is progress toward the virtues that order us to imperfect or to perfect happiness. Aquinas's theory of moral progress to acquired virtue is characterized by a very tight connection between the cognitive and affective dimensions of human agency. Aquinas does not think that the acquisition of the virtues is a matter of mere willpower, as if we could be consistently motivated to act rightly under every existential circumstance. Nor does he think that moral progress depends on the intellect alone, as if knowing what is right were sufficient for willing and doing what is right. Yet he values the cognitive side of moral progress very highly: The main obstacle to moral progress is not the failure to act according to one's own resolve, but rather the failure to realize which ends are worth pursuing. A change of mind regarding the ends of action may be more difficult to accomplish than a change of behavior. This role of the intellect in moral progress nevertheless leaves an important role for the will: One must be *willing* to pay attention to all the resources that enable correct moral thinking. Only then can one attain prudence, and only with prudence is one fully motivated to act according to one's better knowledge.

---

[31] See Osborne, Jr., "Perfect and Imperfect Virtues in Aquinas."

[32] Over the past decades, it has been debated whether for Aquinas the non-Christian can have genuine virtues. For a recent defense that on Aquinas's view they can, see DeCosimo, *Ethics as a Work of Charity.*

Aquinas is optimistic that such progress to natural moral virtue and prudence is possible at any stage of the moral life – not, to be sure, with the individual's own efforts alone, but through those efforts united to external supports consisting in good laws, the example or good advice of others, and healing grace. As to the attainment of the supernatural end, which provides perfect happiness, Aquinas also sees a close connection between different orders of causes. Although the work of God, the attainment of the supernatural end is not disconnected from our own contribution.

CHAPTER 8

Practical Reason and Normativity

Matthias Perkams

8.1 Introduction

In this chapter I want to argue that Aquinas in the *Summa Theologiae* develops a theory of practical reason and normativity that is well suited to integrate two aims central to theories of practical reason – aims that have been formulated by Aristotle and Kant respectively, as we shall see.[1] In short, he thinks that practical reason is competent to find adequate standards for judging any individual action, bringing together both the universal rules of moral acting and all relevant particularities pertaining to the concrete situation, so as to formulate a specified "rule" which does justice to all relevant aspects of the situation; thus, the agent is able, due to her practical reason, to act in a way which would be right in all comparable situations.

In Aristotle, on the one hand, practical reason is basically *phronēsis*, "a state attaining the truth, connected with reason, concerned with action regarding human goods" (NE 6.5.1140b 20f.), which must be "in agreement with right desire" (NE 6.2.1139a 30f.). Thus, the practical is a mode of reason that is intimately connected with desire and takes as its starting point not a theoretical faculty, but moral virtue, that is, a habitual direction toward some "means," which have to be realized in different actions (NE 6.13.1145a 4–6).[2] Because the virtuous habits are

---

I thank Tobias Hoffmann for generously supplying me with important secondary literature, and Chris Manno for correcting my English.

[1] Recent books on Aquinas's theory of practical reason include Rhonheimer, "The Perspective of the Acting Person"; Schröer, *Praktische Vernunft*, and Westberg, *Right Practical Reason*; on the theory of the moral act cf. Pilsner, *The Specification of Human Actions*, and also Kluxen, *Philosophische Ethik*. However, there are many books and articles covering specific topics in this field.

[2] Modern interpreters of Aristotle often extend the task of *phronēsis* to finding the right ends for human life; this may be inferred from an overall interpretation of Aristotle's practical philosophy, but it is stated nowhere explicitly in Aristotle's text. – Aristotle is quoted according to the translation of W. D. Ross (Oxford 1925), adapted to the present purpose, where necessary.

always acquired by acting in certain situations, practical reason is in a certain sense a particular faculty of each human being, depending on certain contingent circumstances, and includes the competence to judge particular situations (NE 6.10.1143a 32–5). Thus Aristotle stresses the likeness *phronēsis* bears to perception (*aisthēsis*: NE 6.8.1142a 27–30) as well as its close connection with experience (e.g., NE 1141b 8–21).

For Kant, on the other hand, only "pure," that is transcendental, practical reason can determine the capacity of the will, because only this type of reason can be free from any empirical influences (*Critique of Practical Reason* 5.15f.).[3] Such a practical reason, which finds its expression in the famous categorical imperative, has to be thought of as closely linked to "its formal condition, that is, … the universality of maxims of the will as law," because otherwise it would be impossible to conceive the idea of its freedom or autonomy (*Groundwork of the Metaphysics of Morals* 4.458). Thus, only a reason that is neither dependent on particular circumstances, nor concerned with particular situations and actions can be called practical. It is therefore not clear, how it can become competent to judge individual actions – Kant delegates this task to a certain "judgment" (*Urteilskraft*: *Critique of Practical Reason* 5.67) – nor can it move the human being to perform them without a "feeling of respect" (*Gefühl der Achtung*: *Groundwork*, 4.400f.).

Thus, the main philosophical theories of practical reason show a remarkable bipolarity: Either practical reason moves the agent by judging particular situations, being a faculty largely dependent upon and formed by particular circumstances, but without a strictly universal form; or it determines a transcendent, non-empirical will, because it is universal in its form and content, while it lacks in itself the competence to judge particular situations. This tension is treated in modern discussions as one basic problem of philosophical ethics: Whereas many modern philosophers, including utilitarians, share Kant's concern for universal rules as a crucial mark of an ethical theory, this approach has been criticized, sometimes with reference to Aristotle, by some philosophical "particularists," who go as far as denying that universal rules can determine how to act correctly in a single case.[4]

---

[3] I quote Kant according to the 1996 Cambridge Edition of his works, having also compared the German original. Page references are to the Akademie edition.
[4] A typical proposal of this kind is Dancy, *Ethics without Principles*; a particularist reading of Aristotle is advocated by McDowell, "Deliberation and Moral Development."

In comparison with these two approaches, Aquinas accepts Aristotle's theory of practical reason and takes over from him the fact that moral cases must always be evaluated according to the particular situation; however, he transforms Aristotle's theory (1) by working out that the agent performing particular actions has to pursue ends that are apprehended by reason as living up to the standard of universality, and (2) by elaborating a theory of human acts as rational entities. As such, actions can be analyzed with ontological categories, if due attention is paid to the particularities of actions, especially to the changeable character of the universal descriptions that can be given of them. In the end Aquinas's theory remains Aristotelian in important respects, insofar as the circumstances or conditions of the particular action remain crucial for determining the applicable moral rules, as long as those rules are still universal in their form. Furthermore it turns out that Aquinas is especially sensitive to showing that individual agents and their moral judgment are the most relevant particular aspects of any action.

From a historical viewpoint, it is not surprising that Aquinas integrates both universal and particular features in his description of an action. As a Christian thinker, he is convinced that there are valid universal norms – for instance, the rules of the Decalogue, which had already been interpreted by many predecessors as the natural law inherent in human reason.[5] As an Aristotelian, on the other hand, he is committed to the particularity of practical reason and its being embedded in a process of striving for certain ends that are connected to the virtues. However, the complicated hermeneutical situation resulting from the necessity of basing his new theory on sources as different as biblical texts (and their medieval interpretations) and the technical treatises of Aristotle, forced him to look upon the problem from different angles, different concepts, and different sources. Thus if we want to reconstruct his whole theory out of the *Summa Theologiae*, we have to take into account not only the Treatise on Human Action (in particular, I-II 18–21), but also certain parts of the treatises on virtues, on prudence, and on law as well as some scattered remarks in other places.[6] Therefore, in what follows I first argue for an intrinsic connection between Aquinas's theory of reason and will on the one hand, and his description of internal and external actions on the other, before addressing the more concrete questions of how the

---

[5] On the history of the concept of natural law cf. the contribution of Jean Porter to this volume.
[6] In keeping with the scope of this volume I restrict my treatment largely to the *Summa Theologiae*, though some useful additions could be taken from other sources.

moral quality of actions can be assessed and how the role of individual agents can be described.

8.2   Practical Reason, Universality, and Particularity

The systematic rigor of Aquinas's approach to action theory can be seen from his presupposition that morality is generally a domain of reason (II-II 47.6), which elaborates upon medieval predecessors and the Aristotelian idea of an *orthos logos* inherent in any virtuous act. A further background assumption is Aquinas's doctrine of the "human act" or "moral act," which states that any action that is performed by a human being as the "master of her own act"[7] is a product of an interaction of reason and will (I-II 1.3c; I-II 18.5c; I-II 57.5 ad 1, ad 2).

Aquinas relates, also on this point more clearly than Aristotle, the connection between reason and action to both steps of the process of decision-making, that is, to the determination of the ends of one's actions and to the specification of that "which is for the sake of the ends" (*ea quae sunt ad finem*). It is true that, like Aristotle, Aquinas holds that the field of practical reason (*ratio practica* or *prudentia*) is for the sake of the ends: "The reason engaged with matters of this sort is the practical reason" (II-II 47.2c). However, the result of *this* reflection has to be measured against *another* rational standard: "If an act issuing from deliberate reason is not shaped by due purpose, it will be against reason merely because of that" (I-II 18.9c).

As this question suggests, the obvious tension that can result from a self-contradiction of reason indicates a second mode of reason that is concerned with the right ends for human acting[8]: "In practical reason certain naturally evident principles pre-exist, which are the ends of the moral virtues" (II-II 47.6.c). More explanations about this can be found in question 61 of the First Part of the Second Part: Every virtue has its stability, insofar as it is a habit, and its direction toward the good, insofar as it is a virtue, whereas "from the fact that it is a moral virtue participating reason, it follows that it observes in all things the limits set by reason" (I-II 61.4c). Thus every virtue in a certain way relates to the "good of

---

[7] The translations from the *Summa Theologiae* are based on the translation organized by the English Province of Dominican Friars, but are usually adapted by the author of this chapter, in order to be more literal and better suited to the terminology used here.

[8] This point is well explained by Hoffmann, "Prudence and Practical Principles." Cf. also Rhonheimer, *Praktische Vernunft*, pp. 405–29, and Porter, *Nature as Reason*, pp. 250–65, who explains very clearly the differences between Aquinas on the one hand and Kant and Hume on the other.

reason" (*bonum rationis*), either as itself being a habit of right practical reasoning, as prudence is, or as concerned with a certain subject matter out of the "rational order" (*ordo rationis*), as with the other moral virtues, which regulate actions or passions according to reason. Especially crucial for the rightness of actions is justice, which concerns, as outward actions do, the relation of one human being with one another (I-II 61.2c).

The ends pursued by the virtues are therefore instantiations of the goals that every human being naturally knows to be true perfections of a good human life (II-II 47.7c), that is of the natural law – discussed in greater detail in Chapter 9 – which consists in universal rules about what activity is good or bad for human beings (I-II 94.2; cf. I-II 10.1). In us, they are found in the so-called synderesis, which is for Aquinas a fixed habit of the first principles (I 79.12). Thus human beings are not dependent on the virtues for knowing those principles, but the acquired habits, which the virtues are, are essential for living according to them (I-II 58.4 ad 3; I-II 95.1c; II-II 47.6 and 7). By this connection with rational principles, the virtues themselves receive a universal outlook; they are not simply expressions of the moral convictions of certain societies, as some modern virtue theorists assume.[9]

The engagement of prudence with that which is for the sake of an end has to do, as in Aristotle, with its typical subject matter, that is, with individual actions. Aquinas works this out by stating a fundamental distinction between theoretical and practical cognition: The former deals, at least as far as its principles are concerned, with eternal and unchangeable objects, while practical reason is concerned with contingent things (I-II 57.5 ad 3; II-II 47.5c). The assumption, that prudence is capable of judging singular cases (II-II 47.3c), receives further clarification by a comparison of prudence with art: Aquinas not only repeats Aristotle's statement that in art a willed mistake is a sign of the artist's excellence, while with prudence, the contrary is true (I-II 57.4c); he also defines the object of art as exterior things, whereas "prudence is about the doing of human acts (*circa agibilia*), which acts are situated within the person acting" (II-II 47.5c). This connection of prudence with what is internal is due to its dependence upon a right appetite, as constituted by the moral virtues, and by its direction toward suitable ends (I-II 57.4c; elaborating upon Aristotle, NE 6.4.1140a 1–6.5.1140 b6; *Met.* 9.6.1048b 18–36; cf. *In VI Ethic.* 3).

---

[9] Cf. esp. MacIntyre, *After Virtue*, pp. 186–8.

8.3   Object and Circumstances: The Inward Act

This focus on inward aspects of a person, which appears here, is also a salient feature of the analysis of human actions in questions 18–20 of the First Part of the Second Part. These questions concern, as their title indicates, "the goodness and moral evil of human acts" (I-II prologue to question 18). In fact they explain mainly the aspects one has to pay attention to in order to evaluate a human act as either good or bad. Thus these questions describe moral actions in a non-moral way, by analyzing how concepts of moral evaluation can be applied correctly to single actions. Aquinas divides his exposition into three questions: treating human acts in general (question 18), internal human acts (question 19), and external acts (question 20). This division reflects the inner structure of Aquinas's theory of the goodness and badness of actions better than some of his remarks, if taken by themselves.

In the first article of question 18, Aquinas introduces the principle of "completeness of being" (*plenitudo essendi*), a typical element of a Neoplatonic ontology: Every being is, on the one hand, good by its very nature, but on the other hand, it still has to reach the completeness that befits this natural goodness in each relevant aspect. If it fails to do so, it falls short of its own completeness. In that case, it is bad insofar as the realization of its ideal state of being is incomplete (cf. also I 5.1c). Now, Aquinas applies this concept not to substances – as Neoplatonists usually do – but to actions which are, in the Aristotelian ontology whose terminology most Neoplatonists share, accidents of a certain sort. Yet by drawing this analogy between actions and substances, Aquinas can apply to actions the whole conceptual scheme that Aristotelianism had developed in order to analyze substances; this means he can identify quasi-substantial and quasi-accidental elements, a quasi-form and a quasi-matter, and he can analyze them according to the scheme of the four causes.

How can such an ontological account, which was developed to treat natural things as instances of universal species, be commensurate with a view that regards actions as wholly singular events? In order to tackle this problem, Aquinas transforms the ontological concepts when applying them to actions by saying that actions are, as moral entities, a specific ontological category which applies to "rational beings" (*entia rationis*: I-II 17.4c).[10] In articles 2–4 of question 18, he introduces three fundamental

---

[10] A thorough explanation of Aquinas's ontology of actions can be found especially in Pilsner, *Specification*.

concepts, which are his basic tools for the analysis of an action: its object, its end, and its circumstances. Generally speaking, the action receives its "species" from its "object" (I-II 18.2c), which means that in this scheme the object takes the place of the substantial form of a natural entity. The circumstances can be compared with accidents, insofar as some accidents are also necessary for the completeness of an entity, in spite of not belonging to its substantial features (I-II 18.3), while the end receives a separate treatment as a third element (I-II 18.4). All three aspects are necessary for an action to be good, as Aquinas explains, interpreting a further quotation of Dionysius: "Each single defect causes evil" (I-II 18.4 ad 3).We should note that all this is in the first line of the introduction of the principal notions by which actions may be explained. More detailed explanations of what exactly the object of an action is, and the role played by the circumstances and the end, remain relatively open at this point.[11]

Article 5 of the same question comes back to the understanding of moral acts as entities constituted by reason. Because, again according to Dionysius, "a human being's good is to live according to reason ... the difference *good* as well as *evil*, considered with regard to the object, is related per se to reason" (18.5c). Thus the evaluation of a human act always depends upon how this action is perceived by reason. Aquinas explains this by stating that the act of human procreation can occur in the moral sphere either through intercourse in marriage or adultery (I-II 18.5 ad 3). This is basically Peter Abelard's teaching that the same outward act can have a different moral value according to the intention of the agent (cf. I-II 1.3 ad 3)[12]; however, in Aquinas the analysis of the internal states of the agent allows for further differentiation by elaborating upon the rational constitution of actions. In order to understand this correctly, one has to look at the third category relevant for describing an action: the circumstances.

Aquinas explains in 18.9–11 that the objects, according to which actions are good or bad, can change according to how the circumstances of the action are evaluated by reason. At this point he states an

---

[11] This openness of the first part of question eighteen had some impact on raising a scholarly debate about whether by "object of an action" Aquinas means a natural thing or an action itself.

[12] In fact, Abelard also advocates that a good outward action is "a good understood and ordered by reason," in the words of Rhonheimer, "Perspective," p. 470. Cf. e.g. Perkams, *Liebe als Zentralbegriff*, pp. 300–24.

ontological peculiarity of actions that is crucial for explaining their ontological distinction in comparison with natural substances:

> Now there is in nature a determination to one point … so we have to
> arrest our examination at some last form, which marks the specific differ-
> ence, after which there can be no other … Rational processes, however, are
> not similarly fixed to one point, but can advance further from any given
> step. Consequently what in one act is regarded as a circumstance acces-
> sory to the object, which defines its species, may in turn be treated by the
> directive reason as the main condition of its object. (I-II 18.10c)

This explanation implies that the stable relation that any natural entity
has to the species it belongs to all the time of its existence does not apply
to reason-based entities, which actions are. Aquinas illustrates the change-
ability of the species-giving objects of actions with the example of a theft
that, because somebody steals from a holy place, becomes by this local
circumstance a sacrilege. This example shows neatly the constitutive function of an individual's reason in this respect: In its evaluation of a concrete situation, it can set aside that theft is a natural kind of wrong action
according to a universal rational rule and reckon this action to another
species of acting.[13] As the example shows, this is not arbitrary, but it is
indispensable for a correct judgment about the situation in question.

What do we learn from all this about what "the object of the act"
means in Aquinas? Already in question 18.2 he defines this object as what
some people call "good of its kind, for instance using what belongs to
you," thus introducing it as the description of an act that is an instance
or token of a universal description of actions. This is confirmed by the
example just quoted: If "theft" and "sacrilege" are possible candidates for
"the object of the act" of taking something away from a holy place, what
is in question is obviously the universal category best suited to describe
this individual act. The same conclusion can be drawn from Aquinas
saying that acts that are indifferent in their species (that is, according to
their object), always receive, as individual acts, a species that is good or
bad according to the agent's intentions. Obviously those individual acts
are, as soon as they are apprehended by practical reason, classified under
the universal concepts "good" or "bad."[14] Consequently, the particular

---

[13] Pilsner, *Specification*, pp. 180–97 offers a useful classification of different ways in which circumstances can determine an action.
[14] Cf. Pilsner, *Specification*, p. 243: "Human actions have numerous species: They are divided essentially into good and evil, and then subdivided into more particular kinds, such as almsgiving, murder, fraternal correction, or theft."

character of each act is due not to its ontological features as a natural object but rather to the practical judgment about a situation that brings together its different features under a unified description. The object of the moral act is exactly this description, which may include a command to perform that action or to omit it, if it is in line with the ends pursued by the rational agent.[15]

8.4   The Will, the End and the Outward Action

The relevance of the end for the description of the act becomes manifest in article 18.6. While discussing the relation between an action's object and its direction toward an end, Aquinas calls the end the object of the internal act, and consequently the formal element of the act, whereas the object of the external act plays only a material role in comparison with that. More explanations on this point can be found in question 20:

> Now since an end is the will's proper object, it is clear that the quality of good or bad possessed by the outward act because of its direction towards the end is present primarily in the will's act and derivatively in the outward act. However, the good or bad possessed by the outward act considered in itself, that is according to the requisite subject matter and circumstances, does not stem from the will, but rather from reason. (I-II 20.1c)

According to this description, the outward act is the action as conceived by reason, while the inward act is an action performed by the will. This is well in line with the above mentioned process of producing actions: Whereas the "end" of the action is the goal pursued by the will (18.6 and 7c), the task of practical reason or prudence is to find out what is best to do for the sake of that end. It is clear from Aquinas's formulation that the outward act precedes the choice or decision of will, insofar as reason presents it to the will as a possible act, and that follows upon it, insofar as the agent really performs this action by such a choice (I-II 20.1 ad 1).[16] For example, somebody may think, before doing anything, about how to express her enmity against the Christian religion, and then she may envisage as a suitable possibility committing a sacrilege, for example by

---

[15] I agree in the relevant points with Rhonheimer, "Perspective," pp. 468–75. There is still some discussion on this point, cf. the overview in Murphy, "Aquinas on the Object and Evaluation of the Moral Act."

[16] "Choice" (*electio*) is for Aquinas the act of the will which brings about a single action. Cf. Perkams, "Aquinas on Choice, Will, and Voluntary Action," pp. 79–85.

taking away a golden cross from a church; if she then chooses or decides to do so, she afterwards performs the outward action which she described beforehand as a sacrilege. Now, a priest may also think about taking away the same cross in order to carry it in a procession. Of course, he neither envisages nor performs a "sacrilege," but the relevant description, i.e., the "object," of his outward act is "performing a liturgical duty." Thus, the same chain of movements may be described correctly in two ways, depending upon the agent's evaluation of the situation. Now the priest will act in most cases for exactly the end "performing a liturgical duty"; however, in certain cases, he may choose the golden cross in order to boast before his friends. In this case, the object of the inward act, i.e., the end of the action, would be "boasting," while the outward action may still be described as "performing a liturgical duty." However, the inward act lends its form to the whole action, such that, from a moral point of view, it will be a bad action.

The same assumption also lies behind the discussion in question 20: The outward act defined by "matter" and circumstances in question 20 is the act that is, according to 18.10, constituted by reason as having a certain object. The fact that Aquinas speaks in question 20 of "matter and circumstances," and not of "object and circumstances," is best understood as a consequence of his conviction that the object of this act depends upon a rational reconstruction that already includes the circumstances.[17]

Thus we can discern a multilayered structure within an action by distinguishing (1) the observable movement in the sensible world, (2) the "outward act" constituted by reason (which may be performed as an observable act, depending upon the will), and (3) the "inward act" of the will, which may include the choice to perform one or more outward acts performed by reason. For Aquinas it is a specific characteristic of rationally constituted beings that they can form a unity of several features that are different under another description, especially as natural beings. This is undoubtedly true for such concepts as "nation," "heap," or "forest" (I-II 17.4c), but especially for human actions. To them Aquinas even assigns two modes of becoming a unity: (1) "An act of a lower faculty is related as matter to an act of a higher one, insofar as the lower acts by the power of the higher faculty that moves it" (I-II 17.4c). This means that both faculties together perform one act that has its form from the higher faculty (I-II 20.3 s.c.); in principle this holds true for any rational act that

---

[17] Indeed in I-II 18.2 ad 2 he already defines the "object" as the "matter with which it deals." Cf. Westberg, "Good and Evil," p. 91.

is conceived by reason in order to reach an end intended by the will. (2) The will's direction toward one end can imply different acts that then form one unity, either because they necessarily supplement each other (I-II 12.3 ad 2) or because achieving one end is required for reaching the next one later on. One can look upon this order of ends either from the perspective of the will's final end, its intention, which unifies all "middle" ends (I-II 12.2c), or from the perspective of a proximate end of a single action that may be directed to more than one further end (I-II 1.3 ad 3). Thus there is more than one way to assign unity to a course of action, and it is up to practical reason to define the limits of the unified action that it proposes to the will.

Now, what are the consequences for the normative evaluation of particular actions? To address this question, Aquinas distinguishes between cases in which the objects of the inward and outward act have an inherent connection and those in which they don't. An example of the latter is when somebody steals in order to commit adultery, while an example of the former (which Aquinas seems to regard as self-explanatory) may be the inherent connection between the end of victory and the tactical disposition within a battle. In the first case the act directed toward the end may be evaluated on its own, such that there may be "two evils in one act" (I-II 18.7c). This sort of divergence between the moral value of the inward and the outward act can be sufficient for transforming an act that is good into one that is bad, as Aquinas shows by the example of someone who helps because he wants to be honored in his society (I-II 20.1c; cf. I-II 21.1 ad 2). In any case where a good inward or outward act is combined with an evil counterpart in this way, the act becomes bad in its entirety:

> One single defect is enough to make any act bad, though for it to be unreservedly good one good point is not enough, since the completeness of goodness (*integritas bonitatis*) is required, (I-II 20.2c)

and this follows from the principle of the plenitude of essence. For example, the priest who takes away a cross from a church for liturgical use does not perform a good action, if the end he personally attains is impressing his friends.

Thus, Aquinas is obviously committed to excluding that actions bad in their species are performed with a good aim, such as, for instance, Robin Hood's theft in order to help the poor. This does not seem to be justified in his eyes (cf. I-II 18.4 obi. 3 with ad 3). However, at least for non-moral cases Aquinas admits explicitly that at times "something is good merely because it is directed towards something else; for instance an unpleasant medicine is good solely because it is health-giving" (I-II 20.3c). Also, regarding moral acts, he stresses that "the good of the end overflows into the outward act," as well as the other way around (I-II 20.3c). He admits, for instance, that it may be possible under certain circumstances that women wear men's clothing, in spite of this being sinful in principle (II-II 169.2 ad 3). However, he does not give a clear explanation of the criteria according to which such exceptions are possible or not.[18] Thus the question of how apparently bad acts can be performed in order to reach a good end deserves a closer look.

8.5 Judging Particular Situations with the Help of Universal Concepts

In keeping with the last paragraphs we can now describe in greater detail the function of practical reason: It considers outward actions suited to an end that is pursued by the will. As soon as the will, in an inward action, chooses to pursue a certain end in this or that way, the outward action will be executed, if there are no obstacles impeding the agent. If this is true, the statement that "moral virtue, which makes the appetite right, is a precondition of prudence" (I-II 57.4c) concerns not only the question of how an already conceived action is brought about, but also of how reason conceives a right action at all. This can be explained by the epistemological side of the moral virtues (cf. I-II 20.3 ad 2), which consists essentially in the connection of the ends pursued by them with natural law (cf. Section 8.2).

Now how can such a virtue contribute to finding the right particular actions? Indeed Aquinas, like many modern defenders of virtue ethics, contends that a virtuous agent is especially competent for determining singular cases.[19] However his remarks on how this works are often relatively unspecified. He stresses that reason should not be obscured by certain passions and states that the virtues make it "connatural" for the agent to act well (I-II 58.5c; 94.6c); he contends that prudence draws certain "conclusions" or "applications" from the universal knowledge of reason (II-II 47.3c and ad 1). While the first point concerns moral psychology

---

[18] A useful discussion of this problem can be found in Jensen, "When Evil Actions become Good," who proposes to distinguish between actions like killing, which are not bad in all cases, and actions like stealing, which are always bad (pp. 762–4).
[19] E.g. Kluxen, *Philosophische Ethik*, pp. 218–25.

rather than finding out what would be the right thing to do, the second one gives the impression that practical reason simply subsumes particular cases under general rules. It is hard to see from this how the individual features of particular actions can become the specific conditions for the moral evaluation of a certain case.

However a clearer account of how practical reason works can be found in his Treatise on Law. Here too Aquinas assumes that the universal principles of practical reason in the natural law, which are known to and valid for all people, are not sufficient for judgments about concrete situations. This is not because one cannot draw correct conclusions from them, but because not all of those conclusions fit the specific moral cases, as the famous example of giving back borrowed arms to a terrorist makes clear (I-II 94.4c). As a consequence, Aquinas draws a fundamental distinction between two sorts of "laws": on the one hand, the rules of natural law or reason in the strictest sense ("do not harm somebody") along with some immediate but likewise universal conclusions ("do not kill anybody"); and on the other hand, some further specifications introduced by human law (I-II 95.2c). If they are to be just, these latter precepts must also be derived from natural law (I-II 95.1c), but they cannot simply be deduced from it.[20] Rather they are determined by a lawgiver whom Aquinas compares with an architect drawing the form of a particular house in a certain way that fits the concrete situation, while respecting the universal features of a house (I-II 95.2c). In the same way the universal precepts of natural law must be realized in different forms by creative acts of the lawgivers (I-II 95.4c), who take into account the specific situation of their countries (I-II 95.3c).

Nowhere in Aquinas, at least as far as I know, is there a similar account about the functioning of practical reason. However, we have good reason to understand the description just given as applying also to prudential judgments. This clearly follows from the assumption that the ends pursued by the virtues are nothing other than actual instantiations of the natural law (cf. Section 8.2): We may also infer the need for prudential judgments from the insufficiency of the natural law to prescribe what is to be done in concrete situations (II-II 47.7c). Indeed, Aquinas presents the act of lawgiving itself as some sort of abbreviation of the process of practical reasoning (I-II 95.1 ad 3). Especially instructive is Thomas's teaching on *epieikeia*, that is, as Aristotle holds, the ability to decide cases

---

[20] Porter, *Nature as Reason*, p. 266f., points out the Ciceronian roots of this idea about the construction of social norms.

in which one has to deviate from the rule of law in order to do what is right (NE 5.1137a 31–38b 3). Here Thomas repeats the example of not restoring borrowed arms to an enemy, thus implying that not only the lawgiver, but any agent, is to make decisions in this way by his own prudential judgment.

One might object here that a practical reason operating according to rules typical for a lawgiver may not be able to judge individual cases in themselves, because laws always apply to more than one case. In order to understand Aquinas's position, we have to look at his concrete argument:

> The more you descend into the detail the more it appears that the general rule admits of exceptions, so that you have to hedge it with cautions and qualifications ... The greater the number of particular conditions accumulated, the greater the number of ways in which the principle is able to fall short, so that it will not be right about returning or not returning [what has been borrowed]. (I-II 94.4c)

According to this paragraph, the singular case, in which a universal rule does not hold for obvious reasons, does not lead directly toward the judgment "I am faced here with a singular case." Rather, the immediate judgment is "regarding this case the universal rule has to be applied in a more specified form." The rational understanding of a particular situation then consists in formulating a more specific rule that includes some qualifications. This new rule – for instance, "we should return borrowed things, but not arms to a dangerous person" – is still universal in its form, even if it holds true only in few cases. Thus it may very rapidly become necessary to specify the rule once again for another situation. However, the situation is still not grasped simply by an intuition, but by a judgment that describes the particular case in a specific way while still relying on universal moral concepts.

This may be explained further by comparison with the doctrine that a circumstance may change the object or the species of a moral act. In this case too, as has been argued in Section 8.3, "object" refers to a type of action: The theft from a holy place in Aquinas's example is not perceived as a singular case, but as a sacrilege, that is as an instance of a type of action that is different from the type that appears at first sight (I-II 18.10c). In the same way, the object of restoring a weapon to a terrorist turns out to be not "returning a borrowed item," but "supporting terrorism." The task of practical reason in both cases is to find the right category to describe the single case, which may appear firsthand to be a simple instance of another case. This implies a flexible use of universal concepts, but no waiver of them.

Now Aquinas seems to mention also some actions that are apparently not good or bad because of a certain rule. Two sets of cases seem to be relevant here: Regarding *epieikeia*, Aquinas adds the specification that such acts "follow what the meaning of justice and the public good demand" (II-II 120.1c). This implies that in those cases the most common rules of justice, such as "rendering to each one his right" (II-II 58.1), break more concrete rules of human law, which are themselves derived from the same principles. Thus we can conclude that practical reason prescribes legitimate exceptions from given laws, if it does so in accordance with even more universal rules of the natural law.

The second relevant case is those actions that are neither good nor bad in their species, whereas in any particular case they are either good or bad, because any human act is necessarily either directed to a good end or not (I-II 18.9; cf. Section 8.3). If an individual act becomes good or bad simply by its relation to the will of a particular human being, this does not mean that no universal rules are at stake here. Rather, the universal rules will determine the inward act, which gives the indifferent outward act its moral form by referring it to some general rule of good behavior; in the cases mentioned here, this takes place automatically, because indifferent acts have no moral value that could withstand being ordered by reason to a certain end.

8.6   Conditions of a Good Judgment

Thus we are reminded again that, at least to a certain degree, any "objective" statement about what is right or wrong can be changed in particular cases by the subjective reason of the individual human being, which is, instead of the eternal law,[21] the "proximate norm" of human acts (I-II 19.4; 21.1). Having learned now that this cannot mean that universal rules can be simply replaced by individual preferences, we have to inspect more closely what the possibilities and the limits of individual decisions are.

One can start by noting a further parallel between acts of lawgiving and prudential judgments of single agents: Just as there may be different just systems of moral law in different countries, there may also be different good wills in different agents. For example, a judge may justly want a criminal to be put to death, whereas the criminal's wife wants equally justly to save his life (I-II 19.10). Aquinas explains this by their different

---

[21] I cannot discuss here the meaning of relevance of *lex aeterna*, which seems to me a crucial but often misunderstood element of Aquinas's theory of law.

rational apprehensions, which result from pursuing different good ends: The judge strives for the execution of the law, whereas the woman's goal is the "private good" of preventing the killing of an innocent person. In principle, these two partial standpoints can both be justified, because there is a fundamental distinction between human and divine willing: Whereas God's end is the universal common good of the whole world, all goods pursued by human agents are necessary particular, even if a human "common good," for example the enforcement of a law, is at stake[22]; this results from the basic plurality of goods relevant for human life (I-II 10.1; I-II 94.2).

Thus there can be no rule fixing ends that every human being has to pursue. Rather this depends upon each individual's personal conditions, upon their public and private duties as well as upon the rules of the society they live in. However, because the human will has to imitate the divine will (I-II 19.9), any particular end pursued by a human person must be based upon a universal perspective that is formally identical with the end pursued by God. If Aquinas calls this end the "good of the whole universe," he means neither the pure concept of good taken absolutely, without which no act of the will would be possible,[23] nor beatitude as the end at least implicitly pursued by all human beings (I-II 1.4–7).[24] Rather, it is the "common good" (*bonum commune*), which is the end of any good action insofar as the action matches the virtue of justice (II-II 58.5f.); however, in God's perspective this is a good of an unlimited universality, which is not accessible to human beings. The necessity to conform all human willing formally to this good makes it even more understandable that every particular rational judgment must have a universal form: If a particular moral judgment disregards the question of what would be right for everybody to do in comparable circumstances, it must lose sight of the universal perspective required for a good action. In this sense, one might think about ascribing to Aquinas a principle of universalization, similar to Kant's categorical imperative.

However, this speculation seems to leave out one crucial element: For Aquinas, a particular moral judgment is not issued by a transcendental

---

[22] The same opposition is crucial for Aquinas's account of the freedom of human acts, as is argued by Henry of Ghent, Quodlibet 1, question 16 (p. 99f. Macken); Porter, *Nature as Reason*, pp. 258–62; Perkams, "Aquinas on Choice," p. 88f.

[23] Cf. Perkams, "Aquinas on Choice," p. 86.

[24] One has to assume that the strivings for beatitude and for the good of the whole universe are for Aquinas closely united to each other, insofar as the latter somehow "takes part" in the former. Cf. e.g. I-II 1.6f.; Müller, "*Duplex Beatitudo*," pp. 66–8.

pure reason, which is defined by being universal, but by the practical reason of a particular agent, who is, including her personal standpoint, her interests, and her goals, herself a crucial "circumstance" of the action (cf. SCG 3.113).[25] Thus a right practical judgment of a human being always includes the sum of a person's individual traits, which are not universalizable in their entirety. For that reason, a non-particular human intellect cannot decide who of the two opposed agents in a given conflict is right, since "the diverse acts of willing of diverse individuals for conflicting good may be good in that they will this to be or not to be for diverse particular reasons" (I-II 19.10c), if both aim at doing something that is useful for reaching the good of the whole universe.

This fact explains why the individual conscience has such a crucial role in Aquinas. For him, conscience too is a rational act, by which a reasonable person evaluates prospective actions and reflects critically upon performed ones (I 79.12). In the second function, conscience is a necessary complement to prudence, whereas in the first one it stands for the binding force of individual practical reason, as Aquinas states in I-II 19.5[26]:

> To believe in Christ is good in itself ... all the same, the will is not borne to this unless it is presented by reason. If the reason presents it as bad, then the will is borne to it in that light, not because it is bad in itself, but because it is accidentally bad due to the way reason apprehends it ... Hence ... every act of will at variance with reason, whether that reason is right or wrong, is always bad.

Thus the apprehension of an action as good by an individual's reason is the first necessary condition for it to be good; there is obviously no universal rule that can overcome this principle.

However, Aquinas supplements this by the important qualification that a will following a mistaken conscience is not good, if the agent is somehow responsible for the ignorance leading to the mistaken judgment (I-II 19.6c). There are even certain false beliefs that render the individual judgment so misguided that it cannot guarantee good actions, unless a thorough change of one's own moral beliefs has taken place (I-II 19.6

---

[25] Cf. Kluxen, *Philosophische Ethik*, pp. 197f. This implies that any right ethical judgment cannot be detached from the individual perspective of the agent; it does not follow that in Aquinas "the first preferential rule" in choosing an action is to secure "the capacity for self-determination of the agent" (Honnefelder, "The Evaluation of Goods," p. 428); this proposal neglects the priority of the common good in Aquinas's ethics.

[26] For further information on the relationship between conscience and prudence cf. Rhonheimer, *Praktische Vernunft*, pp. 383–400.

ad 3).²⁷ Thus the limits of a moral agent's autonomy depend upon the limits of a culpable ignorance of factors determining the moral act: Every agent is responsible for any ignorance that is either directly intended, as when someone intends to dispense with necessary inquiries, or willed indirectly, as when somebody does not know the laws of her own country or the binding rules of her own profession (I-II 6.8; I-II 76.2). The only ignorance that can be excused and that consequently renders the will following it an error of good conscience stems, in Aquinas's eyes, "from ignorance of some circumstance without any negligence."

His examples of this concern always very small particularities: for instance having sex with another's wife while thinking she is one's own (I-II 19.6c), or killing somebody by a shot that was intended to kill a deer (DM 3.6c). However, these examples are on the one hand not very plausible in themselves – everybody should know his partner, and a hunter must not shoot, unless he can be sure not to hurt anybody – and on the other hand admit of no elements of a moral judgment in the strict sense. Instead there is good reason to think that such exculpable errors include more significant aspects of a certain case: An example can be taken from the conflict described in 19.10. Without further specification, in such a situation the woman seems to be, in Aquinas's eyes, not justified in impeding the execution of the judgment (cf. III 18.6c). However, if we come up with a more complex story, we can imagine situations that require specific evaluations, such that each of the two agents may act with a good will despite being ignorant of some important condition of the situation.

This could result from the fact that they have different information regarding the guilt of the condemned person. The woman could know that her husband is innocent or that he acted out of self-defense, whereas the judge may have been deceived by false witnesses in spite of having conducted his investigation correctly; or the woman could have been lied to by her husband or by some friends, in spite of having good reason for trusting them. In both cases the ignorance is provoked by the circumstance of an unforeseeable lie.

Another scenario might arise from divergent beliefs about the legal system according to which the judge is operating: An unjust law, according to Aquinas, "will be no law, but spoilt law" (I-II 95.2c), and it does not "oblige in the court of conscience" (I-II 96.4c). However, it is

---

²⁷ This leads to the complex question of the perplexity of the moral agent; on this see Dougherty, *Moral Dilemmas in Medieval Thought*, pp. 117–32.

complicated to know exactly which laws are or are not unjust, depending on your knowledge of the concrete situation and on your reasoned beliefs about what the requirements of a good law are. Thus the judge may indeed attach great value to enforcing only a just law, but be ignorant of the fact that the law in question has been instituted by a person not authorized to do so.[28] The woman may recognize correctly that the law is unjust, but may be mistaken in the measures to be taken for liberating her husband: She might rightly think that it is just to ask Robin Hood to liberate her husband, while being ignorant that her action accidentally provokes a civil war because of Robin's mutual hatred with Prince John (cf. Aquinas's evaluation of a sedition against a tyrant in II-II 42.2 ad 3).[29]

Thus at least in situations where the moral status of society's rules or of certain agents' motives are themselves questionable, the usual moral rules may not apply, and the individual agent has to decide according to *epieikeia* what has to be done. We can infer that any situations in which actions bad in their species can become good in individual cases, such as the examples of not restoring a borrowed item, are reactions to major disturbances of justice; thus the notion of "bad in its species" is not premoral[30] – because it always applies when no significant disturbance of the moral order can be recognized – nor is the possibility of exceptions restricted to certain types of bad action,[31] nor is the evaluation of an action dependent just upon an intention[32]: It is the particular situation itself, as it is conceived by a sound reasoning, which may necessitate an exception to a valid social rule or a law according to the specificities of the case (cf. I-II 100.8 ad 2).

8.7 Conclusion

In Aquinas, we find a very differentiated theory of human action, which is able to do justice to important concerns of both the universalist and the particularist perspectives.

---

[28] This is one of the criteria rendering a law unjust according to I-II 96.4.

[29] Cf. also the doctrine of the double effect: II-II 64.7c.

[30] As discussed by Westberg, "Good and Evil," p. 95; Jensen, "Evil Actions," p. 749.

[31] As Jensen himself resolves the issue: Jensen, "Evil Actions," pp. 762–4. However, one may ask with Westberg, "Good and Evil," p. 95, if there can be any legitimate exception to the prohibition of some sexual delicts, for instance rape.

[32] Cf. Westberg, "Good and Evil," p. 94.

1 The universal perspective is not only known to every individual by the rules of the natural law but is at work in the operations of any virtuous agent, because acting virtuously is nothing other than realizing the natural law in concrete social contexts and particular situations.

2 However, the realization of the law in human life is possible only via the creative activity of prudence, which is able to judge particular situations by formulating rules which take into account all of the situation's relevant particular aspects without giving up the universal form of rational judgments. This can also be described as the determination of the object of actions due to certain circumstances. In this way, it can be legitimate under certain conditions, to violate, according to the principle of *epieikeia*, certain social norms or even state laws.

3 The irreducible particularity of the practical judgment is due in the end to the individual perspective, which is inherent in Aquinas's very concept of a particular person's reason: Because practical reason is always the reason of a concrete human being with a perspective of her own and a personal history (cf. SCG 3.113), a practical judgment can never be repeated by another agent without a new reflection, even in very similar situations. As long as both act virtuously, that is, make a judgment that is formally universal by being ordered to the goodness of the whole world and that does not break a fundamental rule of the natural law, their very different sentences can be equally just.

It should be added that Aquinas, as a Christian theologian committed to the thesis of original sin, probably would assume that in moral conflicts usually at least one of the parties involved, if not both, is perplexed, that is, her practical reason is so obscured that she has to change her beliefs fundamentally in order to arrive at a good judgment (I-II 19.6. ad 3). For him most conflicts do not result from different justified true beliefs about moral matters, but from different moral failures. The way the world is, it may well be that he is also right about this.

CHAPTER 9

The Natural Law

Jean Porter

Near the beginning of the First Part of the Second Part, Aquinas informs us that this part of the *Summa Theologiae* will be devoted to human actions generally considered, including both an analysis of action as such, and a consideration of the intrinsic and extrinsic principles of human action (I-II 6 intro., I-II 49 intro.). Further on, we are told that the extrinsic principles of action include Satan, who tempts us to evil, and God, who instructs us through law and aids us through grace. This looks like a traditional formulation, and clearly Aquinas does not intend to enter into a discussion of demonology at this point, or to review the doctrine of God so carefully developed in the First Part (I-II 90 intro.). We would expect him to say something more about law and grace, which provide normative criteria in terms of which acts are evaluated, and that is just what he proceeds to do. The natural law plays a central role in this overall account, both as a normative criterion for action, and as the necessary foundation for free judgment and moral accountability.

In this chapter, I will set out Aquinas's theory of the natural law as developed in the *Summa Theologiae*, focusing on the questions devoted to law, natural law, and the Decalogue in the First Part of the Second Part. In the first section, I offer an overview of what Aquinas thinks the natural law most fundamentally is, and how he places it, so to speak, within the wider framework of the *Summa*. In the second and third sections, I take up two specific topics which highlight distinctive and important aspects of Aquinas's overall theory, namely, the unity of the natural law, and the status of moral knowledge.

9.1 What Is the Natural Law?

Aquinas's account of the natural law draws on a wide range of classical and patristic sources, but it is more immediately responsive to the concept of the natural law developed by twelfth- and thirteenth-century scholastic jurists and theologians.[1] These, in turn, are the heirs to a more or less continuous tradition of reflection on natural law or natural right that originates with the Stoics and proceeds through the Roman jurists, patristic theologians, and early medieval theologians and jurists. It would be a mistake to identify the object of this tradition with any one construal of nature or reason, or much less with a specific set of moral injunctions. Rather, the natural law tradition is associated with a distinctive form of normative analysis, in which the conventions of society are interpreted and evaluated in terms of their relation to pre-conventional principles. This approach does not presuppose that the non-natural or conventional is morally evil, but it does presuppose that we do have access to a pre-conventional natural order of some kind, which provides a basis for the normative evaluation of social conventions. This line of analysis implies a distinction between the natural law as such and the social practices or precepts which express it. Perhaps for this reason, the scholastics are hesitant to identify natural law too closely with specific precepts.[2] Rather, with very few exceptions they identify the natural law in its primary sense with basic capacities for moral judgment, or with the foundational principles through which that judgment operates.

Aquinas shares this general view of the natural law, as we will see in more detail below. At the same time, he interprets the natural law in such a way as to underscore its status as a law, that is to say, a normative principle of activity. In contrast to other scholastic theologians, who discuss the natural law in connection with justice, or with virtue generally considered, Aquinas introduces the natural law within the context of a general theory of law, which he defines as "an ordinance of reason directed towards the common good, instituted by one who has responsibility for the community, and promulgated" (I-II 90.4c). Having established what the law is, Aquinas goes on to consider the generally accepted types of law, beginning with the eternal law, and continuing with natural law, divine law, human law, and the so-called law of the tinder, that is, the

---

[1] As Martin Grabmann pointed out almost ninety years ago, we cannot understand Aquinas's theory of natural law unless we place it within the context of earlier and contemporaneous scholastic treatments; see "Das Naturrecht der Scholastik von Gratian bis Thomas von Aquin," p. 67. For other treatments of Aquinas's theory of the natural law as seen in its scholastic context, see Lottin, *Le droit naturel chez saint Thomas d'Aquin et ses prédécesseurs*; Crowe, *The Changing Profile of the Natural Law*; and Porter, *Natural and Divine Law: Reclaiming the Tradition for Christian Ethics*. In my general characterization of the scholastic concept of the natural law, I draw on arguments developed in *Natural and Divine Law*, pp. 63–98.

[2] See Porter, *Natural and Divine Law*, pp. 88–91 for further details.

law of stimulants to sin.[3] Each of these, with the exception of the last, operates in some way as a normative principle for activity, through goal-directed activity or through formulations of normative standards. Even the law of stimulants to sin is connected to a normative standard, insofar as it is a punishment for original sin.

Aquinas's typology of law gives pride of place to the eternal law, which he identifies with the rational principle through which God governs the universe (I-II 91.1c).[4] God's providence, which Aquinas first considers in the First Part as one element of God's activity (I 22.1, 2), is now considered from below, as it were, from the standpoint of creatures whose existence and activities are sustained and directed by God. As we have already been told, every creature exists and operates in accordance with the form of existence in which it was created, and returns to God, its supreme good, through seeking its perfection in accordance with that form (I 5.5c, 6.4c, 103.2c; I-II 1.8c). Correlatively, the eternal law, thus understood, is a normative standard insofar as it is the ultimate source of the intelligible, goal-directed structures of causality through which creatures exist and pursue their proper ends.

In the next article of this question, Aquinas asks "Whether there is in us some natural law?" (I-II 91.2). In order to set up his response, he first cites an objection to the effect that the eternal law is sufficient to govern the human person, and he then goes on in the second and third objections to argue that the human person acts out of reason and will, not law, and correlatively, that the existence of a natural law within us is inconsistent with human freedom. In this way, he indicates that the natural law must be understood in such a way as to account for the naturalness of human activity, without calling into question either rationality and freedom, or the ultimate subordination of human activity to divine providence.

In order to do so, Aquinas situates human activity within a wider context of causal activity more generally:

> [I]t is evident that all things participate in some way in the eternal law, insofar, that is, as they have inclinations to their proper acts and ends through its impression on them. Among the others, however, the rational

---

[3] I-II 91; the last refers to Paul's remark about a "law in my members," later identified with concupiscence, which opposes the "law of my mind," Romans 7:23.

[4] For the patristic and medieval context for Aquinas's account of the eternal law, see Lottin, "La Loi éternelle chez saint Thomas d' Aquin et ses prédécesseurs," pp. 51–67 in *Psychologie et Morale aux XII et XIII siècles*, vol. 2. In my reading of Aquinas's own interpretation of this motif, I am indebted to Bastit, *Naissance de la Loi Moderne: La Pensée de la Loi de Saint Thomas à Suarez*, pp. 77–82.

creature is subject to divine providence in a certain more excellent way, insofar as it becomes a participant in providence, being provident for itself and for others. Hence in the rational creature also there is a participation in the eternal law, through which it has a natural inclination to its due act and end. And such participation in the eternal law on the part of the rational creature is called the natural law. (I-II 91.2c)

Elsewhere, Aquinas says that every creature can be said to love God above all else, or to seek God, insofar as it is inclined to develop and sustain its characteristic form of existence (I 60.5c, I-II 109.3c). We might say that the inclinations mediate the eternal law to creatures, insofar as they embody and express the ordered patterns of activity proper to the kind of creature in question, which, as Aquinas elsewhere observes, represents the creature's specific mode of participation in the divine goodness (I 6.1c). Every creature, including inanimate and non-sentient beings as well as animals, participates in divine providence through the operations prompted by the inclinations, in such a way as to fall under the governance of eternal law. This observation applies to rational creatures, as well as everything else. We too are creatures with a distinctive form of existence, which we are moved to sustain through natural inclinations toward the necessary components of human existence.

Of course, the rational creature will necessarily pursue its final end in a distinctively human way, through choices grounded in rational reflection. For this reason, Aquinas identifies the natural law more specifically with "the light of natural reason," explaining that this light, "through which we discern what is good and evil, which pertains to the natural law, is nothing other than an impression of the divine light in us" (I-II 91.2c). At the same time, by associating the natural law with natural inclinations, Aquinas also underscores the parallels between human action, and the patterns of ordered activity which stem from and express the proper forms of other kinds of creatures, through which they move toward their specific modes of perfection. In this way, he satisfies the criteria set out through the objections cited above. The natural law is a kind of natural principle, since it reflects the characteristically human form of existence and activity. By the same token, it is not inconsistent with human freedom and self-governance, since rational self-governance is the characteristically human form of existence.[5] And finally, this rational self-governance, so far from separating the creature from the eternal law,

---

[5] As Matthias Perkams argues, the natural law in Aquinas is not only not inconsistent with human freedom, it is the necessary principle for autonomy, understood as rational self-governance; see

represents a more excellent kind of participation in divine law, since the rational creature is not only governed by, but is a participant in providential activity.

So far, Aquinas has established that men and women are governed through a natural law, which is distinct from, although dependent on the eternal law. Reading further, he refers to the "light of natural reason, through which we discern what is good and evil, which pertains to the natural law," adding that this is "nothing other than an impression of divine light in us" (I-II 91.2c). Clearly, Aquinas shares in the scholastic consensus that the natural law in its most proper sense is to be identified with a capacity or a principle, that is to say, a foundational norm, for moral judgment, rather than a set of specific divine or rational precepts. At the same time, these comments do not tell us as much as we might hope about what the natural law is.

Aquinas returns to a consideration of what the natural law is in the first article of the question devoted to the natural law, I-II 92.1c, in which he asks whether the natural law is a habit. This article is motived by the traditional identification of the natural law with synderesis, which Aquinas has already interpreted as the habit through which we know the first indemonstrable principles of practical reason (I 79.12c).[6] At this point, Aquinas recalls that earlier discussion, in order to establish that strictly speaking, the natural law is not a habit, but rather, that which is habitually known. This implies that the natural law is a kind of principle or precept, rather than a habit, in accordance with Aquinas's claim at I 79.12c that synderesis is the habit through which we know first principles. Aquinas says as much, observing that "synderesis is said to be the law of our intellect, insofar as it is a habit containing precepts of the natural law, which are the first principles of human operations" (I-II 94.1 ad 2).

At the same time, in the body of this article, Aquinas refers to the natural law in another way, as "something constituted through reason, just as a proposition is a certain work of reason." His point is that we distinguish that which acts from that by which it acts, and he offers the example of someone who speaks appropriately through the habit of grammar. This line of analysis does not contradict the view that the natural law is an innate principle, which serves as the basis for deriving more specific

---

"Naturgesetz, Selbstbestimmung und Moralität: Thomas von Aquin und die Begründung einer zeitgemässen Ethik."

[6] For more on the natural law as synderesis, see Porter, *Natural and Divine Law*, pp. 88–90.

precepts. At the same time, Aquinas appears in this passage to connect the natural law with the activity through which men and women form moral judgments. The natural law, thus understood, is a dynamic and complex reality, closely bound up with the diverse activities of human life.

This is an attractive perspective on the natural law, but if Aquinas had said nothing further, we would be left with a vague and unsatisfactory sense of what the natural law is, and correlatively, how it functions as a normative standard. However, Aquinas goes on to further clarify his understanding of the natural law and its relation to a range of moral considerations in the second article, "Whether the natural law consists of many precepts, or only one?" (I-II 94.2c).

9.2   The Unity of the Natural Law

As the heading indicates, in I-II 94.2 Aquinas takes up the question of whether the natural law is one unified law, or not. After setting out a series of objections in support of the essential diversity of natural laws, he begins his analysis by observing that "the precepts of the law of nature stand in the same relation to practical reason, as the first principles of demonstrations stand to speculative reason, for in either case, they are particular self-evident principles. However, something is said to be self-evident in two senses; in one way, in itself, and in another way, with respect to us." A proposition is self-evident in itself, he explains, if its predicate is in some way implied by the definition of the subject, but a proposition that is self-evident in this way will not necessarily be self-evident to all persons. He goes on to apply his analysis of self-evident propositions to the first principle of practical intellect:

> For just as being is that which first comes under apprehension simply speaking, so the good is that which first comes under the apprehension of practical reason, which is directed towards something that is done; for every agent acts on account of an end, which has the rational character of good. And therefore the first principle in the practical reason is that which is grounded in the rational character of good, that is, "good is that which all things desire." This is therefore the first precept of law, that good is to be done and pursued and evil is to be avoided. And on this are founded all the other precepts of the law of nature, inasmuch as all things to be done or avoided, which practical reason naturally apprehends to be human goods, belong to the precepts of the law of nature.

Here, at last, Aquinas gives us a clear formulation of the first indemonstrable principle of practical reason. We might expect him to continue by explaining how specific precepts of the natural law are derived from these first principles, but that is not what he does:

> Because good has the rational character of an end, whereas evil has the rational character of the contrary, hence it is that all those things to which the human person has a natural inclination, reason naturally apprehends as good, and consequently to be pursued through action, and the contraries of these as evil and to be avoided. Therefore, the order of the precepts of the law of nature is in accordance with the order of natural inclinations.

He continues by enumerating the fundamental human inclinations toward life, reproduction, rational inquiry, life in society, and knowledge of God, each of which is said to be correlated with precepts of natural law. Hence, the precepts associated with these inclinations can all be understood as specifications of the fundamental precept of practical reason, "Good is to be done and pursued and evil is to be avoided." Hence, "All these precepts of the natural law, insofar as they are referred to one first precept, have the rational character of one natural law" (I-II 94.2 ad 1). Aquinas seems to presuppose that we know, at least generally, what the precepts of the natural law are. He certainly does not make any attempt to enumerate them, or much less to justify or derive them, in this article. Rather, he wants to show that these precepts can all be considered as expressions of one unified natural law. Why is this so important to him?

Germain Grisez points out that the question with which Aquinas begins this article was not a standard topic for discussion among the scholastics of his time.[7] While this is true, there was a similar question which was a standard topic, namely, the question whether there are many laws of nature, or only one. On its face, the question whether there are many laws of nature, or only one, seems even odder than the question, whether the precepts of the natural law are one or many. Yet this question was a real issue for the scholastics in the twelfth and thirteenth centuries. It is important to keep in mind that almost any pre-conventional principle of action or judgment could be identified with natural law or natural right, and the relevant textual traditions included a number of different and seemingly incompatible definitions of the natural law. Given this situation, it is not surprising that the scholastics readily spoke in terms

---

[7] Grisez, "The First Principle of Practical Reason: A Commentary on the *Summa theologiae*, 1–2, Question 94, Article 2," p. 169 note 3.

of multiple senses of the natural law.[8] Inevitably, they soon began to try to bring coherence to this diversity of laws. One approach was to identify one of the traditional definitions of the natural law as paradigmatic, and then to explain others in relation to it. For example, the canonist Huguccio of Ferrara, writing about 1188, interprets the natural law as a power of rational judgment, arguing that the other traditional meanings of the natural law should be related to, or understood in terms of, this paradigmatic definition. Another approach organized the various definitions of the natural law in accordance with the different ways of understanding nature. Aquinas's fellow Dominican Roland of Cremona, writing in about 1230, takes this approach, remarking that the manifold natural law should be analyzed in accordance with the different theories of nature established philosophically.

When we turn back to I-II 94.2, it is apparent that Aquinas combines these approaches in order to defend the rational coherence of the natural law. He begins his analysis of the natural law by identifying a first principle in terms of which other precepts of the natural law are to be related. The first principle of the natural law, understood as a starting point for rational judgment, is connected to the rational capacity to distinguish good and evil. In this way, Aquinas's identification of the first principle of the natural law is similar to the interpretation of the natural law as reason, adopted by Huguccio and many others.[9] Within the framework of his taxonomy of human inclinations toward the good, Aquinas then finds a place for other traditional accounts of the natural law. The first inclination, which we share with all other creatures, is associated with the natural law understood as a universal tendency toward existence or goodness mentioned by Roland. The second inclination, to which pertain reproduction and the care of the young, is associated with the natural law as defined by the Roman jurist Ulpian, who identifies natural law with the activities common to human beings and other animals. Finally, the properly human natural law, including those precepts relating to life in society and worship of a divine being, are associated with distinctively

---

[8] In this paragraph and the next, I am again drawing on earlier work on the antecedents of scholastic treatments of the natural law, and the scholastics' own construals of natural law; for further details, including a more extended consideration of texts, see Porter, *Natural and Divine Law*, pp. 66–76, 85–98.

[9] According to Brian Tierney, Huguccio was the first to equate natural law with reason, that is to say with a rational power of moral discernment, but a consensus on this point quickly emerged among canon lawyers; see his *The Idea of Natural Rights: Studies on Natural Rights, Natural Law and Church Law, 1150–1625*, pp. 64–5, and more generally pp. 43–77.

human inclinations to live together and to engage in intellectual activity, which were central to Cicero's conception of the natural law and were subsequently incorporated into scholastic reflection by early canonical commentators on Gratian's *Decretum*.

To sum up the argument so far, there are very striking parallels in both approach and substance between I-II 94.2 and the discussions of the different laws of nature to be found in other scholastic canonists and theologians. These parallels strongly suggest that these discussions form the immediate context for Aquinas's argument in this passage. Furthermore, they indicate that his analysis is motivated by a similar concern to bring coherence to a variety of traditional understandings of the natural law. Accordingly, his aim in I-II 94.2 is to show the rational unity of the natural law through an analysis of the ways in which diverse precepts of the natural law may be said to be expressions of one fundamental precept, directed at the most general end of action, namely, that which is good, abstractly considered as that which is in some way worth pursuing and having.

Aquinas's context explains why he might question the unity of the natural law, but it does not fully explain why he has such a strong stake in establishing that, appearances to the contrary, the natural law can be regarded as one unified standard of judgment. Yet the placement of this article makes it clear that the unity of the natural law plays a central role in Aquinas's overall analysis of the concept. I-II 94.2 follows immediately after the initial identification of the natural law with the first indemonstrable principle of practical reason, as we have just seen, and it is immediately followed by a consideration of the question whether all virtuous acts stem from the natural law – a question that Aquinas answers with a qualified affirmative (I-II 94.3c). These three articles set out Aquinas's fundamental understanding of the natural law, on the basis of which he then goes on to address traditional questions: whether the natural law is the same for all, whether it can be changed, and whether it can be completely extirpated from the human mind (I-II 94.4–6). Structurally, the article on the unity of the natural law serves as a bridge between his consideration of the natural law as a first principle, and his subsequent analyses of the natural law as a principle of virtue and as a foundation for collective and individual moral judgments.

The placement of I-II 94.2 implies that Aquinas has a stake in establishing the unity of the natural law, because he has a stake in defending the unity and coherence of moral judgment. Having established that the natural law is most fundamentally a first principle of reason, analogous to the first principles of speculative reason, he now argues that diverse moral ideals and norms can all be analyzed in terms of injunctions to do what is good or to avoid what is evil in some sphere of activity. Thus, he lays the basis for subsequent arguments that the acts of the virtues and the particular judgments of individuals and communities, if sound, can all be identified in some respect with natural law (I-II 94.3, 4). His arguments in these articles are carefully nuanced, so as not to identify the natural law too closely with particular, contextual judgments (in particular, see I-II 94.3c). He is well aware that our moral judgments, and the ideals and precepts stemming from them, pertain to diverse fields of inquiry and draw on different kinds of rational considerations. Nonetheless, they can all be understood as specific formulations of the first principle of practical reason, formulated in terms of general judgments to the effect that some particular kind of action is good, and to be done, or evil, and to be avoided.

Aquinas's concern to safeguard the unity of the natural law, while at the same time acknowledging its dynamic character, also explains why he analyzes the unity of the natural law in terms of natural inclinations. As we recall, Aquinas identifies inclinations as motions of desire, understood in a broad sense which allows for inclinations among inanimate and nonsentient creatures. The inclinations of a creature stem from its form and move it to act in such a way as to sustain, express, and expand the potential inherent in that form (I 80.1c). The inclinations are therefore not just random desires – they are grounded in the intelligible existence of the creature and serve to express that existence in an active, dynamic way. These observations apply as much to the human creature as to anything else. Our natural inclinations toward life, reproduction, and rational activities of various kinds are rooted in the complex potential of our human nature and move us to express that potential in an orderly way. That is why they provide an ordering principle for the ideals, precepts, and claims that emerge over the course of our lives. At the same time, the inclinations do not, in themselves, generate moral precepts or ideals. These are desires, the motions of appetites, which need to be informed by the virtues in order to operate in morally praiseworthy ways (I-II 50.5c; II-II 108.2c).

9.3 Natural Law, Moral Knowledge, and the Status of Moral Rules

As we have just seen, Aquinas identifies the natural law, properly so called, with the first indemonstrable principle of practical reason.

He apparently believes that there are many precepts of the natural law understood broadly, and he also claims that the ideals of all the virtues can be seen as belonging to the natural law (I-II 94.3c). None of these claims would have been particularly problematic for his contemporaries. Among our own contemporaries, however, Aquinas's views on moral knowledge, and more particularly, on the derivation or justification of law-like precepts, is far from clear. For this reason, Aquinas is accused, or occasionally complemented, for failing to spell out the normative significance of the natural law as he understands it.

These objections are misplaced. Aquinas does have an account of moral knowledge which ties it to the natural law as he understands it. In order to reconstruct that account, it will be helpful to compare his views with those of his teacher, Albert:

> [T]here is a knowledge of the law which is a first potency with respect to the general matters of the law, concerning which it is only necessary to know the terms of the commandment, that is to say, what is stealing and what is adultery, and then through knowledge of these terms, it is evident that one should not steal or commit adultery. Hence, the knowledge of these principles is not acquired except in an accidental sense, namely, through the knowledge of the terms, and not through anything that is prior [to these principles] themselves, as the knowledge of conclusions is acquired. Thus, the knowledge of such principles is placed in us by nature, simply speaking, and is acquired in an accidental way through knowledge of the terms. (*De Bono* V 1.1)

However, the claim that the laws of the Decalogue are self-evident to all was not convincing to everyone. In the words of an anonymous text from this period:

> The law of Moses or Aeschylus[10] does not concern the common conceptions of the soul. For it is not the case that as soon as someone hears, "do not steal," he understands that he is not to steal, and so with respect to the other commandments. Thus, many doubt whether fornication is a mortal sin. But the natural law is concerned with the common conceptions of the soul, as for example, "do not do to another what you do not wish to have done to yourself;" hence, it is by means of the natural law that we understand and are conscious, that is, as soon as we apprehend, we perceive that so it must be done.[11]

---

[10] Aeschylus, the Greek tragedian (d. ca. 456 BCE) was known to the scholastics through Cicero, and they may have known that his plays dealt with the meaning of justice. Thanks to my colleague Brian Daley for this information.

[11] This is taken from an anonymous text excerpted, in Latin, in *Le droit naturel*, p. 125.

When we compare these texts, it is apparent that there was some disagreement in Aquinas's time about the status of what we might call the intermediate precepts of the natural law, such as we find in the Decalogue. However, it also seems that this disagreement does not extend very far. Both Albert and his anonymous interlocutor agree that the natural law is identified with an innate capacity for moral judgment, which can only be exercised within a context of particular formulations or images. It would seem that for both authors, the natural law, considered as a first general principle, is specified in and through the exercise of the natural law considered as a capacity for practical judgment. The remaining disagreements have to do with the level at which the natural law, considered as a capacity, is initially engaged – do we begin with formulations of particular, albeit still very general precepts, or is the natural law, considered as an innate capacity for moral judgment, first engaged at a more basic level?

Aquinas's views on moral knowledge come close to both positions represented here. We have already observed that he moves spontaneously from the natural law as an operative principle, to the first indemonstrable principle of practical reasoning itself (I-II 91.2c). The first principle of practical reasoning is only activated, as it were, through processes of practical judgment, yielding moral judgments which can be formulated as precepts. This line of analysis is confirmed by Aquinas's earlier comment on synderesis, considered as the habitual knowledge of the first principle of practical reason. As such, it plays the same role in practical reasoning that the innate understanding of principles plays in speculative reasoning, providing both the necessary starting points for rational inquiry, and touchstones for evaluating our conclusions (I 79.12c). Elsewhere, he explains how these innate dispositions work:

> [I]ndeed, by the very nature of the intellectual soul, it is appropriate to the human person that, on knowing what a whole is and what a part is, at once he knows that every whole is greater than its part, and similarly in other matters. But what a whole is, and what a part is, he cannot know, except through intelligible species taken from phantasms. And on this account, the Philosopher shows ... that the knowledge of principles comes to us through the senses. (I-II 51.1c)

As this text implies, Aquinas's position presupposes a referential realism.[12] The intellect is capable of spontaneously grasping that the whole is

---

[12] In Coleman, "MacIntyre and Aquinas," Janet Coleman observes that "For Aquinas there is a notion of actual existence that is more basic than logical existence ... For both Aristotle and

greater than its parts because its operations naturally track fundamental logical relations of this kind. In a similar way, the intellect spontaneously grasps that good is to be sought and done, and evil is to be avoided, because it is capable of grasping and formulating the general principle underlying the human creature's operations as a causal agent. Every creature necessarily pursues good and avoids evil in the way appropriate to it, but the rational creature does so knowingly, in accordance with an abstract conception of good which is filled out through judgment grounded in experience.

This line of analysis is confirmed when we turn to I-II 100, comprising Aquinas's analysis of the precepts of the Decalogue, which he, together with nearly all other scholastics, regards as the epitome of the precepts of the natural law, broadly understood.[13] At different points in this question, Aquinas seems to agree both with the anonymous author just cited and with his teacher Albert, claiming that the precepts of the Decalogue are not, and alternatively that they are, self-evident. Yet these claims do not reflect the confusion that they might suggest; rather, they presuppose and develop Aquinas's earlier claim that a proposition may be self-evident in itself, and yet not self-evident to someone who entertains it, or even to someone who affirms it. The precepts of the Decalogue and their further specifications are best understood as falling along what we might describe as a spectrum of more or less apparently self-evident specifications of the natural law understood in its primary sense as a first principle of practical reason.

In the first article of I-II 100, Aquinas would seem to qualify his earlier claim that the natural law is grounded in the first principle that good is to be done and the bad is to be avoided. That is, in addition to this principle, he also identifies Jesus's commandments to love God and neighbor (Matthew 22: 37–9), and correlatively the injunction to avoid harming anyone, as self-evident principles of the natural law. It would appear that he holds that there are several first principles of the natural law, which would seem to undermine the defense of the rational unity of the natural law developed in I-II 94.2. However, the connection between these diverse principles is later clarified in the context of his analysis of the virtue of justice. There, we read that the injunctions to love and to forebear

Aquinas actual existence is intuited as a first principle that is indemonstrable ..." (p. 69). I believe this observation applies to practical, as well as speculative reason, insofar as our conceptions of good and right are grounded in the structures of causality and rational agency.

[13] For details, see Porter, *Natural and Divine Law*, pp. 146–56.

harming others are themselves specifications of the first principle of practical reason as applied to our dealings with other persons, while the first principle more generally construed is foundational for all the virtues, including those which refer only to oneself (II-II 79.1c). This explains why these injunctions are associated specifically with the precepts of the Decalogue, since as Aquinas goes on to say, these are the primary precepts of the virtue of justice (II-II 122.1c). The injunctions to love God and neighbor and to avoid harm, which are said without qualification to be self-evident to all, can be considered as specifications of the first principle to do good and avoid evil, and as such, they do not undermine the rational unity of the natural law.[14]

As Aquinas goes on to analyze the relation between first principles and the precepts of the Decalogue, he develops a position that seems to be closer to that of the anonymous author just cited than to the position of his former teacher Albert. We read that the first principles of practical reason as they pertain to justice are the immediate foundations for the precepts of the Decalogue; the latter are not themselves self-evident, but they can be derived from first principles with only a minimum of reflection (I-II 100.3 ad 1; cf. I-II 95.1c). Hence, they are readily knowable to all persons, and for this reason, Aquinas is prepared to say that they belong to the natural law without qualification (I-II 100.1c). Thus, Aquinas affirms the claim that the precepts of the Decalogue are precepts of the natural law while at the same time denying that they are strictly speaking self-evident to all persons, or foundational for all moral reasoning.

Yet further on in this question, Aquinas does seem at least to imply that the precepts of the Decalogue are self-evident to all. The passage

---

[14] However, the principle of neighbor-love does introduce a normative criterion that cannot be analyzed without remainder in terms of the kind of goodness associated with moral virtue generally considered:

> if we speak of good and evil in general, to do the good and to avoid the evil pertain to all virtue. And in this sense, these cannot be placed among the parts of justice ... But justice, insofar as it is a particular virtue, aims at the good under the aspect of what is due to the neighbor. And according to this, it pertains to particular justice to do the good under the rational character of what is owed in relation to the neighbor, and to avoid the opposed evil, that is, that which injures the neighbor. It pertains to general justice to do the good that is due in relation to the community or to God, and to avoid the opposed evil. (II-II 79.1)

For this reason, moral judgments pertaining to the claims of others cannot be reduced to whatever promotes the good, all things considered – they must always give decisive weight to the claims of the individuals involved.

in question occurs in Aquinas's discussion of whether the precepts of the Decalogue admit of dispensation. Most of Aquinas's immediate predecessors and contemporaries held that these precepts do in fact admit of divine dispensation; Aquinas, in contrast, flatly denies this, on the grounds that these precepts express the intention of their legislator, who is of course God, in such a way that they can never be abrogated:

> For the precepts of the first tablet, which order to God, contain the very order to a common and final good, which is God; and the precepts of the second tablet contain the very order of justice to be observed among human persons, that is, that nothing undue should be done to anyone, and that to each should be rendered what is due. For the precepts of the Decalogue are to be understood in accordance with this rationale. And therefore the precepts of the Decalogue do not in any way admit of dispensation. (I-II 100.8c)

How are we to understand Aquinas's claim that the very order of justice is expressed through the precepts of the Decalogue? It would seem that in his view, these precepts express what it means to fulfill obligations or to inflict undue injury with respect to recurring relations or activities. Understood in this way, the precepts of the Decalogue would indeed be self-evident to anyone who grasps that the actions commanded or forbidden are to be understood in terms of the claim of right that they respect, or the undue injury they inflict. Admittedly, Aquinas does not say even here that the precepts of the Decalogue are self-evident to all, and it might be argued that what he does say is at least consistent with his earlier claim that they follow immediately from first principles, without being universally self-evident. More importantly, Aquinas rests his argument for the binding force of the precepts of the Decalogue on their rational character as immediate implications of the ideal of justice. In this way, he implies that these precepts are in some sense "constituted by reason" (I-II 94.1c), implying an integral, dynamic relation between these precepts and the rational agent who grasps and implements them. Aquinas's subsequent remarks bear this out.

In the third objection, Aquinas offers what seems to be a decisive argument that not only God, but even human persons, can dispense from the precepts of the Decalogue: "The prohibition of homicide is contained among the precepts of the Decalogue. But it would seem that this precept receives dispensation from human persons, for example, when according to the precepts of human law, human persons are legitimately killed, for example, wrongdoers or enemies" (I-II 100. 8 obj.3). He responds as follows:

> [K]illing a person is prohibited in the Decalogue insofar as it has the character of something unjustified; for the precept contains the very rationale of justice. And human law cannot grant this, that a person might licitly be killed without justification. But the killing of malefactors or enemies of the republic is not unjustified. Hence, this is not contrary to a precept of the Decalogue, nor is such a killing a murder, which the Decalogue prohibits ... And similarly, if something is taken from another, which was his own, if it is justified that he lose it, this is not theft or robbery, which are prohibited by a precept of the Decalogue ...
>
> So therefore, these precepts of the Decalogue, with respect to the rational character of justice which they contain, are unchangeable. But with respect to some determination through application to individual acts, whether for example this or that is murder, theft or adultery, or not, this indeed is changeable; sometimes only by the divine authority, namely in those things which are instituted by God alone, as for example marriage and other things of this sort; and sometimes by human authority, with respect to those things which are committed to human jurisdiction. For with respect to those things, human persons act as the vicar of God, not however with respect to all things. (I-II 100.8 ad 3)

Thus, the precepts of the Decalogue are always binding, but that does not mean that we can proceed immediately from these to a correct judgment in every instance of moral choice. In many cases, we will be able to do so, but in other cases we will find it necessary to reflect carefully on the meaning of moral concepts such as murder, theft, or adultery as these apply (or not) in a specific set of circumstances. On this model, moral reasoning proceeds through a process of specification, through which general moral concepts are given concrete meaning through reflection aimed at practical application. The basic moral concepts sketched out in the Decalogue provide immediate starting points for much of this reflection, but at the same time, these concepts are themselves specifications of first principles which comprise the natural law in its primary sense. Because these precepts are formulated in the context of the most fundamental claims and needs of human life, they are quite general and fall within reach of everyone's capacities, even though even these general precepts are too specific to be regarded as strictly speaking self-evident to all. Still more concrete moral norms are derived from these general norms through the same processes of specification, taking account of the complexities of particular cases and the needs and claims of those involved.

The further this process descends to details, the more it is subject both to contingency and error (I-II 94.4c).

Precepts of the natural law thus fall along a spectrum of generality and rational certainty, from the first principle of practical reason, which is completely general and immediately self-evident to all, to the direct and generally accessible applications of this principle comprising the precepts of the Decalogue, and then further to more specific applications, leading finally to determinations of correct action in particular instances of choice. At every level, this process calls for a determination of the concrete meaning of general terms and presupposes a more comprehensive principle as its starting point. Thus even the most general moral precepts of the Decalogue cannot be regarded as strictly speaking foundational first principles. Yet these precepts follow immediately from reflection on the concrete meaning of doing good and avoiding evil, as specified by the twofold precept of love of God and neighbor. Further levels of specification require greater understanding and prudence, which do not fall within the scope of everyone, and that is why these processes require the judgment of "the wise."

Aquinas's initial claim, that the precepts of the natural law do not allow for dispensation, is thus developed in such a way as to qualify what seems at first to be a rigorist view. These precepts are absolutely binding, but that does not mean that they present the moral agent with an externally imposed set of rules, to be implemented mechanically. Rather, these precepts have a point, in terms of which they can be understood, interpreted, and intelligently applied. They represent, in summary forms, the essential demands of justice, and considered as such, they cannot be set aside by God himself. But by the same token, in order to express the claims of justice in actual situations, these precepts must be interpreted and applied in the light of the rationale of justice, which they represent. It is worth noting that on Aquinas's account, the basis for the interpretation of these precepts – that is, their status as intelligible expressions of justice – is also the basis for their authoritative force. These are not divine commands, but rational expressions of exigent moral claims.

Aquinas's account of moral knowledge is thus consistent with what he says about the rational agent, who participates in a certain way in providence, being provident for himself and others (I-II 91.2c). God's providential rule does not reduce men and women to servile status, through commands which they are compelled to obey – rather, he enables them to rule over themselves and others, through endowing them with the capacities to grasp the rational demands of morality and justice, and to act accordingly. The natural law, understood in its primary sense as a first principle of the intellect, comprises one necessary component of the human capacity for rational freedom, accountability, and virtue. It is most fundamentally a principle of dynamic judgment and activity, a source of norms which cannot be reduced to a law-code, and an essential element of human existence.[15]

[15] Portions of this article are adapted from an earlier article, "What the Wise Person Knows: Natural Law and Virtue in Aquinas's *Summa Theologiae*," pp. 57–69, and are used with the permission of the editor of that journal.

CHAPTER 10

Natural Reason and Supernatural Faith

Thomas M. Osborne, Jr.

For Thomas Aquinas, belief is a kind of assent that is based not only on the intellect but also on the will.[1] The nature of his account of the role of human reason in the certitude and rational justification of faith has been contentious. Some scholars have focused on the similarity between Christian belief and other kinds of reasonable belief.[2] These authors disagree over whether for Thomas the certitude of belief primarily depends on the will or on the intellect. Apart from their differing judgments on this last issue, these authors agree that for Thomas Christian belief is reasonable in the same way that other kinds of human belief are reasonable. Others have interpreted Thomas as saying that faith is supernatural in such a way that a special help from God is necessary in order to recognize its reasonableness.[3] This view sharply distinguishes the reasonableness of Christian faith from any other kind of reasonableness. I will explain the once common view that Thomas holds that faith can be justified by human reasoning even though it exceeds the unaided abilities of human reason. Thomas's account of faith in the *Summa Theologiae* indicates how even though without grace or faith someone can assent to the proposition that faith is reasonable, it is impossible without grace to make an act of faith.

My argument is based on three propositions. First, Thomas thinks that faith is certain only because of the way its principles are borrowed from God's own knowledge and that of the saints in heaven. The *Summa*

---

[1] Aquinas, DV 14.1c; ST II-II 2.1c.
[2] Penelhum, "The Analysis of Faith," emphasizes the intellect, whereas Ross, "Aquinas on Belief and Knowledge," and Stump, "Faith and Goodness," focus on the will. Niederbacher, *Glaube als Tugend*, stresses the role of voluntary habits in belief.
[3] Jenkins, *Knowledge and Faith*. Jenkins's account on this issue in some respects resembles that of the early twentieth-century Jesuit Rousselot, in his *Eyes of Faith*. In large part I am presenting something like the alternative accounts that were given by Gardeil, *Credibilité*, and Garrigou-Lagrange, *De Revelatione*, vol. 1, pp. 397–513. For the historical context, see Dulles, *Things Hoped For*, pp. 104–13.

Theologiae is a work of sacred doctrine, which has certitude precisely to the extent that it depends on the certitude of these articles of faith. Second, this certitude of faith differs from that of human science because faith is specified by an object that exceeds the abilities of human reason, namely God as First Truth. The excellence of the object explains how the assent of faith is certain even though it is freely chosen. The knowledge acquired through faith is essentially different from that knowledge of God which is acquired through philosophy. Third, the certitude and supernatural object of faith explain why its act requires a special movement from God and the gratuitous light of faith.

10.1   The Certitude of Faith and Sacred Doctrine

Thomas thinks that both faith and sacred doctrine are habits whereby we assent with certitude to truths that are not known through ordinary human reason. Thomas discusses the nature of sacred doctrine in the very first question of the First Part of the *Summa Theologiae*. Even in this one question Thomas seems to use the term "sacred doctrine" in slightly different ways. In article 1 sacred doctrine seems to be more or less the same as the knowledge possessed through faith. He states that sacred doctrine is necessary because humans are ordered to a supernatural end that exceeds human intellectual ability. Moreover, human reason is weak considered even with respect to what it can know about God through its own powers. However, in article 2 he states that sacred doctrine is a science.[4] For Thomas this term "science" (*scientia*) has a special meaning. It is an intellectual habit of demonstrating conclusions from principles. It is a kind of certain knowledge. Aristotle describes this habit at length in the *Posterior Analytics*. Thomas uses the Aristotelian understanding of the habit of science in order to show a controverted point among his contemporaries, that theology is fully a science. Thomas does not suggest that every believer is capable of possessing such a science. Whereas in article 1 sacred doctrine seems to be a knowledge that is possessed by all the faithful, in article 2 it is a knowledge that is restricted to those who have acquired an intellectual habit.

It can be difficult to see how the two senses of "sacred doctrine" are related.[5] For our argument, it is important to note that even though there

[4] Chenu, *Théologie comme science*; Elders, "Faith and Science," pp. 44–50; Jenkins, *Knowledge and Faith*, pp. 11–98.
[5] Davies, "Is *Sacra Doctrina* Theology?"; Weisheipl, "Meaning of *Sacra Doctrina*."

are different degrees of knowledge about God among the faithful, the certitude of knowledge concerning revealed truths is ultimately based on the same virtue of faith. For instance, there are differences concerning the material object of faith, and in particular the number of truths that are believed. First, Christians whose duties include teaching must explicitly believe in more truths of faith than those who are merely obliged to believe in their teaching.[6] Despite this difference, all Christians are required to know the same central truths of faith, and to have the same motive for their belief in them. After the coming of Christ, all are obliged to believe in the incarnation, since they are bound to know that salvation comes through the passion and resurrection of Christ. This belief in the incarnation requires a belief in the Trinity. All Christians consequently share the same belief in Christianity's central mysteries, even though they have varying degrees of explicit belief about other matters. One cause of this diversity could be the possession of sacred doctrine as a science. Moreover, although there are many material objects of faith, there is only one formal object by which they are believed, namely God as first truth.[7]

Apart from this material diversity in the number of truths that the believer is obligated to believe, there is also diversity in the amount of truths that are capable of being believed. Some truths, called preambles, are merely believed by some Christians even though they are demonstratively known by others.[8] For instance, someone who demonstrates God's existence knows that God exists through human science and not through faith.[9] But most Christians have certain knowledge of God's existence only through faith. Philosophical knowledge of such preambles is available only to a few, over a long period of time, and is subject to error.[10]

Sacred doctrine, as a science about God, is not equally possessed by all the faithful. The restricted character of sacred doctrine is illustrated by its use of philosophy.[11] Thomas states that human reason cannot establish the principles of sacred doctrine, which are revealed by God in Sacred Scripture. In his early *Commentary on Boethius' De Trinitate*, Thomas repeats a widespread contemporary description of the triple role

---

[6] Aquinas, ST II-II 2.6–8.
[7] Aquinas, ST II-II 2.1; DV 14.7. For the importance of this doctrine, see Cessario, *Christian Faith*, pp. 49–83.
[8] Aquinas, In BDT 2.3; ST I 2.2 ad 1. Sparrow, "Natural Knowledge of God"; Elders, "Faith and Science," pp. 57–62; Wippel, "Philosophy and the Preambles."
[9] Aquinas, ST II-II 1.5.
[10] Aquinas, ST I 1.1c; SCG I 4.3–5. For Thomas's development on this issue, see Elders, "Faith and Science," pp. 60–1.
[11] Aquinas, ST I 1.8c and ad 2; II-II 1.5 ad 2; 2.10c and ad 2.

of philosophy as (1) demonstrating preambles, (2) explaining the faith, and (3) addressing attacks on the faith.[12] Thomas repeats each of these points at some place in the *Summa Theologiae*, although in the central discussion, namely question 1, article 8, he focuses on the third. In its response, Thomas notes that the principles of sacred doctrine are like the principles of metaphysics, in that they cannot be proven by any superior science. Arguments are used to respond to those who would deny an article of faith. A well-known example of such a use occurs later in the *Summa Theologiae*, where Thomas argues that the supposed demonstrations of the world's eternity are merely probable arguments.[13] In question 1, article 8 ad 2, Thomas mentions the second member of the traditional threefold distinction, namely that philosophy can be used in explanations. He adds that philosophers can be extrinsic and merely probable authorities for sacred doctrine. In contrast, Sacred Scripture is intrinsic to sacred doctrine and believed on God's authority.

Sacred doctrine's certitude depends on that of its principles, which are borrowed from the knowledge that is possessed by God and the blessed in heaven.[14] Thomas distinguishes between a subalternating and a subalternated science.[15] In a subalternating science, conclusions are demonstrated from principles that are self-known. For instance, the truths of geometry are based on principles that are evident to someone who grasps their meaning. Thomas usually compares the perception of these principles with sight. The natural light of the intellect makes them perceptible in the way that ordinary light makes colors visible.[16] Thomas's contemporaries sometimes attempted to explain knowledge in terms of a light that directly comes from God. Thomas rejects this understanding of the intelligible light, and generally attributes such a light to the agent intellect.[17] In a subalternated science, conclusions are demonstrated from principles that are known not by the light of the knower's intellect, but by the light of the relevant subalternating science. For instance, the science of optics borrows principles from geometry, and the science of music borrows

---

[12] Aquinas, In BDT, 2.1; Elders, *Faith and Science*, p. 52.

[13] Aquinas, ST I 46.1.

[14] Aquinas, ST I 1.2c; In BDT, 2.2c and ad 5.

[15] Elders, *Faith and Science*, pp. 47–8; Jenkins, *Knowledge and Faith*, pp. 52–6, 69–70, 76–7.

[16] Aquinas, ST I 79.3 ad 2; 84.5c; In BDT, 1.1; SCG II 77.4–5. For Aquinas's understanding of this natural light, see Lonergan, *Verbum*, pp. 79–84; Pasnau, *Aquinas on Human Nature*, pp. 302–10; Peifer, *Concept in Thomism*, pp. 116–19.

[17] Elders, "Faith and Science," p. 29, notes the natural light of angelic intellects in *In II Sent.* 9.1.2 ad 4; ST I 106.1 ad 2.

192 THOMAS M. OSBORNE, JR.

principles from arithmetic.[18] The principles of a subalternated science are, or at least can be, accepted on authority. For instance, a physician accepts the authority of the scientists who tell him that there are four elements.[19]

Sacred doctrine is subalternated to the science possessed by God and the blessed in heaven.[20] It might seem strange to describe God's knowledge as "science," and it does not completely fit in with Aristotle's description of science in the *Posterior Analytics*. Later in I 14, Thomas argues that God's knowledge is truly science but it differs from ours in that it is the highest science, since it is perfectly immaterial and infinite. In his discussion of sacred doctrine, Thomas is content to say that sacred doctrine is based on principles that are given to us by God in Sacred Scripture. It is more certain than other sciences precisely on account of the certitude of its principles. Human science is only as certain as its principles, which are known by the light of natural reason, and the human intellect can err.[21] But the light of God's knowledge does not allow for error. Knowledge based on human authority is weak. Sacred doctrine lacks such weakness because God's authority is greater than any human cause of knowledge.[22]

The connection between faith and God's own knowledge can be seen in Thomas's definition of faith as "a habit of mind, by which eternal life is begun in us, making the intellect assent to what is not apparent."[23] Faith in general is a habit of belief in that which is not understood. The theological virtue of faith is distinct from other kinds of faith because of its order to the beatific vision.[24] Faith is about and directed to what is not yet seen. God not only is the object of belief, but his knowledge is the basis of the principles that are believed. Since humans can only reach this supernatural beatitude through God's help, they must attain the requisite knowledge by being taught by God. Thomas writes, "so that we (*homo*) might arrive at the perfect vision of beatitude, it is first required that we believe (*credat*) in God just as the pupil believes the teaching master."[25]

---

[18] Aquinas, ST I 1.2
[19] Aquinas, In BDT, 2.2 ad 5.
[20] Aquinas, ST I 1.2c; In BDT, 2.2 ad 5; *In prol. Sent.* 1.3, qla 3, sol. 2. For interpretations of the early *Sentence* commentary passage, see Jenkins, *Knowledge and Faith*, pp. 69–70; Chenu, *Théologie comme science*, pp. 80–5.
[21] Aquinas, ST I 1.5c.
[22] Aquinas, ST I 1.8 ad 2.
[23] *[H]abitus mentis, qua inchoatur vita aeterna in nobis, faciens intellectum assentire non apparentibus.* Aquinas, ST II-II 4.1c. See also DV 14.2.
[24] Aquinas, ST II-II 4.1c.
[25] *Unde ad hoc quod homo perveniat ad perfectam visionem beatitudinis praeexigitur quod credat Deo tanquam discipulus magistro docenti* (ST II-II 2.3c). See also DV 14.10; In BDT, 3.1. Elders, *Faith and Science*, pp. 57–8; Jenkins, *Knowledge and Faith*, pp. 68–9.

Sacred doctrine is based on the articles of faith, which are known by God and the blessed in heaven. Humans need to know such truths in addition to the naturally knowable truths in order to reach their supernatural end. The Christian begins with a faith that should eventually be replaced by the beatific vision.

Even though faith differs from opinion because it is a kind of knowledge, it also differs from the knowledge that is science because its object is obscure. Faith's certitude is based on God's authority. Thomas writes:

> [F]aith is certain knowledge, inasmuch as the intellect is determined through faith to something knowable. But this determination to one does not proceed from the vision of the believer, but from the vision of the one who is believed. And thus, inasmuch as it lacks vision, it falls short of the nature of the knowledge which is in science; for science determines the intellect to one through vision and the understanding of first principles.[26]

In science, the object is evident in such a way that assent is compelled.[27] An individual might choose to consider or not consider what he knows through science, but the self-evident principles and the demonstrated conclusions must be assented to when they are considered in themselves or as demonstrated. Similarly, the blessed in heaven do not choose to believe what they see in the beatific vision.

Opinion is similar to science in that someone with opinion can choose whether or not to consider its objects.[28] The difference is that in opinion, when the object is considered, the assent will be weak. The object's obscurity makes the believer's assent uncertain. Faith is subject to choice not only in the consideration of the object, but also in the assent itself. The difference between the Christian's faith and a heretic's belief shows how faith is distinct from opinion.[29] The Christian with faith believes in the articles of faith because they are revealed by God through Sacred Scripture and the teaching of the Church. In contrast, the heretic believes in only some articles, and only on account of his own judgment. Consequently, the believer and the heretic might believe in exactly the same propositions about the Trinity, but the first has faith and the

---

[26] *[F]ides cognitio quaedam est inquantum intellectus determinatur per fidem ad aliquod cognoscibile. Sed haec determinato ad unum non procedit ex visione credentis, sed a visione eius cui creditur. Et sic, inquantum deest visio, deficit a ratione cognitionis quae est in scientia: nam scientia determinat intellectum ad unum per visionem et intellectum primorum principiorum* (ST I 12.1 3 ad 3).

[27] Aquinas, ST I-II 67.3c.; II-II 2.9 ad 2.

[28] Aquinas, ST II-II 1.4c.

[29] Aquinas, ST II-II 5.3; DV 14.10 ad 10. In DV 14.3 ad 5, Aquinas argues that faith is distinct from opinion and science because it comes from the will.

second has opinion. The difference is not in the clarity of the object, but in the nature of the assent. The heretic does not believe in the articles as revealed. The authority of Sacred Scripture and the Church gives certitude to the believer's assent.

Faith also has more certitude than human science. Thomas distinguishes between the ways in which knowledge can gain certitude on account of its cause and on account of the believing subject. On account of its cause, faith is more certain than science since the First Truth has the greatest certitude. However, human science can be more certain than faith on the subject's part, since the articles do not compel the subject's belief. Nevertheless, doubt in the articles is unfounded. Such doubt comes not from the articles believed but from human weakness. Similarly, heretics can have complete certitude on their part even though they lack the certitude that comes from true faith.[30]

Thomas compares faith with science and opinion in order to shed light on its distinct character, which is its basis on God's testimony. We learn more about faith by seeing how it is both like and unlike the other two. Under normal conditions, the intellect requires a clearly perceived object for its assent to be certain. Moreover, the intellect can assent to a truth on the basis of human authority, but such human faith will be weaker than scientific assent. In contrast, supernatural faith is more certain than science even though its object is unseen. Sacred doctrine shares in this certitude because of its dependence on faith.

Human sciences have certitude ultimately because of the way in which the self-evident principles are grasped by the human understanding. Such principles do not rely on other arguments or testimony. Sacred doctrine relies on faith, which ultimately rests on principles that are not fully grasped by the believer. Consequently, the certitude of sacred doctrine and faith needs to be explained differently. This explanation is based on the way in which faith by its very nature exceeds human abilities.

10.2   Faith as Essentially Supernatural Knowledge

In order to understand the peculiar certitude of faith, it is important to consider not only the general distinction between faith and human science, but also the narrower distinction between faith and that human science which is concerned with our knowledge of God from his effects. Thomas thought that the philosophers had attained such knowledge

[30] Aquinas, *Quodlibet* 6.4.

without revelation. In what way does faith differ from such naturally certain knowledge of God?

Faith exceeds human reason because of its formal object, which is God as the First Truth. This formal object sets faith and sacred doctrine apart from any natural knowledge, including the natural knowledge of God. Faith is also specifically distinct from the knowledge of God's essence through the beatific vision. God's essence is clearly known only to himself and to the angels and saints in heavens. Such knowledge is impossible for angels and humans in this life, and to any created intellects if they are relying on their own natural powers.

According to Thomas, "the known object is in the knower according to the mode of the knower."[31] The known object cannot have a mode of being that exceeds that of the knower. But since God is subsistent being, his being exceeds any creature's mode of knowing; no creature on its own can know God's essence.[32] Such knowledge is impossible even for angelic intellects, whose subsistent natures are nevertheless distinct from their own act of being. Since their mode of being is immaterial, their proper object is an immaterial created quiddity. They can have evident knowledge of created immaterial natures but not of God. The difficulty is even greater for the human intellect whose being is joined to matter. In this life, human knowledge of even immaterial objects is ultimately based in sense perception. The proper adequate object of the human intellect is the essence of a material thing, although humans can arrive at a confused knowledge of the immaterial.

Both angelic and human intellects can know God's essence because they are able to be raised by God above their natural abilities. In contrast, the physical senses common to humans and other animals are limited to the perception of particular physical objects, and they cannot even know natures. Intellects have an ability to be raised to such knowledge that the senses lack. The human ability to be raised to such knowledge is sometimes described as an "obediential potency," since it is a potency to being raised by God.[33] Thomas states that God raises an intellect to the vision of his essence through a created light of glory.[34] This light elevates the knower so that God can make himself known, even if in an imperfect way on account of the limited nature of the created light.

---

[31] *Cognitum autem est in cognoscente secundum modum cognoscentis* (ST I 12.4c). I have omitted the "autem." For the meaning and importance of this axiom, see Wippel, "What is Received."

[32] Aquinas, ST I 12.4c. See also ST I 62.1c; I-II 5.5c; DV 8.3c.

[33] Dougherty, "Self-Evidence," pp. 169–75.

[34] Aquinas, ST I 12.2c, 5c, and 7c; II-II 5.1 ad 1; DV 8.3, 10.11c and ad 7, 13.2c; SCG III 58.3; *Quodlibet* 7.1.1.

According to Thomas, this light of glory can only be given in the next life.[35] His argument for this conclusion resembles the previous argument for the insufficiency of the created intellect's natural powers, since both are based on a premise about the knower's mode of being. This later argument is that, since in this life our being is connected with the body, and the beatific vision is a direct vision of the immaterial, we cannot have the beatific vision in this life even with the help of grace. This argument in one way differs from the first because it applies to human and not to angelic intellects, since it argues from the way in which human knowledge depends on the senses. Moreover, this argument argues for a stronger conclusion to the first because it is about both natural powers on their own and powers that are assisted by grace.

This argument is also distinct because its conclusion follows only for the ordinary course of events.[36] God sometimes does give the beatific vision to those in this life. For instance, Moses and St. Paul saw God's essence even though they were joined to the body. Nevertheless, they did not use their senses in this vision. It is not contradictory for someone with a mode of being that is joined to the body to see the divine essence. However, it would entail a contradiction if someone were able to know God's essence in the same way that we ordinarily know other essences in this life, which is by using sense information and images.

Like the beatific vision, faith's primary object is God in himself. But faith differs from the beatific vision on account of its obscurity. Philosophy contains some truths about God. It differs from faith in that it is a scientific knowledge of God from his sensible effects. This knowledge of God belongs primarily to metaphysics. In his proemium to his *Commentary on the Metaphysics*, Thomas explains that metaphysics is called theology because it considers God and other substances that exist apart from matter.[37] The subject of this science is common being (*ens commune*). Metaphysics is concerned with God at least insofar as he is a cause of this common being.[38] In the *Commentary* Thomas states that in one way metaphysics is divine because God himself has this science and it is about God.[39] In fact, only God himself has it to the highest degree.

---

[35] Aquinas, ST I 12.11.
[36] Aquinas, ST I 12.11; I-II 175.3.
[37] Aquinas, *In Met.* proemium.
[38] Wippel, *Metaphysical Thought*, pp. 11–22; Elders considers the relationship between natural theology and metaphysics in *Faith and Science*, pp. 111–16.
[39] Aquinas, *In I Met.* 3.64.

The philosophical knowledge of God is a limited knowledge acquired from his sensible effects. It is true knowledge in that it answers the *Posterior Analytics'* question of whether a thing is (*an est*).[40] Since the knower reasons from effects to cause, the science proceeds by means of the kind of argument (*quia*) that proves that the cause exists but does not give a reason why the cause exists. According to this kind of proof, we can know whether God exists and eventually those conclusions that necessarily follow from the fact that he is the first cause of everything. According to such philosophical inquiry, he is named and understood either as distinct from creatures, in relation to creatures, or as exceeding all creatures. Any creaturely limitations are negated of God because God supersedes all created perfections.

Thomas does not always explicitly state which propositions about God can be demonstrated by philosophers and which can be known only through faith. Demonstrations must be based on principles that themselves have such features as priority, primitiveness, universality, and necessity. Consequently, what at first looks like a demonstrative syllogism might be a dialectical syllogism. For instance, in the *Summa Contra Gentiles*, Thomas uses natural reason to argue for the resurrection of the body, which cannot be demonstrated.[41] Readers at times disagree about whether a particular philosophical argument in either *Summa* is demonstrative or merely probable. For instance, in *Summa Theologiae* I 22 and 25, Thomas primarily uses natural reason to show what theology holds concerning God's providence and omnipotence. But in *Summa Theologiae* II-II 1.8 ad 1, Thomas states: "[W]e hold many things about God through faith which the philosophers were not able to investigate by natural reason: for instance, concerning his providence and omnipotence, and that he alone is to be worshipped."[42] Two influential commentators give plausible and conflicting interpretations of this passage. Thomas de Vio Cajetan (1468–1534) suggests that philosophers could not have

---

[40] Aquinas, ST I 1.7 ad 1; 12.12; 13.11 ad 5; In BDT 1.2c, 6.3–4. See Martin, *God and Explanations*, pp. 80–93; White, "Prelude to the Five Ways," pp. 37–43, and 44, note 4. Wippel, *Metaphysical Thought*," pp. 502–43, shows at the very least a verbal change in Aquinas's opinion concerning the quidditative knowledge of God. Doyle, "Theological Truth," pp. 578–9, distinguishes between our knowledge of "what God is not," which is a negative knowledge of God's essence through *propter quid* demonstrations, and our knowledge that "God exists," which is a positive statement known through a *quia* demonstration.

[41] Aquinas, SCG IV 82.5–9. For the use of probable arguments, see SCG I 9.3.

[42] [M]ulta per fidem tenemus de Deo quae naturali ratione investigare philosophi non potuerunt: puta circa providentiam eius et omnipotentiam, et quod ipse solus sit colendus. See also Aquinas, DV 14.9 ad 8.

demonstrative certitude about these matters, whereas Domingo Banez (1528–1604) states that Thomas is distinguishing between what can be demonstrated about these same matters through nature and through revelation.[43]

Whatever the limits of philosophy, it is clear that philosophers know through reason alone some truths that most believers know only through faith. Although the propositions believed are the same, the habits by which they are believed differ specifically. In the very first article of the *Summa Theologiae*, Thomas states that there is a similar difference between the theology that is part of philosophy and that which is part of sacred doctrine.[44] Both astronomers and natural scientists can prove the same proposition that the earth is round. The sciences are distinguished by the way in which such propositions are demonstrated. An astronomer uses mathematics to demonstrate its roundness, and the natural philosopher considers the nature of matter. Similarly, the philosopher knows that God exists and other preambles through the light of natural reason, whereas the Christian believer knows them through the light of divine revelation.

Since philosophy is about what we can know through sensible effects, in this life we lack quiddative knowledge of God. Unlike philosophy, sacred doctrine and faith are directly about God's essence in itself rather than simply as known through his effects. However, only in the next life will we be able to know what God is, and then because our intellects have been elevated by the light of glory. Faith, and consequently sacred doctrine, is about what we know of his essence through revelation. Since this essence cannot be seen, faith remains obscure and its object cannot compel our assent.

10.3   Faith Requires a Supernatural Cause

The obscurity of faith's object explains why an act of faith requires special assistance from God. Ordinary human certitude comes from the grasp of self-evident first principles or demonstrated conclusions. When we grasp the principles or the demonstrations, we are not free to withhold our assent. Faith's object does not compel assent. Such assent cannot be explained in the way that other certain knowledge can be explained, even

---

[43] Cajetan, In II-II 1.8; Bañez, In II-II 1.8, 41e–42d. For contemporary discussions of these issues, see Wippel, "Demonstrating God's Omnipotence"; Shanley, "Demonstrating God's Providence."
[44] Aquinas, ST I 1.1 ad 2.

if such knowledge is also about God. In this final section we will show that, according to Thomas, even the judgment that such certain assent is reasonable is insufficient for the assent itself. The evidence for faith does not compel faith, at least in humans. The judgment that one should believe is different from that judgment which is an act of belief. Such an act of faith ultimately depends on God's supernatural movement of the will and intellect.

Even though its object is obscure, faith is reasonable.[45] Thomas writes: "[T]o believe is an act of the intellect assenting to divine truth on account of the will's command moved by God through grace, and thus it is subject to free choice in its order to God."[46] The formal object of faith is God as First Truth, and materially it includes propositions that are revealed by God. If the object of faith were evident, then the act of faith would be less free then an act of demonstration is. It is reasonable to assent to what God reveals even though revelation does not make the object of assent evident.

This obscurity of the object is at least necessary for the freedom of human assent, although it is insufficient for the freedom of the demons' assent. The demons know both that God has revealed the articles of faith and that God cannot lie. Consequently, they know that the articles of faith are true. Nevertheless, these revealed truths are obscure to demons as well.[47] They believe in the Trinity only because their assent is forced by the evidence of signs that indicate its truth. The exact nature of this coercion by evidence is perhaps unclear both in the *Summa Theologiae* and in earlier texts.[48] Nevertheless, Thomas consistently holds that the demons do not believe through choice. In contrast, Christians freely believe and therefore can have merit.

Why does the evidence compel the demons and not Christians? It is somewhat unclear whether humans simply fail to grasp the evidence in the way that demons do, or whether for humans the obscurity of

---

[45] The classic text is Aquinas, SCG I 6.

[46] *[C]redere est actus intellectus assentientis veritati divinae ex imperio voluntatis a Deo motae per gratiam, et sic subiacet libero arbitrio in ordine ad Deum* (Aquinas, ST II-II 2.9c). See also ad 3, 4.1 ad 5; III 7.3 ad 2.

[47] Aquinas, ST II-II 5.2. Jenkins, *Knowledge and Faith*, pp. 170–2; Penulhum, "Analysis of Faith," pp. 145–6; Niederbacher, *Glaube als Tugend*, pp. 118–19.

[48] It is interesting to compare this text with earlier texts on this issue, such as *In II Sent.* 7.1.2 ad 4; *In III Sent.* 23.3.3 sol. 1; DV 19.4 ad 4. Thomas also addresses the point in ST I 64.2 ad 5. In this latter text, the Leonine says that the demons' belief is *non voluntate*, whereas the Piana edition has *non voluntarie*. For the texts and possible readings, see Waldschmidt, *Notion and Problems of Credibility*, pp. 24–36.

the object is somehow sufficient for the freedom of human assent. The human intellect is weaker than the demonic, and it thinks by reasoning from one truth to another. In the *Summa Theologiae*'s discussion of demonic belief, Thomas states that for humans, the obscurity is not merely in the object, but in the evidence for its truth. This discussion perhaps implies that humans are unable to fully grasp this evidence. In his earlier *Commentary on Boethius' De Trinitate*, Thomas suggests that signs could never be sufficient to force human belief.[49] He states that human assent can only be compelled by principles and demonstrations from them.

Thomas denies that an act of Christian belief is lightly made. Even though faith cannot be demonstrated, it can be seen to be reasonable through preaching and miracles. Although such preaching and miracles do not make the object of faith apparent, they do show that the articles are worthy of belief. Thomas states: "[T]he believer would not believe unless he saw that those things [which fall under faith] should be believed, either on account of the evidence of signs or on account of something of this sort."[50] Miracles are signs that show the rationality of faith. They are supernatural effects that lead the observer to knowledge of the supernatural cause. In a biblical commentary Thomas even refers to them as "demonstrations of faith" and compares them to demonstrations in science.[51] Natural reason can know that God can never lie, and that he performs miracles in proof of revelation. We know through natural reason that some miracles, such as raising someone from the dead, can only be performed by God and not by demons.[52]

Miracles and prophecy provide the main evidence for faith, whereas philosophical demonstrations and arguments primarily remove impediments.[53] Consequently, in the context of the rationality of an act of belief, miracles are far more important than the demonstration of such preambles as God's existence. In particular, Christ's miracles were sufficient for showing his divinity and making unbelief culpable.[54] Thomas even states that "miracles diminish the merit of faith, inasmuch as

[49] Aquinas, In BDT 2.1 ad 5.

[50] *non enim crederet nisi videret ea esse credenda, vel propter evidentiam signorum vel propter aliquid huiusmodi.* Aquinas, ST II-II 1.4 ad 2. Cf. 2.9 ad 3. For later theological issues concerning miracles and other motives of credibility, see Garrigou-Lagrange, *De Revelatione*, vol. 1, pp. 514–19.

[51] Aquinas, *In 2 Ad Thessalonicenses*, 3.1.65. Gardeil, *Credibilité*, p. 104.

[52] Aquinas, ST I 114.4; DP 6.5; *In Ioannem*, 10.5.1431; *In 2 Ad Thessalonicenses*, 2.2.49; *In II Sent.*, d.7 3.1 ad 2; *In III Sent.*, d. 16 1.3.

[53] Aquinas, ST II-II 2.9 ad 3; 2.10 ad 2; 6.1c; SCG III 154.8–10.

[54] Aquinas, ST III 43.4c; *Quodlibet* 2 4.1 ad 4; *In Ioannem* 15.5.2054–5.

through them is shown the hardness of those who do not wish to believe those things which are proved through the divine Scriptures, except on account of miracles."[55] In this and related passages, Thomas seems to be referring to unbelievers who already accept the authority of Scripture, such as Jews and heretics.[56] On this plausible reading, because such unbelievers have Scripture, they have sufficient basis for believing in what is taught by Christ and the Church. According to Thomas, miracles would then be needed to overcome their moral faults.

On account of such signs, prophecy, and similar evidence, revelation can be judged worthy of belief even apart from an act of faith.[57] In his early *Sentence Commentary*, Thomas states in adults that the judgment that one should believe and an accompanying will to believe often precedes faith and its acts.[58] It is clear (against Jenkins and Rousselot) that the special light of faith is unnecessary for the judgment of credibility, even though such a judgment might often presuppose a previous cooperation with grace or be part of such cooperation.

Thomas distinguishes between exterior causes of belief, such as miracles and preaching, and interior causes.[59] Miracles and preaching on their own cannot cause an act of faith. Many lack faith who hear the same preaching and see the same miracles that believers do. Exterior aids such as preaching are necessary to know what to believe, but they do not on their own cause belief. But the beginning of faith cannot be primarily caused by the believer's free choice, since God's grace would then be unnecessary. Thomas identifies this position with the heresy of Pelagianism.[60] The beginning of faith (*initium fidei*) must come from God and not from humans, although God moves the believer's intellect and free choice to an act of freely chosen belief. Thomas has theological reasons for holding that even though faith is rational, natural human abilities are insufficient for faith.

---

[55] *miracula intantum diminuunt meritum fidei, inquantum per hoc ostenditur duritia eorum qui nolunt credere ea quae Scripturis divinis probantur, nisi per miracula.* ST III 43.1 ad 3.

[56] Waldschmidt, *Notion and Problems of Credibility*, pp. 49–50.

[57] Aquinas, ST II-II 2.1 ad 1; *In III Sent.* 23.2.2 sol. 2 and ad 3; *In 1 ad Corinthos* 14.4.857. For later theological developments of this issue, see Garrigou-Lagrange, *De Revelatione*, vol. 1, pp. 497–503.

[58] Aquinas, *In III Sent.* 23.2.5 ad 4–5. Gardeil, *Crédibilité*, p. 27.

[59] Aquinas, ST II-II 6.1; SCG III 154.4. For the distinction between exterior and interior causes, see also ST I 111.1 ad 1; DV 18.3c. For the insufficiency of free choice, see especially *In Ad Ephesos* 2.3.95–6. For these causes in their historical context, see Lang, *Entfaltung des apologetischen Problems*, pp. 76–83.

[60] He means what would come to be described as "Semipelagianism." For later scholastic debates over Semipelagianism and the *initium fidei*, see Garrigou-Lagrange, *De Revelatione*, vol. 1, pp. 417–22. For Aquinas's development on grace, see Bouillard, *Conversion et grâce*, pp. 92–122.

Thomas's understanding of reason's insufficiency for faith is based on his position that the object of faith is essentially supernatural because its formal object is supernatural. He argues:

> Since someone (*homo*), in assenting to those things which belong to faith, is elevated above his/her nature, it is necessary that this be in him/her from a supernatural principle moving interiorly, which is God. And therefore faith with respect to assent, which is the principle act of faith, is from God interiorly moving through grace.[61]

Thomas in this article argues that all acts of faith, including those that have been preceded by evidence, require a supernatural illumination of the intellect and an efficient causality of the will. Although God efficiently causes all good human acts and the being of sinful acts, through a special movement he supernaturally produces good acts such as faith which exceed the ability of unaided human nature.[62] In an act of faith, God efficiently moves the will so that it freely chooses and commands an intellectual assent which has certitude and a formal object that are supernatural. Similarly, although God enlightens the intellect and moves all cognitive acts, in a special way he enlightens and moves the intellect to assent to those acts that exceed natural powers, whether through the light of prophecy or through the light of faith.[63] An act of faith, although it is an act of the agent's own intellect and in some way will, requires an additional divine illumination and motion that is unnecessary for natural acts of knowledge and willing. Evidence is neither sufficient nor even necessary. God's movement and illumination could replace the arguments through miracles.[64]

The light of faith plays a similar role in the assent of faith to that which natural light of reason plays in the assent to self-evident principles.[65] This light of faith is needed both for belief in revealed articles and to avoid error.[66] Thomas also compares it to the habit of virtue by which someone judges correctly concerning the ends of virtue.[67] The light of

---

[61] *[C]um homo, assentiendo his quae sunt fidei, elevetur supra naturam suam, oportet quod hoc insit ei ex supernaturali principio interius movente, quod est Deus. Et ideo fides quantum ad assensum, quod est principalis actus fidei, est a Deo interius movente per gratiam.* Aquinas, ST II-II 6.1.c.

[62] Aquinas, ST I-II 109.2. For God's more general movement of free choice, see ST I-II 10.4; DM 6.3c and ad 3. For other texts and a discussion, see especially Oderberg, "Divine Premotion"; Osborne, "Knowledge through Causes," pp. 227–32.

[63] Aquinas, ST I-II 109.1.

[64] Aquinas, *Quodlibet* 2 4.1c and ad 2–3; In Ioannem 15.5.2055. Gardeil, *Crédibilité*, pp. 136–8.

[65] Aquinas, In BDT, 1.2c; 2.3c. For additional texts and discussion, see Cessario, *Christian Faith*, pp. 76–9; Jenkins, *Knowledge and Faith*, pp. 161–210; Stolz, *Glaubensgnade und Glaubenslicht*, pp. 84–103.

[66] Aquinas, ST II-II 1.4 ad 3.

[67] Aquinas, ST II-II 2.3 ad 2. For the connection between the light of faith and virtue, see especially Stolz, *Glaubensgnade und Glaubenslicht*, pp. 84–95.

faith is distinct from the light of natural reason because it makes possible an assent to supernaturally known first principles, namely the articles of faith. Unlike the light of reason, it does not make its objects evident. Such evidence is made possible only in the next life by the light of glory. A Christian with both faith and charity can understand the object of faith better through the gift of the Holy Spirit that is called "understanding."[68] But the act of faith itself is first made possible by the light of faith.[69]

Thomas's understanding of the role of reason in faith is necessarily connected with his thesis that the formal object of faith is the First Truth itself. But he also states that faith can be judged to be reasonable even without the light of faith. We can know that we should believe without making an act of belief. Nevertheless, miracles and preaching do not compel assent. The supernatural character of faith makes it necessary for us to have supernatural light in order to believe. The certitude of faith is caused not by the reasons for belief, but by the supernatural illumination and movement of the believer by God.

For Thomas, faith is a reasonable and certain knowledge of propositions that serve as the foundation for sacred doctrine, which satisfies the criteria of an Aristotelian subalternated science. Faith and sacred doctrine are more certain than human sciences because they are founded on God's own knowledge. However, despite their certitude, the objects of belief cannot be proven through any human science or even be made evident in such a way as to compel assent. Recent scholarly literature has either neglected Thomas's position that God in a special way causes an act of faith, or has suggested that the judgment of credibility itself requires faith. Although believers often make judgments of credibility with the assistance of faith and the light of grace, such supernatural assistance is not necessary for such judgments. Although the act of faith can be shown to be reasonable to someone who lacks the relevant assistance of grace, every act of faith depends on such special assistance from God, and especially the light of faith. This light of faith and God's movement of the believer's will are necessary for an act of faith not on account of faith's irrationality, but because its formal object exceeds human capacities.

---

[68] Aquinas, ST II-II 8.5c and ad 3. See also I-II 68.8 ad 2.
[69] Jenkins, *Knowledge and Faith*, p. 196, seems mistaken in thinking that the gift of understanding is prior to faith, and that both the light of faith and the gift of understanding must be prior to judgments of credibility. For the gift of understanding, see Still, "Gifted Knowledge," pp. 177–84.

The Significance of Christology in the Summa Theologiae

Michael Gorman

11.1 Introduction

According to Christian belief, the Big Picture looks something like the following: There is exactly one God – a personal being who is infinitely intelligent, infinitely powerful, and infinitely good, who in fact possesses every possible perfection, and who is utterly transcendent and independent of everything else. Mysteriously, this one God is somehow tri-personal: The Father, the Son, and the Holy Spirit are each divine, and each is distinct from the other, and yet somehow together they are just one God. This God has created everything else that exists, including (and to us most importantly) us. We humans were meant to use our rationality and will to love and serve God and to live in harmony with our fellow creatures, but instead we sinned and put ourselves into a damaged state from which we cannot emerge without help from God himself. For our sake, then, the second divine person – the Son – retaining his divinity, became human as well and lived out a life that culminated in his death by crucifixion, his rising from the dead, and his ascension into heaven. This divine-human person, Jesus Christ, is the cause and source of the unmerited help that God offers to all humans. Although Christians have not always agreed on just how that help gets conveyed to us, they do agree that being in a right relationship with Christ is the key to living a holy life in this world and reaching a glorious fulfillment in the next.

From this brief and limited sketch, it is easy enough to gather that a central part of Christian theology will be the study of Christ, i.e., Christology. Aquinas's theology is no exception. Making use of a now-standard distinction, we can say that Aquinas talks about the *person* of Christ, who and what he is, but also about the *work* of Christ, what he does to bring about human salvation.[1] Naturally, Aquinas uses his own

---

[1] While Aquinas and other medievals understand these as distinct topics, they also recognize their interconnection. For example, Aquinas sees Christ's ontological constitution as making possible the

creative philosophical and theological intelligence as much as he can, but this should not obscure the fact that in the main, he proceeds in a fairly traditional way. In his understanding of the person of Christ, he follows the main line of Christian orthodoxy laid down in the Church councils of the fourth and fifth centuries, holding, as we will see in a bit more detail below, that Christ is one person with two natures, divinity and humanity. He also follows the mainline Christian tradition in focusing, in his account of Christ's work, on Christ's suffering and salvific death on the cross, as well as on the sacramental system through which the redemption won by Christ is conveyed to us.

The *Summa Theologiae* contains a large and detailed treatment of Christ: Third Part, questions 1–59. Using traditional terminology, we can call this the *Summa's* "Treatise on Christ." Interestingly, however, some of Aquinas's Christological ideas show up outside of the Treatise as well. What's more, some of his non-Christological ideas play an important role within the Treatise. The purpose of this chapter is to give an account of Aquinas's Christological thinking in the *Summa*, both inside and outside the Treatise on Christ, and also to show how that thinking interacts with his thinking on other topics.

First, I make a few remarks on how the Treatise on Christ (or "the Treatise") fits into the structure of the *Summa*. Second, I explain the main Christological claims that Aquinas makes in the Treatise. Third, I discuss the significance of the fact that some elements of Aquinas's Christology are found outside the Treatise. Fourth, I discuss the way in which some of Aquinas's non-Christological ideas function within the Treatise, and how they get modified there. Beyond the obvious goal of spelling out some basic elements of Aquinas's Christology and how it fits into the *Summa*, I hope in all this to make some points about Aquinas's pedagogical strategies and about the interaction of philosophy and theology in his thought.

11.2   Christology in the Structure of the *Summa Theologiae*

As is often noted, the *Summa Theologiae* is a highly structured work, and Aquinas himself makes a point of this in the work's main prologue. It is reasonable then to wonder where Christology shows up in the *Summa*, and why it shows up there.

---

salvific role he is to play. For a very helpful discussion, including discussion of Aquinas, see Adams, *What Sort of Human Nature?*

The first and most obvious point has already been noticed: There is a "Treatise on Christ" in the *Summa*, a treatise which takes up the first fifty-nine questions of the Third Part. A simple fact will make clear how strongly Aquinas's Christological remarks are concentrated there: According to the *Index Thomisticus*, the word *Christus*, in one or other of its grammatical variants (*Christi, Christo*, etc.) appears 6,606 times in the *Summa Theologiae*; fully 87 percent of those appearances are in the Third Part, and of those, 74 percent are found in the Treatise on Christ. This is not surprising, of course, but it helps us to focus our minds on the fact that Christology is not likely to be a recurring theme in the *Summa* in the same way that nature or form or causation might be. A solid 64 percent of the appearances of *Christus* are crammed into only 12 percent of the questions actually written by Aquinas (i.e., not counting the supplement to the Third Part).[2]

At the same time, that still leaves us with 2,209 appearances of *Christus* outside of the Treatise, and 799 of them come before the Third Part. That last figure should be a bit surprising. In the prologue to the *Summa*, already mentioned, Thomas makes a point of saying that he will introduce topics in the correct order. To say *Christus* almost 800 times before getting to the discussion of Christ might seem, well, a bit precipitous.

Below we will look at the nature of these Christological references outside the Treatise on Christ. For now, let us focus more on the positioning of that Treatise within the *Summa*. The most natural way of thinking about the Treatise's positioning is by looking at what Aquinas himself has to say about it. Two passages stand out in particular.

After having explained, in *Summa Theologiae* I 1, what theology is and how it proceeds, Aquinas begins in I 2 to engage in the actual work of theology itself. In the prologue to that question, he sketches out the main divisions of the *Summa*: Part I considers God (and the procession of creatures from him); Part II considers the movement of rational creatures to God; and Part III considers Christ, the way by which humans aim toward God. On this telling, one might say that the *Summa* is about God, his creatures, and how his rational creatures move toward him, and

---

[2] A more thorough analysis would discuss appearances of *Iesus* and – much harder to collect – references to Christ by some other name or description. I don't think such analysis would change the general picture here much at all; for what it's worth, there are only 250 occurrences of *Iesus* and its variants in the whole of the *Summa*, and of course some significant number of these appear in expressions like *Iesus Christus* and hence were already accounted for when we enumerated appearances of *Christus*.

Christ appears at the conclusion and culmination as the way by which those rational creatures so move.

> This way of thinking is confirmed by a look at the prologue to the Third Part:
>
> > Having considered [in the Second Part] the final end of human life, and virtues and vices as well, it is necessary for the consummation of the entire theological enterprise that we turn our consideration to the one who is the Savior of all and to the benefits he brings to humankind.[3]

Without going so far as to say that the First and Second Parts of the *Summa* are merely preparatory, we can see that Christology is essential to the *Summa* and even, in a sense, its highpoint. The work finds its completion in the discussion of Christ and his gifts: These are, so to speak, what the *Summa* had been aiming toward the whole time.

Another way of thinking about the placement of the Christological Treatise has to do with Aquinas's desire, expressed in the overall prologue to the *Summa*, to present his ideas in an order that will be helpful to the reader's growth in understanding, as opposed to an order forced by the requirements of textual commentary (as happens when one comments on Scripture, say, or on Peter Lombard's *Sentences*). Given that Christ is both divine and human, and that he aims to bestow grace upon us, it makes sense that Aquinas would, before discussing Christ, first explain divinity, humanity, and grace, and so he does: God himself is discussed in I 1–43, human nature is explained in I 75–102, and grace is discussed in I-II 109–14.

In his discussions in the Treatise, Aquinas does not merely presuppose earlier discussions as a sort of general background; he sometimes exploits them with ruthless efficiency. For example, Aquinas holds that because Christ is both divine and human, he has both divine and human ways of knowing. In III 9, Aquinas examines Christ's knowledge in a general way, establishing that in addition to divine knowledge, Christ also has three kinds of human knowledge: the beatific vision, infused knowledge, and garden-variety acquired knowledge. One would expect that from here, Aquinas is going to discuss each of these four kinds of knowledge, but in the prologue to III 10, Aquinas informs us that he need not bother discussing Christ's divine knowledge, inasmuch as divine knowledge was already discussed back in the First Part. Likewise, although he is not

---

[3] *[N]ecesse est ut, ad consummationem totius theologici negotii, post considerationem ultimi finis humanae vitae et virtutum ac vitiorum, de ipso omnium Salvatore ac beneficiis eius humano generi praestitis nostra consideratio subsequatur* (ST III, prologue).

explicit about it, he seems to engage in a similar strategy when discussing Christ's human knowledge. Questions 10–12 of the Third Part concern the three modes of Christ's knowing, and in those questions Aquinas raises specific issues about how Christ has these kinds of knowledge, without saying very much about what those kinds of knowledge actually are; apparently this is unnecessary inasmuch as they were discussed earlier (see, for example I 84–9 for acquired knowledge).[4]

So far we have seen two ways of thinking about the positioning of the Treatise on Christ: It is the culmination of the work, and it comes after the material that it cannot be understood without. Still other ways of thinking about the *Summa*'s structure have been proposed. One way sees a progressive narrowing of topic in the *Summa*: The First Part concerns God and all of creation; the Second Part concerns God and humans; the Third Part focuses on God and just one human, namely, Christ. Another way, somewhat similar to the first, sees a narrowing of focus with regard to God's presence: The First Part concerns God's universal presence; the Second Part concerns God's presence in those humans sanctified by grace; the Third Part concerns God's presence in one particular human, namely Jesus Christ. Still another way exploits the classic theme of *exitus* and *reditus*: The First Part concerns humans' coming forth from God and the natural principles that make possible their return; the Second Part focuses on their actual return by means of supernatural grace; the Third Part focuses on the fullness of their return in glory.[5] Various things can be said for and against these proposals; I mention them here only to bring out the fact that the *Summa* is an immensely complicated work whose structure can be looked at in various ways.

11.3   Christ in the Treatise

Having considered the positioning of the Christological Treatise in the *Summa* as a whole, let us turn now to considering the structure and content of that Treatise itself. As Aquinas explains in its prologue, the Third Part was intended to discuss three main topics: Christ the savior, the sacraments by which we reach salvation, and the eternal life which we arrive at by rising from the dead through him. (Of course the Third Part

---

[4] For discussion of the placement of the Christological Treatise in light of Aquinas's pedagogical intentions, see Laporte, "Christ in Aquinas's 'Summa Theologiae'," pp. 239–47.

[5] These proposals come from Corbin, Persson, and Torrell, respectively; for discussion, see Laporte, "Christ in Aquinas's 'Summa Theologiae'," pp. 226–31.

was not completed; Aquinas died partway through the discussion of the sacraments.)

Anyone familiar with Aquinas's work will expect the Christological Treatise to be highly organized, and this expectation will not be disappointed. Broken down only to the second level of division, we have the following:

1   The incarnation itself (questions 1–26)

    1.1 Fittingness of the union of humanity and divinity (question 1)
    1.2 Mode of union (questions 2–15)
    1.3 Consequences of the union (questions 16–26)

2   What Christ did and suffered (questions 27–59)

    2.1 His entry into the world (questions 27–39)
    2.2 The progress of his life (questions 40–5)
    2.3 His departure from the world (questions 46–52)
    2.4 His exaltation after his life in the world (questions 53–9).

In the first main part of the Treatise, Aquinas looks at the person of Christ, who is someone in whom humanity and divinity are joined, discussing the fittingness of that union, its nature, and its consequences. In the second main part of the Treatise, Aquinas looks at the course of Christ's life, dividing it up chronologically: Christ's entry into the world, his life within the world, his death, and his post-mortem exaltation in heaven. We can thus understand the Treatise's structure according to the person-and-work schema already mentioned. We can also consider the interesting suggestion by John Boyle that the second division can be seen as a commentary on Christ's life as portrayed in Scripture, with the first division providing the conceptual apparatus needed for the proper understanding of that Scriptural portrayal.[6]

Each of the secondary divisions is, of course, further subdivided. For example, Aquinas examines the mode of union (questions 2–15) from three angles: in itself (question 2), with respect to the divine person that assumes human nature (question 3), and with respect to the human nature that was assumed (questions 4–15). Aquinas divides the consequences of the union (questions 16–26) into consequences pertaining to Christ in himself (questions 16–19), consequences pertaining to Christ's relationship to God the Father (questions 20–4), and consequences

---

[6] See Boyle, "The Twofold Division."

pertaining to us (questions 25–6). Or to consider one last example, Aquinas divides his treatment of Christ's departure from the world into a consideration of Christ's suffering (questions 46–9), death (question 50), burial (question 51), and descent to the dead (question 52), with the treatment of Christ's suffering being divided into treatments of the passion itself (question 46), its causes (question 47), and its salvific fruits (questions 48–9).

It should be clear that a complete discussion of the Treatise would take us far beyond the limits of this chapter. What I will do here is simply spell out a few of the key claims that Aquinas makes.

In his discussion of the union in itself (III 2), Aquinas makes clear his view that the incarnation is the event by which the second person of the Trinity, a divine person, takes to himself or "assumes" a human nature. The result of this assumption is that the human nature is joined to Christ "in person," i.e., in such a way that there is (still) only one person: What happens with the incarnation is not that Christ and some distinct human person come to work together very closely, but that Christ himself becomes human. (Because the union yields only one person or "hypostasis," it can be called a "hypostatic union," a term often seen in Christological discussions.) At the same time, the human nature is *not* joined "in nature" to Christ's divine nature: Each nature retains its own status as the nature that it is. The result is that Christ is one person existing in two distinct natures: He is at root divine but he is also – as a result of the incarnation – human.[7]

Turning now to what Aquinas says about the assumed human nature (III 4–15), let us consider some of his ideas about Christ's grace (questions 7–8). Aquinas wants to say that Christ is holy and a sharer in the divine life, and indeed that he is these things in a maximal way. Aquinas could in a sense affirm all this solely on the basis of the fact that Christ is divine, but he wants also to say that they are true of Christ *as human*: Christ is a maximally holy human being, a human being who shares, humanly, in the divine life as much as possible. Now because Christ is divine, it is, of course, altogether fitting that his humanity be holy, but his human holiness is not constituted by the fact of his being divine: There must be something about the humanity itself in virtue of which it is holy. It must have its own property of holiness, and not simply be joined to something else that is holy. Now since nothing created is ever

---

[7] For much more on Aquinas's metaphysics of the incarnation, see Gorman, *Aquinas on the Metaphysics of the Hypostatic Union*.

holy by right, and since Christ's human nature is a creature, his human nature needs to receive holiness and participation in God's life as a free gift, i.e., as a "grace" (III 7.1), a grace that makes Christ humanly holy. But this is not all that that grace does. Aquinas holds that Christ has grace that enables him – even in his humanity – to be a source of grace for others. This is part of what it means to say that Christ is "the head of the Church" (see III 8.1). Aquinas is careful to add (III 8.5c) that the grace by which Christ is maximally holy is not a different grace from the grace by which he is the head of the Church: They are the same essentially, but distinct in conception.

So Christ is both divine and human, and his humanity is graced in a way that enables him to transmit holiness to others not only in virtue of being divine, but also by means of his humanity. This leads to the next point, Christ's salvific passion (III 48–9). In III 48, Aquinas looks at Christ's suffering from at least four different angles: as meritorious (48.1), as satisfying for sin (48.2), as a sacrifice for sin (48.3), as redeeming from sin (48.4).

To focus on just one of these ideas: In III 48.2c, Aquinas says that to render satisfaction for an offense is to offer to the offended party something at least as lovable to that party as the offense was hateful. Christ's suffering was, for three reasons, more lovable than human sin is detestable: because of the great love with which it was accepted; because the life he gave up was so valuable, inasmuch as it was the life of someone both divine and human; and finally on account of the greatness of the suffering he endured. Of course Aquinas doesn't mean that the suffering is lovable in itself. He means that Christ's suffering, although not the only possible way for salvation to take place, was the best way (III 46.3), and it is exceedingly good and lovable that Christ be willing to bring about our salvation in the best way, even at such great cost to himself.

We have looked at only three elements of the Treatise on Christ: the basic idea of Christ as one person with two natures; the idea of Christ as possessing a graced humanity that serves to transmit grace to other humans; and finally the idea of Christ as dying a salvific death. These have been chosen because they allow some of the interconnectedness of Aquinas's Christology to become clear. That Christ is so grace-filled, and that he can suffer so charitably and therefore so effectively, make the most sense when understood in light of his constitution as both divine and human. Or, to put it differently and in terms of a point noted earlier about the structure of the Treatise, the deeds and sufferings described in III 27–59 are best understood in light of the ontological account of the incarnate person given in questions 1–26.

Having given this sketch of a few of the main claims of the Treatise on Christ, I will now turn to look at some of the ways in which Aquinas discusses Christ outside of that Treatise.

11.4   Christ outside the Treatise

As already noted, there are numerous references to Christ outside the treatise devoted to him. In short, Aquinas not only makes Christological points for Christological purposes in the Christological part of the *Summa*, he also makes them *en route* to making non-Christological points in non-Christological parts of the *Summa*. A few passages will illustrate this fact.

Prior to the Treatise, there are many passages where Aquinas mentions facts about the person and work of the incarnate Christ on the way to proving some other point. Starting with passages that invoke ideas about the person of Christ, let us look at I 25, which is devoted to God's power. In 25.6, Aquinas asks whether God can make better the things that he has made. He answers that God cannot make things of a certain nature better in terms of their essential principles, because natures do not work like that: Natures do not come in degrees, so if something is a human being, for example, then it is as human as it can be, and cannot be improved upon in that respect. On the other hand, there are two ways in which God can do better. First, he can always add more to the accidental perfections of his creatures, e.g., by making humans wiser than they are. Second, he can always make things that are by nature superior to the things he has made – e.g., he can make angels instead of humans. But the fourth objection gives a few examples of creatures that cannot be improved on: Christ's humanity, the beatific vision, and the Blessed Virgin Mary. In his response, Aquinas concedes that there is a sense in which each of these cannot be improved on: Each has an unsurpassable dignity due to a certain unity with the infinite good, namely, God. The details of this argument are not important for us here: What is important here is only the fact that Aquinas is taking for granted, already in the First Part, his views about the goodness and perfection of Christ's human nature as joined to divinity.

A few more examples of pre-Treatise invocations of the person of Christ will now be discussed in less detail. In I 20.4, Aquinas asks whether God always loves better things more. Objection 2 raises the issue of whether God loves Christ's humanity more than he loves the angels, and Aquinas says in the reply that indeed he does, on account of that humanity's union to divinity. In II-II 14.1, Aquinas asks about the meaning of the "sin against the Holy Spirit" mentioned in the New Testament. In explaining in the reply various proposed interpretations of that difficult expression, Aquinas takes it for granted that Christ is both human and divine. In II-II, 174.4, Aquinas asks whether Moses was the greatest of the prophets. The answer is yes, but one of the difficulties that needs to be handled, expressed in objection 1, is that in the *Glossa Ordinaria,* David is said to be the most excellent prophet. Aquinas relativizes the sense in which David had better prophetic insight by noting that it applied only to the lesser matter of Christ's incarnation as human, in comparison with which Moses's insight into divinity is a better ground of superiority. There is much to be said about all of these passages; for our purposes here, the point is only that Aquinas is, outside of and prior to the Treatise on Christ, appealing to ideas about Christ's ontological make-up that he will not officially present or argue for until much later in the *Summa.*[8]

In addition to bringing in points about Christ's constitution as a divine and human person, Aquinas also brings in, prior to the Treatise, ideas about Christ's saving work. For example, in *Summa Theologiae* I 73.1, Aquinas asks whether – as Scripture seems to attest – God completed his works on the seventh day of creation. Aquinas says, unsurprisingly, that God does indeed complete his works on the seventh day, but he adds that this concerns only the creation of things in their kinds: The bringing of things to their perfection went on beyond that point. The first objection points out that there are other "completions" of divine work mentioned in Scripture: the end of the world, and Christ's incarnation, which happened "in the fullness of time," and the completion indicated by Christ's shout "it is finished" on the cross. Aquinas says in response that nature was completed when the world was first founded, and will reach its final glorious consummation at the end of time, but that the grace that leads to that glory arrived in its fullness at the time of Christ. Leaving aside the various important issues here, what matters for present purposes is that in this passage from the First Part, Aquinas takes

---

[8] Still more examples: ST I 29.1 ad 2, where a discussion of personhood raises a question about Christ's human nature; I 62.9 ad 3, where a question about whether angels can progress in merit leads to a remark about Christ as the only person with the beatific vision who can also progress in merit; II-II 18.2 ad 1, where a discussion of whether the blessed can hope leads to a discussion of whether Christ could hope; II-II 174.5 ad 3, where a discussion of whether the blessed can be prophets leads to a discussion of whether Christ could be a prophet.

for granted and discusses Christ's salvific work of grace, a topic that will not be officially introduced until the Third Part.

For another example, in discussing the Jewish ceremonial laws, Aquinas says in I-II 101.2 that all worship in this life involves figures and images, due to our inability to behold God immediately in this life. Once Christ has come, the way to God has been revealed, so only the ultimate goal needs to be portrayed figuratively, but in the Old Testament period, Christ had not yet been revealed, and therefore Old Testament worship contained symbolic representations of not only the goal but also of the way to that goal, i.e., Christ the savior. For example, in I-II 102.3, Aquinas considers whether there were good reasons for the ceremonial precepts being as they were, with objection 2 raising doubts about why certain animals were sacrificed and not others. Aquinas gives a number of reasons why the animals were correctly prescribed, and the last reason is that the prescribed animals represented Christ. He says, for example, that the lamb represents Christ's innocence, and that a dove and a turtledove were both sacrificed so as to represent Christ's two natures.[9]

So far we have looked at some passages in which Aquinas anticipates his Christological discussions in *Summa Theologiae* III 1–59. Now let us turn to a few passages where he brings in Christological points *after* that treatise. I will give one passage concerning Christ's person, and one passage concerning his work.

As already noted, the second main division of the Third Part, sadly never finished, was devoted to discussion of the sacraments. Questions 73–83 concern the Eucharist, and question 76 is concerned with Christ's presence in the Eucharist. The first article asks whether "the whole Christ" (*totus Christus*) is contained in this sacrament. Because the Eucharist involves the conversion of bread and wine into Christ's body and blood, one might well suspect that only these parts of Christ, and not Christ in his entirety, is present there. Aquinas answers by making a distinction between what is present in the sacrament by sacramental power and what is present in the sacrament by natural concomitance: Christ's body and blood are present in the sacrament by the power of the sacrament, but since his soul is joined to them, it must be present there too, concomitantly with them. And – this is what is most important for our discussion here – not just his soul, but his divinity as well: "Wherever

---

[9] For other examples of references to Christ's saving work prior to the Treatise, see ST I-II, 112.1 ad 1, where a discussion of grace leads to a mention of Christ as cause of grace, and indeed as cause both as God and man; I-II 114.6, where a discussion of merit leads to the remark that Christ can merit grace for others insofar as he is head of the Church.

Christ's body is, there must be his divinity as well."[10] The point for us is that Aquinas draws on what he had earlier established about the union of divinity and humanity in Christ to make a point about the sacraments.

Now let us look at a post-Treatise passage where Aquinas calls on what he has established about Christ's saving work. *Summa Theologiae* III 60–5 is a discussion of sacraments in general, prior to discussion of individual sacraments such as baptism and the Eucharist. In question 62, Aquinas discusses the principal effect of the sacraments, which is to convey grace, and in 62.5, he says that sacraments receive their power to convey grace from Christ's passion. Grace removes sin and perfects the soul for the purposes of divine worship, and both of these arise out of Christ's self-offering on the cross, which takes away sin and is a perfect sacrificial offering. For our purposes here, the thing to focus on is the way in which Aquinas can appeal, in his discussion of the sacraments, to points he had made earlier about Christ's suffering. Interestingly, and not surprisingly, Aquinas also refers back in this article to points he had made about Christ's person, inasmuch as he says that Christ's divinity is the main cause of grace and that his humanity is an instrumental cause of it.

In this section, we have seen that Aquinas appeals to Christological ideas outside the Treatise on Christ: He does so both with regard to ideas concerning Christ's person and with regard to ideas concerning his deeds and sufferings, and he does so both before and after the Treatise. That Aquinas does so *after* the Treatise is not surprising – it is simply one more example of his adoption of a pedagogically helpful order, an order which, as we saw earlier, was important to him. But that he does so *before* the Treatise deserves special comment. It might be rather surprising to see Aquinas take things "out of order." But what was the alternative? Think of grace. Grace is one principle of human action and is discussed by Aquinas at the end of the First Part of the Second Part. Grace is caused by Christ. As the *Summa* now stands, Aquinas discusses grace before he discusses Christ, and this requires him to say something about Christ prematurely, inasmuch as his discussion of grace needs to mention Christ as grace's cause. Aquinas could have discussed grace after the Treatise on Christ, but that wouldn't have worked perfectly either: In discussing the effects of Christ's passion, he would have had to mention grace, which means he would have had the opposite problem, namely, discussing grace prematurely. There's no way to write a work like the *Summa* that would permit a perfectly satisfactory front-to-back reading. This is not to say

[10] *[U]bicumque est corpus Christi, necesse est et eius divinitatem esse* (III 76.1 ad 1).

that there's no such thing as a good pedagogical order, but only that there are limits to how far one can go, limits that must always be kept in mind.

11.5 Non-Christological Ideas in the Treatise

In the previous section we saw how Aquinas discusses Christological ideas outside the Treatise on Christ. Now we will consider how he discusses non-Christological ideas within the Treatise on Christ. I want to make three general points here. First, Aquinas makes use of non-Christological and indeed non-theological ideas when engaging in Christological analysis. Second, he sometimes modifies these ideas for Christological purposes. Third, the fact that he does so reveals ways in which, in his mind, philosophy does not give us an entirely complete picture of what is possible. This means that examining the interplay of philosophy and theology in the Treatise can reveal some larger points about Aquinas's way of thought.

The first point, that Aquinas draws on non-Christological and non-theological ideas, is perhaps unsurprising, and it can be explained with reference to things already noted. To pick the most obvious example, Aquinas says that Christ is one person with two natures, and in developing this, he needs to make use of the notions of person and nature, which are not themselves specifically theological or Christological notions at all, but instead ideas that can be, and are, developed in purely philosophical contexts. Other examples include his appeals to divine and human knowledge: These he develops quite independently of Christology, and then makes use of them in order to make sense out of Christology.

The second point is less obvious and requires more discussion. I will focus my remarks on a particular issue concerning substantial natures. For Aquinas, forms are principles of existence: Something exists in the way that it does in virtue of the forms that it has. This encompasses both accidental and substantial forms: Socrates exists as white, accidentally, in virtue of his accidental form of whiteness, and he exists as human, substantially, in virtue of his substantial form.[11] And what holds for substantial forms also holds, *mutatis mutandis*, for substantial natures, like humanity. What's more, this normally encompasses two facts: A human nature explains why a human substance is human, and it also explains why it subsists as a substance (rather than inhering, like an accident).

---

[11] *Quod autem facit actu esse substantiale est forma substantialis, et quod facit actu esse accidentale dicitur forma accidentalis* (*De Principiis Naturae* 1, lines 43–6, *Opera Omnia*, Leonine Edition 43, p. 39).

Now Christ has a human nature. Should we say that his human nature is responsible both for his being human, and for his subsisting as a substance? Aquinas holds that we should *not* say this:[T]he Son of God does not have existence *simpliciter* from his human nature ... but only existence as human.[12] Christ's human nature is a principle in virtue of which he exists as human, but it is not a principle in virtue of which he exists *simpliciter*, in the primary sense, i.e., as a substance or person. It's easy enough to see why: If Christ's human nature were a principle in virtue of which he existed as a person, then he would be not one person but two: a divine person by his divine nature, and a human person by his human nature.

Notice what this means for Aquinas's use of non-Christological material in his Christology. On the one hand, he does use this material; on the other hand, in at least some cases, such as the one we just considered, he modifies the material to make it more suitable for Christological inquiry. If he had taken the pre-made philosophical notion of a substantial nature and insisted on using it in the form in which it comes from philosophy, he would have had to say that Christ's human nature made him, Christ, a person, and this would have contradicted the claim that the two natures are "united in person" and therefore the idea that Christ is only one person. So Aquinas has to modify his way of thinking about human nature to allow for the possibility that a human nature can, at least in some cases, make something human without making it a person.[13]

The third point flows from the second one. Aquinas modifies the ideas he draws from philosophy to make them suitable for Christological work. His doing so, however, reflects light back onto philosophy. In this case, we can say that Aquinas's Christological ideas imply that it is not strictly true that a substantial nature is a nature in virtue of which its possessor subsists: It is usually that sort of thing, to be sure, but if a substantial nature were united in person to an already-existing substance, then that second nature would not be a principle of subsistence. Christology, in other words, has revealed as possible something whose possibility does not show up in purely philosophical discussions: the possibility of a substantial nature doing only some of what a substantial nature is naturally fitted to do.

---

[12] *Non enim ex natura humana habet Filius Dei quod sit simpliciter ... sed solum quod sit homo* (III 3.1 ad 3).

[13] I have discussed this point about Christ's human nature at some length elsewhere: see Gorman, "Incarnation"; see also Chapter 4 of Gorman, *Aquinas on the Metaphysics of the Hypostatic Union*.

Using the example of what is brought about by a substantial nature, I have just spelled out the three points I wanted to make about Aquinas's use of non-Christological ideas in the Treatise. Let me now give a different example. In his discussion of the human soul, Aquinas insists that each human has only one soul: Socrates does not have, say, a rational soul to account for his rationality, an animal soul to account for his animality, and a vegetative soul to account for his being alive. Instead, he has one soul that is responsible for all of these (I 76.3). For our purposes, what is most important is the first of Aquinas's arguments for this position, namely, that since unity comes from form, and since a soul is a substantial form, then if Socrates had more than one soul, he would not be absolutely one thing (*unum*). Here again, what applies to a substantial form applies in its own way to a substantial nature: A being that had more than one substantial form would not be one thing (*unum*).

If we applied this to the case of Christ, then it would seem necessary to say that Christ, who has two natures, is not absolutely one thing, but instead somehow two things joined in a certain very special way. But this is definitely not Aquinas's view. In III 17.1, he considers the view that we should say that Christ is one person, *unus* in the masculine gender, but not one thing, *unum* in the neuter gender, on the grounds that there are in Christ two substances or supposits, one divine and one human, that together make up one person. Aquinas rejects this as an inadequate account of the hypostatic union (see III 2.3), and therefore he says: Because we posit one person and one supposit in Christ ... it follows that we should say that Christ is not only "one person" in the masculine, but also "one thing" in the neuter.[14] I think it is fair to say that Aquinas is insisting here that Christ is one thing, *unum*, just as an ordinary human, like Socrates, is one thing. So again it must be that Aquinas is modifying his philosophical ideas a bit. Apparently he does not actually hold what we would have thought he holds, namely, that a substance cannot have two substantial natures – apparently he holds that a substance can have two substantial natures, if the situation is right. In III 3.1 ad 2, he says:

> [M]ore than one nature can come together accidentally in a created person – as when both quantity and quality are found in the person of one man. But it is proper to a divine person, on account of its infinity, that

---

[14] *Quia vero nos ponimus in Christo unam personam et unum suppositum, ut ex praedictis patet, sequitur quod dicamus quod non solum Christus est unus masculine, set etiam est unum neutraliter* (III 17.1c).

there be in it a coming-together of natures not only accidentally, but also substantially.[15]

Here Aquinas uses "nature" to cover both accidental and substantial natures. He says that of course more than one "nature" can be found in a normal created human – Socrates can be both white and tall. But only in the case of a divine person can there be more than one substantial nature, and this is because the divine person is infinite.

For our purposes, what is important to focus on is the following. First, as in the first case we examined, Aquinas uses his philosophical ideas about nature and person when discussing Christology. Second, he has to adapt his ideas for use in that Christological context. The idea that substantial natures and substances come in a one-to-one correspondence needs to be modified to make room for Christology; the more precisely stated view is that this one-to-one correspondence is characteristic of *created* substances. Third, Christological inquiry has revealed a possibility that would not have been apparent to ordinary philosophy, namely, that there should be a substance or supposit with more than one substantial nature.

I want to give one more example that focuses on the idea that Christology reveals possibilities that philosophy does not. Aquinas sometimes makes pessimistic claims about what human beings can know, saying that generally speaking we have only incomplete knowledge of the essences of things and must at times make do with a grasp of their accidents.[16] But Aquinas holds that Christ's human knowledge – even his acquired knowledge – extends as far as human knowledge can extend. For example, Aquinas holds that by observing the stars and planets, Christ could – by his acquired human knowledge, the same type that you and I have –gather all their powers and their influences on earthly things (III 12.1 ad 2); or again, Aquinas holds that Christ knew all languages perfectly (II-II 172.1 ad 3), despite the fact that he only needed the language useful for his own preaching mission to the Jews. In other words, Aquinas's pessimism about non-miraculous human cognitive powers is a pessimism in practice, not a pessimism in principle.

One final point before concluding this section: I have suggested that in laying out certain philosophical principles – one nature per substance, for example – Aquinas is often stating things in a way that he doesn't strictly

---

[15] *Quia etiam in personam creatam possunt plures naturae concurrere accidentaliter: sicut in persona unius hominis invenitur quantitas et qualitas. Hoc autem est proprium divinae personae, propter eius infinitatem, ut fiat in ea concursus naturarum, non quidem accidentaliter, sed secundum subsistentiam* (III q. 3.1 ad 2). See also III 2.3 ad 1.

[16] ST I 29.1 ad 3; ST I 77.1, especially 77.1c, ad 5, and ad 7.

believe, or rather that he is stating things that he believes only with an unstated qualification, e.g., one nature per *created* substance. Why would he proceed in such a way? The answer, I think, is that he wants not to be pedantic. A debate over whether humans have more than one soul is no time to bring up the issue of the incarnation; that, I think, is sufficient to explain why Aquinas doesn't state these qualifications until he needs to, namely, in theological texts.

11.6 Conclusion

In this chapter I have explained a number of points concerning the significance of Christology in the *Summa Theologiae*: I have tried to indicate its importance in that work, how it fits into it structurally, some of its content, and how it influences and interacts with non-Christological ideas. I want to conclude with a remark about how to read the *Summa*. As noted already, it is not really possible for Aquinas to present his material in a way that would allow for a simple front-to-back reading. Sometimes, points Aquinas makes presuppose points he will not make until much farther on. In such cases, we won't entirely understand the earlier passage without the later passage. To use an example described above, Aquinas asks whether God's power involves his being able to make better anything that he has made, and our understanding of Aquinas's answer will not be complete until our reading of the Treatise on Christ makes clear what he meant by his reference to Christ's humanity.

That examining the Treatise will shed some light on the First Part's discussion of divine power does not mean, of course, that we will end up having to rethink the First Part's basic teaching on divine power. That would be a much more radical way for a reading of a later passage to influence a reading of an earlier one. But it is my suggestion that in the *Summa*, things that come later *do* sometimes require us to rethink the core content of what came earlier. For example, our understanding of Aquinas's views on Christ's humanity forces us to rethink Aquinas's views on substantial natures. In short, it's not merely that earlier parts will be seen more clearly when later parts have been read; it's also that, sometimes, the reading of later parts will force us to thoroughly reconsider some of what we thought we had learned from earlier parts. This stands as a warning to those who might hope to read just the "philosophical parts" of the *Summa*. In the *Summa* as in baseball, it ain't over til it's over.[17]

[17] I would like to thank Sophie Oriani for comments on an earlier version, and Taylor Abels for his help in preparing the manuscript for publication.

CHAPTER 12

From Theology to Philosophy: The Changing Status of the Summa Theologiae, 1500–2000

Jacob Schmutz

"Like another Bible" (*Quasi altera Biblia*): This is how the German Protestant polymath Daniel Georg Morhof (1639–91) described the status enjoyed by the *Summa Theologiae* in his time, at least in Catholics lands (Morhof, *Polyhistor*, p. 86). In 1567, Aquinas had been declared the fifth "Doctor of the Church" by Pope Pius V, which made him the first medieval author put on a par with the Church Fathers. Two centuries earlier, the very existence of the *Summa* itself had been used as an argument for elevating its author to sanctity: Each article is a miracle of its own, according to the canonization bull (Mandonnet, "Canonisation," p. 39). No other single work of theology – besides the Bible – received more attention throughout the entire early-modern period than Aquinas's *Summa*. In his still valuable 1924 catalogue, Anton Michelitsch (1865–1958) listed hundreds of early-modern commentaries on the *Summa*, mostly printed ones, for just the 1500–1800 period, and his list could easily be multiplied by ten or more today if we took into account the still largely unmapped early-modern manuscript production.[1] Even in Protestant lands, Aquinas had his unexpected supporters: Some Lutherans saw in the *Summa* a real antidote to the rising wave of Roman Jesuitism dominating early-modern Catholic theology. Like the Bible, the *Summa* had become one of the first global books. It was available in all South American, coastal African, and South Asian mission libraries, and even outside the Catholic world: Jonathan Edwards (1703–58) discussed some of its themes at colonial Yale, and Theophylact Lopatinsky (d. 1742), taught on the *Summa* in Moscow Academy, in an attempt to renovate orthodox theology.[2] Most impressively perhaps, Ludovico

I wish to thank Sylvio H. De Franceschi (Paris), Leonhard Hell (Mainz), Aza Goudriaan (Amsterdam), and Henrik Wels (Münster) for precious suggestions that helped inspire this chapter.

[1] Michelitsch, *Kommentatoren*; also Kennedy, *Catalogue*, Berger and Vijgen, *Thomisten-Lexikon*.
[2] He composed a manuscript *Scientia sacra* (1706–10). On this context, see Plested, *Orthodox Readings*, pp. 173–4.

Buglio (1606–82), a Sicilian Jesuit who died in Beijing, translated the First and Third Parts of the *Summa* into Chinese – almost three centuries before its first comprehensive translation into English.

This editorial bounty raises several questions: First, what made Aquinas such an important figure, apparently eclipsing all other medieval theologians during the early-modern and contemporary period? Second, why, among his massive production of philosophical, theological, and biblical commentaries, was the *Summa Theologiae* singled out? Third, can we identify a beginning and an end to this vast movement, and what were the major fault lines in the history of its reception? Histories of Thomism abound: The first appeared as early as the seventeenth century, and arguably the best – an almost 900-page historical survey by the Austrian prelate Karl Werner (1821–88; *Der Heilige*) – even predates the official "rebirth" of Thomism following Leo XIII's famous encyclical *Aeterni Patris* (1879). Almost all recent surveys of post-medieval Thomism follow a "Decline and Rebirth" paradigm,[3] strongly influenced by Jacques Maritain's (1882–1973) disparaging comments on the "demon of mediocrity" that had seduced early-modern commentators, obscuring the true Thomas Aquinas (Maritain, *Antimoderne*, pp. 119–21). The entire period is often dismissed as degenerate: The Dominican Yves Congar (1904–95), a key figure of the Second Vatican Council, denounced the most influential *Summa* commentary of the eighteenth century written by a fellow Dominican as a "system of abstractions and prefabricated solutions" (Congar, *Situations*, p. 55).[4]

In what follows, I shall propose a very different narrative: First, I will argue that Thomism *never* declined, but that it remained a powerful current even in the heyday of the Enlightenment. Second, I will claim that the eighteenth century, often presented as the "waning" (Curran, "Christianity," p. 64) of Thomism, is in reality the true key to understanding the conditions and forms of its later nineteenth-century "revival." Third and last, I will have to explain why, among Aquinas's huge intellectual production, it was the *Summa* that ensured his persistence as an authority during these centuries. To establish these points, attention must also be given to material history: the place of Aquinas in the Gutenberg galaxy and the institutional decisions governing the

---

[3] Among those accessible in English, see: Torrell, *Aquinas's Summa*, pp. 93–130; Cessario, *History*; McGinn, *Aquinas's Summa*, pp. 117–209.

[4] Congar's target here was the vast *Summa* commentary (19 vols., Liège, 1746–51) compiled by the French Dominican Charles-René Billuart (1685–1757).

teaching of scholastic theology and philosophy. Finally, we will have to enquire a bit more closely about his readers, who were not all, as we shall see, aspiring priests in the hallowed halls of Catholic seminaries.

12.1   The Historical Triumph of Aquinas

From a medieval point of view, Aquinas's triumph was in no way evident: Within his own Dominican tradition, it took time and many disputes for his authority to emerge.[5] English Dominicans in particular proved firm adherents of nominalism during most of the late medieval period. On a strictly textual level, the *Summa* had long been overshadowed by Peter Lombard's *Sentences*, which formed the basis of theology instruction until the sixteenth century. Therefore, the emergence of a *Summa*-centered Thomism initially seemed to be a highly regional phenomenon. In Cologne, Henry of Gorcum (c. 1378–1431), a student of John Capreolus in Paris and later vice-chancellor of the university, as well as his pupil John Tinctor (d. 1469), started using the *Summa* for teaching purposes. In 1483, the Dominican *studium generale* of Cologne confirmed this practice, and Konrad Köllin (d. 1536) is now commonly remembered as one of the first great early-modern commentators on the *Summa*. Likewise, in Paris, this use of the *Summa* long remained a Dominican affair: Peter Crockaert (1465–1514), a Flemish student of the Scottish nominalist John Mair, imposed the *Summa* at the *studium generale* of Saint-Jacques in 1509, abandoning the *Sentences*, a move confirmed by the 1523 General Chapter of the Dominican order held in Valladolid. Francisco de Vitoria (1492–1546), returning from Paris the same year, is often remembered as having been the first to impose this practice in Spain. In reality, the older Constitutions (1422) of Pope Martin V had already stipulated that the "Thomistic" chair could use the *Summa* (while the "primary" chair had to use the *Sentences*), and the powerful Archbishop of Seville (today mainly remembered for his inquisitorial zeal), Diego de Deza (1443–1523), a Dominican who had previously taught at Salamanca, had imposed the *Summa* in his newly founded college of Saint Thomas (1517).[6]

A second step in this triumph of Aquinas's *Summa* was its progressive adoption *outside* the Dominican order, in three concentric circles of

---

[5] For this history, see Roensch, *Thomistic School* and Robiglio, *La sopravvivenza*.
[6] On this evolution, see: García Villoslada, *Universidad*, pp. 279–307; Guelluy, "L'évolution"; Goris, "Thomism"; Lécrivain, "La Somme"; Barrientos García, "La teología"; Toste, "Commentaries"; Lanza and Toste, "The Sentences" (for the Spanish context).

scholastic education: among the new religious orders, in the faculties of theology of the new universities, and also in the seminaries of the secular clergy, which became increasingly important in the early-modern period. Why Aquinas, and not one of the other medieval authorities that enjoyed great respect, in particular successors in the late medieval faculties of theology, such as John Duns Scotus, Gregory of Rimini, or Gabriel Biel? In the general humanist onslaught on the technical language of medieval scholasticism, it is interesting to note that Aquinas was usually the only one spared. Even Lorenzo Valla (1407–57), the most powerful Renaissance critic of abstruse scholastic language, managed to find some kind words for Aquinas in a *Praise* delivered at the Minerva, not without expressing reservations about Aquinas's defense of rational theology (Valla, "Praise," p. 22).

To save Aquinas from the wreck of medieval scholasticism, it was essential to portray him as the true medieval heir to the Church Fathers, in particular Augustine. The strongest case was made by Sixtus of Siena (1520–69), a converted Jewish Dominican of the Italian Renaissance, who used the Pythagorean doctrine of metempsychosis to argue that Augustine's soul had migrated into Aquinas's body (*Bibliotheca*, p. 560). This Augustinian image was also at the heart of Aquinas's reception at the Council of Trent (1545–63), which proved decisive in redefining theological identity within the Catholic world for the following centuries. Franciscan, Augustinian and humanistically minded theologians were numerous and powerful at the Council. It therefore became important for the Dominican faction in particular to present Aquinas as a true Augustinian – and not as a scholastic – in order to gain preeminence over the other medieval authorities and also to make him the best herald against the competing Protestant interpretation of the Church Fathers. Historically anterior to both humanism and late medieval nominalism, Aquinas was presented as a safe haven against Biblical literalism and predestinarianism. This was the context of Pope Pius's declaration of Aquinas as Doctor of the Church in 1567, just after the end of the Council. As a result, post-conciliar histories all enshrined the role of Aquinas: According to a rapidly popularized legend, in particular by the influential Church history of Cesare Baronio (1538–1607), the Council itself is said to have been celebrated with two books on the altar, the Bible and the *Summa* (Baronius, *Martyrologium*, p. 112).[7]

---

[7] For a contemporary historical sketch of this "triumph" of the *Summa* and of Aquinas's authority, see Camblat, *Opusculum secundum*; a good general historical survey for the seventeenth century is provided by De Franceschi, "L'empire thomiste."

Not all theologians shared such enthusiasm. The Franciscans and other congregations fought for their own scholastic heroes. And if we look at the young Society of Jesus (established 1540), we find numerous voices rejecting Aquinas during the long debates leading to their famous *Ratio Studiorum* (1599). Alonso Pisano (1528–98), a Spanish Jesuit active in Poland, wrote that he believed it inopportune to use the *Summa* as a manual for instruction in moral theology. Theology should go back to revelation and not restrict itself to the words of a specific teacher; he added that Aquinas's scholastic *habitus* would be rejected by many "Northerners" and that he would be useless to convert Protestants, who despised him as "a simple monk who knew neither Greek nor Hebrew" (Theiner, *Die Entwicklung*, pp. 368–73). These reservations were eventually overcome, and the *Ratio* adopted the *Summa* of Aquinas as the key text from which to conduct theological studies, although in practice a wide *delectus opinionum* was tolerated among Jesuit teachers. It constituted the fundamental material for four years of scholastic theology, as opposed to only two dedicated to Sacred Scripture.[8] A similar movement can be observed in all the new congregations and in the reforms of the old ones, which almost all adopted Thomas Aquinas as an authority. This was particularly so for the reformed Carmelites and the Benedictines, who all became staunch and solid Thomists. Some smaller but often locally influential congregations took the same pro-Thomistic stance, such as the *Teatini* in Italy or the French Cistercian reform of the *Feuillants*. This provoked a sometimes violent "scholastic war" (*bellum scholasticum*) that raged during most of the early-modern period, either between Thomists and their opponents or between Aquinas's own competing interpreters (Schmutz, "*Bellum*"). In time, the triumph of Aquinas became so complete that many attempted concordist syntheses between Aquinas and Bonaventure (a Capuchin speciality), or Aquinas and Giles of Rome (for the Hermits of Saint Augustine). Eventually, only the Franciscan-Scotist tradition would remain an anti-Thomistic fortress, but sometimes rebuilt according to a Thomist plan: the Neapolitan Franciscan Angelo Volpi (d. 1647) composed a multi-volume Scotist *Summa Theologiae Scoti* (1622–46) but organized its contents as Aquinas did, and Girolamo da Montefortino (1662–1738) composed a work that completely mimics the *Summa* in Scotistic terms.

---

[8] For the history and organization of the theological curriculum, see Theiner, *Die Entwicklung*, pp. 148–64; Schmutz, "Les normes."

A similar movement would eventually win within the major universities. They were in no way uniform, and the use of the *Summa* was initially just a barometer of Dominican or Jesuit influence: The first one to have accepted the *Summa* as textbook was the Italian university of Pavia, which in 1480 started nominating its Dominican professors on the condition that they read the works of Aquinas. It was at this university that the famous Tommaso de Vio (Cajetan, 1468–1538) started teaching in 1497, using the *Summa* after having previously taught on the *Sentences* in Padua in 1493.[9] His role was certainly important in giving institutional support to the use of Aquinas in the *studia*, but the majority of universities did not follow his lead. During most of the sixteenth century, their teaching practices remained closely attached to the *Sentences*. It was only in the aftermath of Trent that this situation progressively changed, when many universities were prompted to establish new "bodies of doctrine" (*corpus doctrinae*), in which the thought of Thomas Aquinas constituted a key element. In Spain, these tendencies were also actively supported by more down-to-earth political maneuvers that had little to do with doctrine, namely the close-knit institutional ties between the Dominican order and the Spanish royalty, to whom it provided an efficient armada of inquisitors, censors, bishops, and confessors. The 1561 new statutes of the University of Salamanca stipulated in rather paradoxical fashion that holders of the Morning and Evening Chairs should read the *Sentences* according to the order of the *Summa* of Aquinas (Barrientos García, "La teología," p. 69). The pro-Dominican policy would gain even more momentum with the new chairs endowed by the powerful Duke of Lerma (1552–1625) at the universities of Salamanca, Valladolid, and Alcalá; among the holders of these chairs, we would find some of the seventeenth century's most illustrious Thomists. In Louvain and Douay, a similar phenomenon could be observed with the creation of new chairs explicitly dedicated to Thomism in addition to those of *Sentences* and of Holy Scripture.[10] In France, the new statutes of the University of Paris (1598–1600) still mentioned the *Sentences* as a textbook, but in practice it was dropped as of the beginning of the seventeenth century, and the *Summa* was the only text in use. The regulations for the three types of theology examinations (*baccalaureus, licentia,*

---

[9] On this Paduan revival of Thomism, see Gaetano, *Renaissance Thomism.*

[10] On the Louvain context, see Brants, "La création" and Martin, "L'introduction." For Salamanca, see Belda Plans, *La Escuela,* with references to the numerous studies by the unsurpassed Spanish Dominican scholar Vicente Beltrán de Heredia (1885–1973).

and *tentativa*) were all based on parts of the *Summa*. In Rome, special chairs were endowed at the Casanatense in order to explain the *Summa*. Thus, it seemed that the triumph could not have been more complete, as the French Jesuit Pierre Labbé (1596–1678) put it in an often printed *elogium*: "[N]othing rises after the *Summa*, be it not the splendor of glory" (Labbé, Elogia).[11]

As a material consequence of this massive change in teaching, the market for editions and commentaries on Aquinas's works skyrocketed. We still lack a comprehensive study explaining the background to and promotion of the *Summa's* numerous editions, and we can here mention only some of the most important ones. Three years after he was declared Doctor of the Church, the so-called *Piana* edition was published in Rome (1570, named after Pope Pius V), the first comprehensive new early-modern attempt, reprinted in a 1593 Venetian edition in 18 volumes.[12] Before that, the first complete edition had been published in Basel in 1485. Almost every important printing town of Europe would have its own edition, but only a handful made real progress: We can mention the 1569 Antwerp edition (reprinted 1570) by the Louvain humanist and logician Augustin Hunnaeus (1522–78), which long remained standard; the 1612 Antwerp edition by Cosme Gil Morelles (d. 1636); the little-known but precious Douay edition, based on an older 1496 Roman edition and new collations of manuscripts kept in Northern France, which was counterfeited by Paris printers in 1622; the Lyons edition, promoted by the Parisian Dominicans starting in the 1630s (published 1655), and finally the new edition by the French Dominican Jean Nicolaï (1663–85), and the Venice edition by Bernardo Maria de' Rossi (1687–1775). Of particular interest are the numerous "derivative works" produced around the *Summa* that also distinguish the early-modern reception from the medieval tradition. Spanish artists excelled in representing the triumph of Aquinas and the *Summa Theologiae*.[13] We find the first attempts to offer a vernacular translation, such as Léonard de Marandé (fl. 1620–50)

---

[11] This *Elogium* was often reprinted and included in many other works of scholastic theology. Note that Labbé composed an equally influential praise of John Duns Scotus, an evident sign of the Jesuit's freedom of theological opinion.

[12] First attempts to list the Renaissance editions can be found in Échard and Quétif, *Scriptores*, pp. 322–3 and Touron, *La vie*, pp. 779–84. See also De Franceschi, "L'empire thomiste," pp. 321–2.

[13] See for instance Diego Velázquez's *Temptation of St Thomas Aquinas* (1632), Museo de Arte Sacra, Cathedral of Orihuela (Spain) or Francisco de Zurbarán's *Apotheosis of St Thomas Aquinas* (1631), an altarpiece of the Dominican convent of Seville, now at the Museo Provincial de Bellas Artes, Sevilla (Spain).

in France, who tried to accommodate the *Summa* to the "impatient French mind," by immediately translating the conclusions rather than the initial objections (Marandé, *La Clef*). The *Summa* was submitted to all the pedagogical innovations of the Renaissance: It was either completely rewritten in the form of axioms or in syllogistical form to facilitate the student's capacity to draw firm conclusions from premises (Ochoa, *Omnes*; De' Medici, *Explicatio*), or transformed into a huge didactic poem (Gravina, *Rhytmicum*; Penon, *Hymnus*). French Dominicans also attempted an impressive visualization of the *Summa* in a series of explanatory diagrams.[14]

12.2 Thomistic Hermeneutics

Once his central authority was admitted, the following centuries were mainly marked by an ongoing debate between the interpreters of Thomas Aquinas about the right meaning of his *littera* and his intention. This became an important hermeneutical problem: How to understand Thomas after three centuries of non-Thomistic theology had completely modified the very language of theology. In a precious work for historiography, Xante Mariales (ca. 1580–1660), a Venetian Dominican, attempted for the first time a complete overview of the conflicting interpretations of the *Summa* among all recent commentators (Mariales, *Bibliotheca*). There was not one Thomism, but a multiplicity of varieties: As the Spanish Jesuit Cristóbal de Ortega (1597–1686) observed: "Dominican Thomists … are largely different from the Thomists of our Society" (Ortega, *De Deo*, p. 2). The debate would rapidly degenerate into a war of invectives: *Spurious Thomista, pseudo-Thomista*, etc. were common names thrown at opponents; partisans claimed being *vere Thomista, rigidus Thomista*; historical distinctions were made between *Thomista antiquior, vestutior* (Ortega, *De Deo*, pp. 39, 80, *passim*), or a *Thomista iunior*. Especially during the first part of the seventeenth century, the Jesuit commentators excelled in giving "liberal" interpretations from Aquinas, using him more as "light" (*lux*) than as a "leader" (*dux*). The famous Coimbra commentators have expressed it in a striking metaphor: Aquinas's doctrine should be considered a "Lesbian Rule" (*regula lesbia*), referring to the flexible leaden rule used by the ancient builders

---

[14] See for instance a striking anonymous manuscript from the Convent of the Faubourg Saint-Honoré: *Abrégé de théologie et de métaphysique sous forme de tableaux* (s. XVII), Paris BNF, Ms. lat. 18166.

from the Greek island of Lesbos, mentioned by Aristotle (NE 5.10). Among all medieval authorities, his doctrine is commendable because it accounts for unusual cases as well as new terrain in theology.[15]

On the opposite side, the theologians of the Dominican order and their Carmelite allies rapidly took over the role of the "wardens" of the true doctrine. The Salmantine Domingo Báñez, often celebrated as a "rigorous" or "staunch" Thomist, famously lamented that the "Thomists of our time either do not read Aquinas, or just do not care about him" (*Commentaria*, vol. III, p. 796). This protestation of orthodoxy should not, however, be taken at face value and obscure the fact that the Dominicans introduced many novelties – starting with the famous *praemotio physica*, perhaps the seventeenth century's most discussed concept, introduced to explain the relationship between the first divine cause and secondary human free agency.[16] As of the 1640s, the competing Jesuits and Jansenists would challenge the Dominican "right" to embody true Thomism, both groups seeking a "Thomistic refuge"[17] in order to advocate for the orthodoxy of their views which had come increasingly under attack from the papacy and from one another, especially in the decade-long debates about the compatibility between human freewill and divine grace. With so many "Thomists," guidelines were needed: In 1693, Tirso González de Santalla (1624–1701) drafted for the Roman inquisitors a *Parallelism of True and False Thomism* (Serry, *Historiae*, coll. 373–80), whose aim was to disqualify the use of Aquinas by the Jansenists and advocate for the Thomist orthodoxy of the Jesuits.

What role did the *Summa* play in this enduring quest for Thomistic orthodoxy? If Thomism could become a "Lesbian Rule," it was because Aquinas had written so much over his career and so one could easily find competing opinions in his work. "This is what I can hardly suffer," protested the French Jansenist philosopher Antoine Arnauld (1612–94), "when in order to explain the true feelings of Saint Thomas, one looks for them in places different from his *Summa*" (Arnauld, *Lettres*, p. 169). To remedy the numerous violent doctrinal disagreements, it was thus necessary to enshrine the *Summa* as the absolute touchstone for orthodoxy. "*In Summa correxit*"; "*Neque in Summa hoc dixit*": These were

---

[15] The metaphor of the Lesbian Rule was often used by Renaissance writers to attack the opportunism of lawyers, bishops, or even popes. In philosophy, its use seems to date back to the Collegium Conimbricense, *De Anima*, p. 67.
[16] On the concept and debate, see key texts in Beltrán de Heredia, *Domingo Báñez*, and studies by Hübener, "Praedeterminatio," and Knebel, *Wille*, with most of its bibliography.
[17] For the Jansenist strategy, see De Franceschi, *La puissance*.

already common expressions used by Domingo de Soto (1495–1560), the acclaimed Salamanca Dominican commentator and Tridentine theologian, when he tried to solve some vexed issues on the value of sacraments (Soto, *Commentariorum*, p. 852).[18]

12.3   Dismantling the *Summa*

A striking fact is that a great number of early-modern *Summae* published during the early-modern period in the name of Aquinas did not respect the order of their original model. First, they largely dismantled the *Summa* into different units that became increasingly isolated from each other. Second, they distinguished within the *Summa* between matters that were dependent upon revelation and matters that could be investigated by pure reason. A material consequence is that the *Summa* was often not printed as a whole: When Peter Schöffer (ca. 1425–1503), one of Gutenberg's trainees and later rivals, produced its very first printing, in Mainz (1467), it contained only the Second Part of the Second Part.[19] This indicates that the work's treatment of morality was seen as the most important element in the German pre-Reformation and humanist context, and this would remain an important trend. The "practical" parts of the *Summa* (on human actions, virtues and vices, sacraments) certainly won the statistical battle between what became known as the two parts of theology, namely the *theologia speculativa* (based on the First and Third Parts, i.e., God and Christology) and the *theologia practica* (most of the rest, dealing with humans). Although Aquinas had clearly stressed that the *theoretical* end of contemplation was the highest goal of theology (and also the highest human good), "his argument is not seen as convincing by all," observed the Spanish Jesuit Juan Maldonado (1533–83; "De constitutione," p. 251), like many who insisted on the practical dimension.

Rather than a model to follow, Aquinas's *Summa* thereby became something like a quarry from which to extract the building blocks

---

[18] This passage by Soto has often been quoted in later treatises on confession and moral theology. Aquinas would often be attacked on this issue, especially in France: See for instance de Launoy, *Veneranda*, pp. 229–30, where he clearly opposes Peter Lombard's authority against the "errors" of Aquinas, who claims that it is not necessary that the act of confession should be preceded by contrition.

[19] First attempts to list the Renaissance editions can be found in Échard and Quétif, *Scriptores*, pp. 322–3 and Touron, *La vie*, pp. 779–84. For a tentative list of later editions, see De Franceschi, "L'empire thomiste," pp. 321–2.

of a new literary genre of post-Tridentine scholasticism, the *Cursus Theologicus*, divided into "parts" which did not at all correspond to the parts of Aquinas's *Summa*.[20] The fundamental division between theoretical and practical theology was reflected in a new nomenclature, such as the progressive introduction of the neologism "fundamental theology" (*theologia fundamentalis*) to designate the first speculative parts of theological education, later also dubbed "dogmatic" theology (*theologia dogmatica*).[21] The practical parts became an autonomous discipline under the title *theologia moralis*,[22] which explains why the Second Part of the Second Part received such extraordinary attention during these centuries. Moral theology gave birth to a number of subdisciplines, such as casuistry (or cases of conscience), which sparked an immense debate throughout the seventeenth and eighteenth centuries, with a succession of polemics between probabilists and anti-probabilists.[23] Several traditions added a third, more apologetical and defensive part, absent as such in Aquinas: "polemical theology" (*theologia polemica*). The theological unity between theory and practice, advocated by Thomas Aquinas in the *Summa*, had become a scattered field.

An even more radical questioning of the *Summa's* structure consisted in completely rearranging its order in commentaries: not starting with God, but starting with the treatise on faith, extracted from its original spot in the Second Part of the Second Part and placed at the outset of the theology course. This move can be interpreted as a typically modern process of subjectivizing theology: Faith, as the subjective capacity to assent to supernatural mysteries, is more important than the objective nature of these mysteries themselves (God, the Trinity, Incarnation, etc.). This way of reorganizing theology was championed, for instance, in the *Marrow of Theology* (1650), a small but very influential treatise published by a secular Sorbonne-educated priest, Louis Abelly (1603–91). In the following decades, numerous theology courses in both print and manuscript form started explicitly with the *De Fide*, as for instance the three-volume course (1736) by the French Jesuit Paul Gabriel Antoine (1679–1743). This trend continued in the eighteenth century, when "fundamental

---

[20] See on this Farley, *Theologia* and Hell, *Entstehung*, pp. 57–66.

[21] See: Stirnimann, "Fundamentaltheologie"; Niemann, "Fundamentaltheologie" and Niemann, "Zur Frühgeschichte"; and Filser, *Dogma*.

[22] On this general movement, see the (very Jesuit-centered) investigation by Theiner, *Die Entwicklung*; Vereecke, *Etudes*; Mahoney, *The Making*.

[23] The classic presentation remains Deman, "Probabilisme"; recent studies include Schüssler, *Moral*, and Gay, *Morales*, all with excellent bibliographies.

theology" courses included long preliminary sections justifying the rational nature of religion in general (*demonstratio religiosa*), before turning to the more specific Christian revelation and Catholic Church (*demonstratio christiana* and *demonstratio catholica*, respectively). This became the key method of theologians wishing to rebuke Enlightenment critiques of religion as "irrational" or "superstition." In Vienna, the Italian-born Dominican Pietro Maria Gazzaniga (1722–99), started his theology course (1777) in highly Ciceronian fashion, insisting on the practical function of religion rather than starting with the existence of a transcendent God, in order to seduce readers used to the criticism of revealed religion by Spinoza, Toland, or Voltaire.

A second way of dismantling the *Summa* consisted in distinguishing between its revealed and non-revealed contents. It is usually overlooked by historiography that huge chunks of the *Summa* were exfiltrated into *philosophy* courses, rather than serving as a basis for *theology* courses. This specifically philosophical use of the *Summa* concerned not just natural theology (such as discussions on matter and form, eternity and time, potency and act) mainly extracted from the First Part, but also the *Summa's* discussions of ethics. For instance, when Jan van Malderen (1563–1633), taught the First Part of the Second Part in Louvain, he conspicuously left out the treatise on passions (questions 22–55), claiming it "belongs to philosophy" (*Commentaria*, p. 179). The survival of "philosophical" ethics courses in other countries, such as in the French colleges or Italian universities, should therefore not be mistaken for a form of Aristotelian resilience: On the contrary, most of them were nothing more than abridgments and commentaries of the ethical parts of Aquinas's *Summa*. A vivid example is the ethics course drafted by Eustachius a Sancto Paulo for his acclaimed philosophy course, aptly entitled *Summa Philosophica* (1609), famous for earning the praise of Descartes as one of the best of his own time. A close look at its structure shows that it consists mainly of a selection of headings taken from the Second Part, with special concern not to include specifically theological subjects, such as the cardinal virtues or the gifts of the Holy Spirit.

Complete philosophy courses (*cursus philosophici*), such as Eustachius's were plentiful in the early-modern age. Religious congregations, provinces, and individual colleges commissioned such textbooks, and they became the standard for teaching everywhere. Some of them openly mimicked the organization of Aquinas's *Summa* by their division into four parts (considering that the Second Part is in reality composed of two parts). A Milanese Jesuit, Cosmo Alamanni (1559–1634), was probably the first to have suggested this new presentation, dividing his philosophical textbook into parts called *Ia, Ia-IIae, IIa-IIae,* and *IIIa* (Alamanni, *Summa philosophiae*). The model was followed by another more orthodox Thomist, the French discalced Carmelite Philippus a Sanctissima Trinitate (1603–71), who claims to have "derived" an entire philosophy course from Aquinas's theological *Summa* (*Summa philosophica*, Ad lectorem). Among the Dominicans, Antoine Goudin (1639–95) wrote a similar *Summa of Philosophy According to the Firm Principles of Aquinas* (1670), which was to prove tremendously influential into the nineteenth century, when one of the German promoters of "neo-Thomism" (Plassmann, *Vorhallen*) used it as a model. In the German lands, the Benedictines transformed the University of Salzburg into a flagship of philosophical Thomism, as illustrated by the work of Ludwig Babenstuber (1660–1726; *Philosophia*).[24] In the eighteenth century, a plea for "neo-Thomism" was made by the Master General Joan Tomàs de Boixadors (1703–80) in the form of an encyclical epistle to his order, *De Renovanda et Defendenda Doctrina Sancti Thomae* (1757). Several textbooks answered this call, and contributed to transforming the *Summa* into a work of *philosophy* and not *theology*. This was the case with the Dominican Salvatore Maria Roselli (d. 1784) for his lectures at the Roman Minerva, and of Vincenzo Buzzetti (1777–1824), a professor at the Collegio Alberoni in Piacenza, an institution which is often seen as the cradle of neo-Thomism.[25] By extracting from Aquinas's *Summa* enough to fill a complete textbook of philosophy, all these authors contributed to establishing a firm "Aristotelian-Thomist" paradigm, presenting the Angelic Doctor as the best exponent of Aristotle's perennial philosophy, and therefore as the best antidote against philosophical novelties such as Cartesianism, atomism, mechanistic physics, or modern forms of skepticism.

12.4 Is the *Summa* Theological?

An even more radical stance was taken by early-modern readers of Aquinas: They did not attempt to "derive" philosophy from the *Summa Theologiae*, but questioned its very theological nature. The suspicion came

---

[24] On the Salzburg tradition, see Bauer, *Metaphysik*.
[25] On this tradition, see: Narciso, "Neotomismo"; Narciso, *Salvatore Roselli*; Rossi, *Il movimento*. For a general presentation of these now widely forgotten manuals, see: Colombo, "La manualistica"; Schmidinger, "Der Streit."

from all those who believed that Aquinas's work was giving too much weight to human rationality in its scrutiny of divine nature and the history of salvation. This approach included a broad and improbable coalition of humanists, partisans of a purely pastoral conception of theology, early Protestant reformers, and Catholic critics of scholastic methods in theology. Arguably the most famous criticism came from Luther, who transformed *thomista* into a bad word, to be thrown at somebody who "prostitutes" human reason to the devil and misunderstands the practical nature of the theology of the cross: There is only one place for *speculative* theology, namely "with the devil in hell," claimed the German reformer in a famous table-talk (Luther, *Table Talk*, p. 22). Thomism, as the paramount example of a theology which claims to be *magis speculativa, quam practica*, as asserted in the first question of the First Part (1.4c), is widely accused of "extinguishing the faith." True Christian theology had to shy away from the *theologia philosophica* dear to the "popish schools" (*in scholis Pontificiorum*), as the reformed Utrecht theologian Peter van Mastricht (1630–1706) expressed it (van Mastricht, *Theologia*, p. 8). They missed the practical dimension of theology, which was at the heart of the Reformation, and as a result, their work should be considered not Christian and theological, but quasi-pagan and philosophical. If any medieval scholastic authority had to be used, then many Protestant academic theologians usually preferred to turn toward alternative sources, such as Bonaventurian skepticism or advocates of the practical character of theology, such as John Duns Scotus or a later Dominican such as Thomas of Strasbourg.[26]

Not all reformed theologians shared such harsh judgments. Many showed a more conciliatory attitude toward Aquinas through an interesting polemical argument: Because he had become the paramount authority for the Catholics, it could be profitable for the Protestants to show that Aquinas's views were akin to those of the reformers, thereby efficiently debunking the Catholic claim to be the true and universal church. This strategy was pursued by the Alsatian Lutheran Johann Georg Dorsche (1597–1659),[27] who tried to show similarities between Aquinas and the Augsburg Confession in a 600-page volume offering very close readings of the *Summa* (*Thomas Aquinas*), anticipating from that point

---

[26] See for instance Meisner, *Philosophia*, p. 855, who invokes the authority of Bonaventure, claiming that it is sometimes better to doubt than to define at all cost.

[27] See also, in a similar vein, Reiser, *Vindiciae*. In this context, see Zeller, "Orthodoxie"; Donnelly, "Calvinist Thomism."

of view the twentieth-century Protestant appropriation of Aquinas: "In many ... articles we can happily and successfully use Aquinas against the Papists," commented another later reformed bibliographer (Serpilius, *Commentatores*, p. 177). But the most revealing use of the *Summa* in the Protestant academies came from those who saw its value in its *philosophical* nature, once it was admitted that its theology was useless. A good example of this attitude was Petrus van Mastricht's own teacher in Utrecht, Gisbert Voetius (1589–1676). He did not shy away from recommending the *lectio ipsius summae Thomae* when it came to acquire a basic understanding of scholastic theology, "at least in its principal places and questions" (Voetius, *Exercitia*, p. 61).[28] Voetius believed Aquinas was a lesser evil for religious orthodoxy than the new dualistic philosophy of Descartes. This Protestant use "decatholicized" Aquinas's *Summa* and produced the perception that it could be treated as a work of philosophy.

A similar attitude became noticeable in Catholic lands. Their heralds were those who did not believe the classical Tridentine claim that Aquinas was the best exponent of the Church Fathers, but that it was better to go back to the Fathers themselves. Cornelius Jansenius (1585–1638), arguably the seventeenth century's most important theologian, said about contemporary scholastic theologians that they were more "illuminated by Aristotle than by the Holy Spirit" (Jansenius, *Augustinus*, p. 14). This anti-scholastic attitude gave birth to a new form of theology, *positive theology*, often seen as one of the most important innovations of early-modern Catholic theology.[29] Rather than rationally deriving conclusions from a limited set of revealed propositions, as in Aquinas, positive theology endeavored to establish vast catalogs of all the Biblical, patristic, and historical sources and arguments about a specific point of doctrine or dogma. French theologians – often Jansenist or crypto-Jansenist – led the way in this return to the *ancienne théologie*. While positive theology required immense erudition, mastery of ancient languages, and critical skills to establish theology's historical sources, at the same time it commended a certain form of fideism. Accordingly, the French historian Louis Le Gendre (1655–1733) offered a down-to-earth explanation of the century-long success of the *Summa*: Scholastic theologians

---

[28] On Voetius's conciliatory attitude toward Aquinas and the Catholic scholastics, see Goudriaan, *Orthodoxy, passim.*

[29] On the development of positive theology, see: Guelluy, "L'évolution"; Tshibangu, *Théologie positive.* On its origins, see: Andrés Martín, *La teología*, pp. 181–7, 303–7; Hofmann, *Theologie*; Stirnimann, "Fundamentaltheologie"; Quinto, *Scholastica*, pp. 238–47.

are just a lazy bunch! It is indeed easier and faster to read the *Summa* and pretend to be wise than to know the Bible and the Church Fathers in detail (Le Gendre, *Les mœurs*, p. 98).

But in spite of this widespread onslaught against scholasticism, almost all – including Jansenius himself – refrained from directly attacking the authority of Aquinas, untouchable as doctor of the Church. The most sophisticated method for challenging the theological value of the *Summa*, while at the same time upholding the authority of Aquinas, was yet to come: It was simply to *deny* that he was the *author* of this terrible work of scholasticism entitled *Summa Theologiae*. In a century saturated with debates about forgery and authenticity (Grafton, *Forgers*), the first to have used this strategy was the Gallican Jean de Launoy (1601–78). After having discovered a manuscript panegyric by Peter Roger, composed in 1323, which did not mention the *Summa*, he concluded that the *Summa* had not been written by Aquinas but must have been the work of some later medieval degenerate scholastic. It led to an important dispute, with an effective rebuttal by the French Dominican Noël Alexandre (1639–1724).[30] Another controversy erupted about the alleged plagiarism of Aquinas, given the *verbatim* correspondence between the *Summa* and some passages of the *Speculum Morale* attributed to Vincent of Beauvais (who died before Aquinas), which had been printed in 1624. Jacques Echard (1644–1724), one of the fathers of Dominican bibliography and historical criticism, resolved this knotty problem with a vibrant demonstration. But the most flamboyant strategy was the work of Jean Hardouin (1646–1729), the eccentric librarian of the Jesuit College of Louis-le-Grand in Paris. Not only did he consider the work to be spurious, but he even doubted the existence of its author (as he did likewise for most of pre-modern literature). In a four-volume manuscript critical discussion of the *Summa*, he admirably summarized the general spirit of all those Catholics who believed that the *Summa* had little to do with theology, attributing it to an atheist: "He entitled his work *Summa of Theology*, whereas in reality it is nothing else than a purely philosophical summa (*summa mere philosophica*)." Its author "had no knowledge of the true God," which explains "why in the body of the articles, which always starts with the formula *I respond by saying*, he always makes use of

---

[30] See Launoy, *Veneranda*, pp. 289–90, where he speaks about *Beatus Thomas, vel alius quis sub illius nomine scripsit* (a passage highlighted in De Franceschi, "L'empire thomiste," p. 319); Échard, *Sancti Thomae Summa*. See a good reconstruction of the debate in Zahora, "Thomist Scholarship" (who does not, however, mention the Launoy episode).

arguments that are only supported by natural reason or by the philosophy of Aristotle, Avicenna and others" (Hardouin, *Censura*, vol. I, f. 5v).

12.5 Transforming the *Summa* into a Philosophical Classic

The paradox of regarding the *Summa* as a work of philosophy also characterizes its reception in the nineteenth and twentieth centuries. In 1879,
Pope Leo XIII officially started the vast movement now known as "neo-
Thomism" with the encyclical *Aeterni Patris*.[31] Its pastoral tone should
not overshadow the fact that *philosophy* was at the heart of the project,
and not *theology*. After a century marked by the rise of liberalism and
socialism and politics, the development of idealism and materialism in
philosophy, and the explosion of science into a realm of increasingly
disconnected disciplines, the encyclical intended to restore an imagined
medieval unity of knowledge.

A first immediate outcome was the start of the so-called Leonine edition, which is still underway today, an attempt at a critical edition of
Aquinas's complete works. Among the first printed volumes stands the
Summa (vols. IV–XI, 1882 ff.), in a version which to this day remains
an embarrassment to Dominican scholarship.[32] The second immediate outcome was a confirmation of the "philosophical turn" taken by
Thomism.[33] The desired program of dialogue with modern science has
probably best been carried out by the Institute of Philosophy founded
by Cardinal Désiré-Joseph Mercier (1851–1926) in Louvain, who used
Thomism as an encompassing paradigm to organize modern studies of
chemistry, physics, and mathematics with a general reflection on human
finality and happiness. This new philosophical Thomism would also soon
take a repressive form: In 1914, Pius X issued the famous *24 Thomistic
Theses*, drafted by the French Dominican Édouard Hugon (1867–1929),
as a preceptive list of what all Catholic institutions should teach in
courses of philosophy (they were integrated into Canon Law in 1917).

---

[31] On the origin of the encyclica and the neo-Thomist movement, see in particular the essays by
Coreth, Neidl and Pfligersdorffer, *Christliche Philosophie*, which contain very complete bibliographies; Bonansea, "Pioneers," for a good summary of the Italian context; Scheffczyk, *Theologie* for
Germany; and general studies by McCool, *Catholic Theology, Unity, Neo-Thomists*; Prouvost,
Thomismes. The real authorship of the encyclical remains a matter of debate to this day: Some have
argued for the Corsican Dominican Tommaso Zigliara (1833–93), and others have attributed its
drafts to the Jesuits Joseph Kleutgen (1811–83) and Matteo Liberatore (1810–92). All were prominent professors of philosophy. On this debate, see Boyle, "A Remembrance."
[32] See the remarks in Pasnau, *Treatise*, p. 413, and Bataillon, "Recherches."
[33] A point well made by Weisheipl, "Revival."

These theses were very general principles for describing reality, all of which could be traced back to some philosophical distinctions used in the *Summa*: potency and act, matter and form, analogy between uncreated and created being, the immortality and subsistence of the soul, etc. New "Aristotelico-Thomist" textbooks were published in large numbers, including the first ones in English, such as the quickly produced translation of the *Foundations of Thomistic Philosophy* (1931) by the French Dominican Antonin-Dalmace Sertillanges (1863–1948) and *Modern Thomistic Philosophy* (1934–35) by R. P. Phillips.[34] The same period witnessed massive translations of the *Summa*, such as the famous edition produced by the Fathers of the English Dominican Province (22 vols., 1912–33).

Of course, the *Summa* also remained a theological classic, and the nineteenth and early twentieth centuries were not short of linear commentaries. French romantic Catholicism played an important role here as early as in the 1820s, defending in particular the heritage of Charles-René Billuart (1685–1757) who had started his theology course with a treatise on the *cardinal*, and not *theological* virtues.[35] The size of some of these commentaries was intimidating, such as the 25 volumes by the Servite Alexis Lépicier (1863–1936) or the 21 volumes by the Dominican Thomas Pègues (1866–1936). Pègues, known for his royalist and anti-modern positions, also produced a catechism-style abridged version of the *Summa* (Pègues, *Catechism*). Some of them were strongly linked to the anti-modernist mentality: Louis Billot (1846–1931), a French Jesuit famous for his reactionary ideas, provoked a considerable debate by arguing that atheists are ultimately incapable of morality – the exact opposite of what Francisco de Vitoria (1492–1546) and so many early-modern commentators had tried to defend during the Renaissance (Billot, *De personali*, pp. 24–32; Billot, "La providence"). But these vast scholastic commentaries were rapidly denounced as an improper way to do theology in the twentieth century. A striking example was the work of Marie-Dominique Chenu (1895–1990), one of the fathers of the so-called *Ressourcement*-theology and a student of Reginald Garrigou-Lagrange (1877–1964), the "sacred monster of Thomism" (Peddicord, *Monster*). In a book condemned by the Vatican in 1942, Chenu violently attacked the "systematization" of theology that had "obscured" the innovative and

---

[34] For a sampling of these Thomistic teaching texts produced in English in the first half of the twentieth century, see Haldane, *Modern Writings*.
[35] On the work of Billuart and its important legacy, see De Franceschi, "L'exténuation."

spiritual approach that had characterized Aquinas himself (Chenu, *École*, p. 123). He issued an invitation to a complete reconsideration of the historical context and the literary style of the *Summa*, uncovering its forgotten neo-platonic structure (Chenu, *Toward Understanding*; Hankey, *God in Himself*). This marked a generalized ebbing of the *Summa* in Roman Catholic theology, in favor of a "new theology" inspired by the Bible, the Church Fathers, and the tradition, that would eventually come to full expression after the Second Vatican Council.[36] John Paul II's encyclical *Fides et Ratio* (1998) can so far be considered as the last Thomistic act of the Vatican.

This relative theological disavowal of the *Summa* did not affect its growing reception as a purely *philosophical* work, fulfilling in a certain way Jean Hardouin's seventeenth-century prophecy. The fact that the *Summa* was at the heart of the thought of Étienne Gilson (1884–1978), Jacques Maritain, Gustav Siewerth (1903–63), or Josef Pieper (1904–97), who all considered themselves *philosophers* and not *theologians*, transformed the work into a classic of the discipline. Since the 1930s, and to this day, self-declared Thomists have constituted an easily identifiable and vibrant intellectual community in philosophy departments of numerous Catholic universities, including North America. But what is more interesting is the success of the *Summa* outside of strictly confessional circles. Starting in the 1940s, Richard McKeon (1900–85), himself a former student of Gilson in Paris, introduced sections of the *Summa* as part of a renewed liberal arts curriculum in the University of Chicago. In 1952, Mortimer Adler (1902–2001) imposed the *Summa* as the only medieval title (with Dante and Chaucer) of the *Great Books of the Western World* series, between Augustine and Machiavelli. Likewise in Chicago, Yves Simon (1903–61) popularized the idea of Aquinas as a Neo-Aristotelian at the Committee on Social Thought, gaining a powerful secular conservative following. In Oxford, Peter Geach (1916–2013) was famed for keeping "always to hand" a pocket edition of the *Summa* (Kenny, "Form," p. 65) and for using it in his classes on logical or metaphysical themes. Geach's method is often considered the birth of "analytical Thomism,"[37] which has led to stripping the *Summa* of most of its

---

[36] For a good synthesis, see Schoof, *Survey*, and more recently Mettepenningen, *Nouvelle Théologie*; for post-Vatican II, see contributions in Fourcade and Avon, *Nouvel Âge*. On the place of Thomism at Vatican II, see Komonchak, "Thomism."

[37] For a synthesis of analytical Thomism, see Paterson and Pugh, *Analytical Thomism*; on current debates and disagreements, see Kerr, *After Aquinas*.

theological overtones: Anthony Lisska argues for instance that the "existence of God is, in a structural sense, neither a relevant concept nor a
necessary condition for Aquinas's account of natural law" (Lisska, *Natural
Law*, p. 230) – a sentence that certainly made Billot and others turn in
their graves.

This philosophical reading of Aquinas and its promise for a fully
rationalized "theism" has also made considerable progress in reformed circles during the last decades, with the blessing of Karl Barth (1886–1968):
He admitted that although Aquinas's thought does "not point us to the
Reformation," it was essential to dissociate him from "typical ... post-
Tridentine Catholicism" and "Roman Jesuitism"; as a result, "there is a
lot that the Evangelical theologian can learn in Thomas' [*Summa*] as a
well-chosen compendium of all preceding tradition" (Barth, *Dogmatics*,
p. 316). Strongly Lutheran-educated Norman Kretzmann (1928–98)
became a leading historian of medieval rational theology, and self-
declared Episcopalian or Anglican professors of philosophy such as Brian
Leftow, Marilyn Adams, or Peter van Inwagen do not hesitate to use
Aquinas in their treatments of the important questions of philosophical
theology. The *International Handbook of Protestant Education* (Jeynes and
Robinson) now dedicates a chapter to Aquinas.[38]

12.6   Conclusion

In his acclaimed essay on good taste, the Italian Enlightenment thinker
Ludovico Antonio Muratori (1672–1750) ensured that among all scholastics, theology had kept its "majesty" only in Aquinas, but that it
had degenerated subsequently, due to the arid and nasty style of later
scholastics who made unnecessary conceptual complications (Muratori,
Riflessioni, p. 112). Muratori was one of those who contributed to popu-
larizing the powerful paradigm of the late medieval "decline" which I
set out to challenge in this chapter. In reality, the history of Thomism
has rather been a steady stream of commentaries: There was certainly
no eighteenth-century "waning," and the late-nineteenth-century neo-
Thomism was not so much a "renewal" as a reenactment of a number of
seventeenth-century options.

In navigating this stream, the *Summa* was a vessel that has been con-
tinuously adapted, and sometimes even completely deconstructed and

---

[38] For a critical assessment of these Protestant appropriations, see Vos, *Aquinas, Calvin*.

rebuilt in different ways. Today's philosophy students will have difficulties in recognizing the fact that it was initially drafted with a pastoral goal for the instruction of Dominican "beginners." Its success proved uninterrupted, but for highly contradictory reasons: Whereas post-Tridentine theologians saw it as a synthesis of the Church Fathers, nineteenth-century scholasticism transformed it into a monument of rationalism. One reason, however, seemed to have convinced all those who see in Aquinas the "arbiter" of all theological and philosophical disputes of their age: its permanent quest for moderation and conciliation between extremes, which lies at the heart of its scholastic method of objections, conclusion and responses, and which consistently allowed Thomism to be presented as some sort of middle way between extremes – such as naturalism and supernaturalism, fideism and rationalism, voluntarism and intellectualism, legal positivism and naturalism, libertarianism and compatibilism, realism and idealism, etc. As noted by Massoulié, "between opposing doctrines, the middle path is always Saint Thomas' doctrine" (Massoulié, *Divus Thomas*, p. 7).

Bibliography

Adams, M.M., *What Sort of Human Nature? Medieval Philosophy and the Systematics of Christology* (Milwaukee, WI: Marquette University Press, 1999)
  Some Later Medieval Theories of the Eucharist: Thomas Aquinas, Giles of Rome, Duns Scotus, and William Ockham (Oxford: Oxford University Press, 2010)
Aertsen, J.A., *Medieval Philosophy and the Transcendentals: The Case of Thomas Aquinas* (Leiden: Brill, 1996)
Andrés Martín, M., *La teología española en el siglo XVI* (Madrid: Edica, 1976)
Anscombe, G.E.M. and P.T. Geach, *Three Philosophers* (Oxford: Basil Blackwell, 1961)
Avo, N. (ed.), *The Sermon-Conferences of St. Thomas Aquinas on the Apostles' Creed* (Notre Dame, IN: University of Notre Dame Press, 1988)
Barnwell, M., "The Problem with Aquinas's Original Discovery," *American Catholic Philosophical Quarterly* 89/2 (2015), 277–91
Barrientos García, J., "La teología de la Universidad de Salamanca en los siglos XVI y XVII," in L.E. Rodríguez-San Pedro Bezares and J.L. Polo Rodríguez (eds.), *Saberes y disciplinas en las Universidades Hispánicas* (Salamanca: Ediciones Universidad de Salamanca, 2004), pp. 51–96
Barth, K., *Church Dogmatics I/2*, translated by G.T. Thomson and H. Knight (Edinburgh: T. & T. Clark, 1956)
Bastit, M., *Naissance de la loi moderne: La Pensée de la loi de Saint Thomas à Suarez* (Paris: Presses Universitaires de France, 1990)
Bataillon, L.-J., "Recherches sur le texte de la prima pars de la Summa theologiae de Thomas d'Aquin," in J. Hamesse (ed.), *Roma, Magistra Mundi: Itineraria Culturae Medievalis. Mélanges Offerts au Père L.E. Boyle à l'occasion de son 75ᵉ Anniversaire* (Louvain: Fidem, 1998), pp. 11–24
Bauer, E., *Thomistische Metaphysik an der alten Benediktineruniversität Salzburg* (Innsbruck: Tyrolia, 1996)
Belda Plans, J., *La Escuela de Salamanca y la renovación de la teología en el siglo XVI* (Madrid: BAC Maior, 2000)
Beltrán de Heredia, V., *Domingo Báñez y las controversias sobre la gracia: Textos y documentos* (Madrid and Salamanca: CSIC and Biblioteca de Teólogos Españoles, 1968)
Berger, D. and J. Vijgen (eds.), *Thomisten-Lexikon* (Bonn: Nova & Vetera, 2006)

Billot, L., *De personali et originali peccato. Commentarius in Primam Secundae (qq. 71–89) Quarta editio* (Prato: ex officina libraria Giachetti, Filii et Soc., 1910)

"La providence et le nombre infini d'hommes en dehors de la voie normale du salut," *Etudes* 161 (1919), 129–49; 162 (1920), 129–152; 163 (1920), 5–32; 164 (1920), 385–404; 165 (1920), 515–35; 167 (1921), 257–79; 169 (1921), 385–407; 172 (1922), 513–35.

Boland, V., *Ideas in God according to Saint Thomas Aquinas* (Leiden, New York, and Köln: E. J. Brill, 1996)

Bonansea, B.M. 1954, "Pioneers of the Nineteenth-Century Scholastic Revival in Italy," *The New Scholasticism* 28/1 (1954), 1–37

Bouchard, C., "Recovering the Gifts of the Holy Spirit in Moral Theology," *Theological Studies* 63 (2002), 539–58

Bouillard, H., *Conversion et grâce chez S. Thomas d'Aquin* (Aubier: Montaigne, 1944)

Boyle, L.E., O.P., "A Remembrance of Pope Leo XIII: The Encyclical *Aeterni Patris*," in V.B. Brezik (ed.), *One Hundred Years of Thomism. Aeterni Patris and Afterwards* (Houston, TX: Center for Thomistic Studies, 1981), pp. 7–22

The Setting of the Summa Theologiae of Saint Thomas Aquinas, *The Etienne Gilson Series*, vol. 5 (Toronto: PIMS, 1982)

Boyle, J., "The Twofold Division of St. Thomas's Christology in the Tertia Pars," *The Thomist* 60 (1996), 439–47

"St. Thomas and the Analogy of *Potentia Generandi*," *The Thomist* 64 (2000), 581–92

Bradley, D.J.M., *Aquinas on the Twofold Human Good: Reason and Happiness in Aquinas's Moral Science* (Washington, DC: The Catholic University Press of America, 1997)

Brants, V., "La création de la chaire de théologie scolastique et la nomination de Malderus à l'Université en 1596," *Analectes pour servir à l'histoire ecclésiastique de la Belgique* 4 (1908), 46–54

Broggio, P., *La teologia e la politica: Controversie dottrinali, Curia romana e Monarchia spagnola tra Cinque e Seicento* (Florence: Leo S. Olschki, 2009)

Brower, J.E., *Aquinas's Ontology of the Material World: Change, Hylomorphism, and Material Objects* (Oxford: Oxford University Press, 2014)

"Aquinas on the Problem of Universals," *Philosophy and Phenomenological Research* 92 (2016), 715–35

Brown, B.F., *Accidental Being: A Study in the Metaphysics of St. Thomas Aquinas* (Lanham, MD: University Press of America, 1985)

Calder, T., "Is the Privation Theory of Evil Dead?," *American Philosophical Quarterly* 44 (2007), 371–78

Cates, D.F., *Aquinas on the Emotions: A Religious-Ethical Inquiry* (Washington, DC: Georgetown University Press, 2009)

Cessario, R., O.P., *Christian Faith and Theological Life* (Washington, DC: The Catholic University of America Press, 1996)

A Short History of Thomism (Washington, DC: The Catholic University of America Press, 2005)

Chase, M., "The Medieval Posterity of Simplicius' Commentary on the *Categories*: Thomas Aquinas and Al-Farabi," in L.A. Newton (ed.), *Medieval Commentaries on Aristotle's Categories* (Leiden–Boston: E. J. Brill, 2008), pp. 9–29

Chênevert, J., "Le verbum dans le Commentaire sur les Sentences de saint Thomas d'Aquin," *Sciences Ecclesiastiques* 13 (1961) 191–223 and 359–90

Chenu, M.-D., "Le plan de la somme théologique de Saint Thomas," *Revue Thomiste* 47 (1939), 93–107

La Théologie comme science au XIIIᵉ siècle, 3rd ed. (Paris: Vrin, 1957)

Toward Understanding Saint Thomas, translated by A.-M. Landry and D. Hughes (Chicago, IL: H. Regnery Company, 1964)

"Les passions vertueuses: L'anthropologie de saint Thomas," *Revue philosophique de Louvain* 72 (1974), 11–18

Une École de Théologie : le Saulchoir (Kain-lez-Tournai: Le Saulchoir, 1937; repr. Paris: Editions du Cerf, 1985)

Coleman, J., "MacIntyre and Aquinas," in J. Horton and S. Mendes (eds.), *After MacIntyre: Critical Perspectives on the Work of Alasdair MacIntyre* (Notre Dame, IN: University of Notre Dame Press, 1994), pp. 65–90

Colombo, G., "La manualistica," in R. Fisichella (ed.), *Storia della teologia*, vol. 3. (Bologna: Edizioni Dehoniane, 1996), pp. 309–36

Congar, Y., *Situations et tâches présentes de la théologie* (Paris: Éditions du Cerf, 1967)

Coreth, E., W. Neidl, and G. Pfligersdorffer (eds.), *Christliche Philosophie, vol. 2: Rückgriff auf scholastisches Erbe* (Graz, Vienna & Cologne: Styria, 1988)

Crosby, J.F., "Is All Evil Really Only Privation?," *Proceedings of the American Catholic Philosophical Association 2001* 75 (2002), 197–209

Crowe, M., *The Changing Profile of the Natural Law* (The Hague: Martinus Nijhoff, 1977)

Curran, C.E., "Roman Catholic Christianity," in J. Neusner (ed.), *God's Rule: The Politics of World Religions* (Washington, DC: Georgetown University Press, 2003), pp. 61–84

Dancy, J., *Ethics without Principles* (Oxford: Oxford University Press, 2006)

Davies, B., "*Is Sacra Doctrina* Theology?," *New Blackfriars* 71 1990, 141–7

Thomas Aquinas's 'Summa Theologiae': A Guide and Commentary (Oxford and New York: Oxford University Press, 2014)

Davies, B. and B. Leftow (eds.), *Thomas Aquinas: Summa Theologiae Questions on God* (Cambridge: Cambridge University Press, 2006)

DeCosimo, D., *Ethics as a Work of Charity: Thomas Aquinas and Pagan Virtue* (Stanford, CA: Stanford University Press, 2014).

De Franceschi, S.H., "Thomisme et thomistes dans le débat théologique à l'âge classique: Jalons historiques pour une caractérisation doctrinale," in

Y. Krumenacker and L. Thirouin (eds.), *Les écoles de pensée religieuse à l'époque moderne* (Lyon: Université Jean Moulin-Lyon III, 2006) pp. 65–109

Entre saint Augustin et Saint Thomas: Les jansénistes et le refuge thomiste (1653–63) (Paris: Nolin, 2009)

"L'empire thomiste dans les querelles doctrinales de l'âge classique. Le statut théologique de Thomas d'Aquin au XVIIe siècle," *XVIIe siècle* 62/2 (2010), 313–34

La puissance et la gloire: L'orthodoxie thomiste au péril du jansénisme (1663–1724) (Paris: Nolin, 2011)

"L'exténuation de la querelle de la grâce au miroir de la Somme de théologie. Le *Cursus theologiae* (1746–51) du P. Billuart et l'opposition entre thomistes et molinistes," *Revue des sciences philosophiques et théologiques* 100 (2016), 353–84

Deman, T., "Probabilisme," in A. Vacant and E. Mangenot (eds.), *Dictionnaire de théologie catholique*, vol. 13. (Paris: Letouzey & Ané, 1936) col. 417–619

Den Bok, N., *Communicating the Most High: A Systematic Study of Person and Trinity in the Theology of Richard of St. Victor* (Paris and Turnhout: Brepols, 1996)

Dewan, L., O.P., "St. Thomas and the First Cause of Moral Evil," in L. Dewan (ed.), *Wisdom, Law and Virtue: Essays in Thomistic Ethics* (New York, NY: Fordham University Press, 2007), pp. 186–96

Dixon, T., *From Passions to Emotions: The Creation of a Secular Psychological Category* (New York, NY: Cambridge University Press, 2003)

Donnelly, J.P., "Calvinist Thomism," *Viator* 1 (1976), 441–55

Doolan, G.T., *Aquinas on the Divine Ideas as Exemplar Causes* (Washington, DC: The Catholic University of America, 2008)

Dougherty, M.V., "Aquinas on the Self-Evidence of the Articles of Faith," *The Heythrop Journal* 46 (2005), 167–80

Dougherty, M. V., *Moral Dilemmas in Medieval Thought: From Gratian to Aquinas* (Cambridge: Cambridge University Press, 2011)

Doyle, J., "St. Thomas Aquinas on Theological Truth," in K. Emery, Jr., R.L. Friedman, and A. Speer (eds.), *Philosophy and Theology in the Long Middle Ages: A Tribute to Stephen F. Brown* (Leiden/Boston: Brill, 2011), pp. 571–89

Dulles, A., *The Assurance of Things Hoped For: A Theology of Christian Faith* (New York, NY: Oxford University Press, 1994)

Elders, L., *Faith and Science: An Introduction to St. Thomas's Expositio in Boethii De Trinitate* (Rome: Herder, 1974)

Emery, G., "La procession du Saint-Esprit a Filio chez S. Thomas d'Aquin," *Revue Thomiste* 96 (1996), 531–74

Trinity in Aquinas (Ypsilanti, MI: Sapientia Press, 2003)

"The Procession of the Holy Spirit *a Filio* according to St. Thomas Aquinas," in *Trinity in Aquinas*, translated by Heather Buttery (Naples, FL: Sapientia Press, 2006), pp. 209–69

Farley, E., *Theologia: The Fragmentation and Unity of Theological Education* (Philadelphia, PA: Fortress Press, 1983)

Filser, H., *Dogma, Dogmen, Dogmatik: Eine Untersuchung zur Begründung und zur Entstehungsgeschichte einer theologischen Disziplin von der Reformation bis zur Spätaufklärung* (Münster: LIT, 2001)

Flew, Anthony, "Theology and Falsification," in A. Flew and A. MacIntyre (eds.), *New Essays in Philosophical Theology* (London: SCM Press, 1955)

Fourcade, M. and D. Avon (eds.), *Un nouvel âge de la théologie? 1965–80* (Paris: Karthala, 2009)

Friedman, R., "Relations, Emanations, and Henry of Ghent's Use of the *Verbum Mentis* in Trinitarian Theology: The Background in Thomas Aquinas and Bonaventure," *Documenti e studi sulla tradizione filosofica medievale* 7 (1996), 131–82

Intellectual Traditions at the Medieval University: The Use of Philosophical Psychology in Trinitarian Theology among the Franciscans and Dominicans, 1250–1350 (Leiden: Brill, 2013)

Gaetano, M., *Renaissance Thomism at the University of Padua, 1465–1533*, Ph.D. Dissertation (Philadelphia, PA: University of Pennsylvania, 2013)

García Villoslada, R., *La Universidad de París durante los estudios de Francisco de Vitoria* (Roma: Universitas Gregoriana, 1938)

Gardeil, A., *La Crédibilité et l'apologétique*, revised edition (Paris: Gabalda, 1928)

Garrigou-Lagrange, R., O.P., *De Revelatione per Ecclesiam Catholicam Proposita*, 4th ed., 2 vols. (Rome: Ferrari, 1945)

Gasson, J.A., "The Internal Senses – Functions or Powers? Part I," *The Thomist* 26 (1963), 1–14

Gay, J.-P., *Morales en conflit: Théologie et polémique au Grand Siècle (1640–1700)* (Paris: Éditions du Cerf, 2011)

Geach, P., "Identity," *Review of Metaphysics* 21 (1967), 3–12

Gelber, H., *Logic and the Trinity: A Clash of Values in Scholastic Thought, 1300–1335*, Ph.D. Dissertation (Madison, WI: University of Wisconsin, 1974)

George, R.P., *Making Men Moral: Civil Liberties and Public Morality* (New York, NY: Oxford University Press, 1993)

Gondreau, P., *The Passions of Christ's Soul in the Theology of St. Thomas Aquinas* (Münster: Aschendorff Verlag, 2003)

"The Passions and the Moral Life: Appreciating the Originality of Aquinas," *The Thomist* 71 (2007), 419–50

Goris, H., "Thomism in Fifteenth-Century Germany," in P. van Geest, H. Goris, and P. Leget (eds.), *Aquinas as Authority* (Louvain: Peeters, 2002)

Gorman, M., "Incarnation" in B. Davies and E. Stump (eds.), *The Oxford Handbook of Aquinas* (Oxford: Oxford University Press, 2012), pp. 428–35

Aquinas on the Metaphysics of the Hypostatic Union (New York, NY: Cambridge University Press, 2017)

Goudriaan, A., *Reformed Orthodoxy and Philosophy, 1625–1750* (Leiden: E.J. Brill, 2006)

Grabmann, M., "Das Naturrecht der Scholastik von Gratian bis Thomas von Aquin," in Vol. I of *Mittelalterliches Geistesleben: Abhandlungen zur Geschichte der Scholastik und Mystik*, 3 vols. (München: Hueber, 1926), pp. 65–103

Grafton, A., *Forgers and Critics: Creativity and Duplicity in Western Scholarship* (Princeton, NJ: Princeton University Press, 1990)

Grant, W.M., "The Privation Account of Moral Evil: A Defense," *International Philosophical Quarterly* 55 (2015), 271–86

Grisez, G., "The First Principle of Practical Reason: A Commentary on the Summa Theologiae, 1–2, Question 94, Article 2," *Natural Law Forum* 10 (1965), 168–201

Guelluy, R., "L'évolution des méthodes théologiques à Louvain, d'Erasme à Jansénius," *Revue d'histoire ecclésiastique* 37 (1941), 31–144

Gunten, A.F., "In principio erat verbum. Une évolution de saint Thomas en théologie trinitaire," in C.J. Pinto de Oliveira (ed.), *Ordo Sapientiae et Amoris: Image et message de Saint Thomas d'Aquin à travers les récentes études historiques, herméneutiques et doctrinales: hommage au professeur Jean-Pierre Torrell O.P. à l'occasion de son 65e anniversaire* (Fribourg: Editions Universitaires, 1993), pp. 119–41

Haldane, J. (ed.), *Modern Writings on Thomism*, vol. 2 (Bristol: Thoemmes-Continuum, 2004)

Hankey, W.J., *God in Himself. Aquinas' Doctrine of God as Expounded in the Summa theologiae* (Oxford: Oxford University Press, 1987)

Hause, J., "Aquinas's Complex Web," in S. Hetherington (ed.), *What Makes a Philosopher Great? Arguments for Twelve Philosophers* (London: Routledge, 2017), pp. 86–103.

Hell, L., *Entstehung und Entfaltung der theologischen Enzyklopädie* (Mainz: von Zabern, 1999)

Hofmann, M., *Theologie, Dogma und Dogmenentwicklung im theologischen Werk Denis Petau's* (Bern etc.: Peter Lang, 1976)

Hoffmann, T., "Aquinas on the Moral Progress of the Weak Willed," in T. Hoffmann, J. Müller, and M. Perkams (eds.), *The Problem of Weakness of Will in Medieval Thought* (Leuven: Peeters, 2006), pp. 221–47

"Prudence and Practical Principles," in T. Hoffmann, J. Müller, and M. Perkams (eds.), *Aquinas and the Nicomachean Ethics* (Cambridge: Cambridge University Press, 2013), pp. 165–83

Hoffmann, T., J. Müller, and M. Perkams (eds.), *Aquinas and the Nicomachean Ethics* (Cambridge: Cambridge University Press, 2013)

Honnefelder, L. "The Evaluation of Goods and the Estimation of Consequences: Aquinas on the Determination of the Moral Good," in S.J. Pope (ed.), *The Ethics of Aquinas* (Washington, DC: Georgetown University Press, 2002), pp. 426–36

Hübener, W., "Praedeterminatio Physica," in *Historisches Wörterbuch der Philosophie*, vol. 7 (Basel: Schwabe & Co., 1976), col. 1216–25

Hughes, C., *On a Complex Theory of a Simple God* (Ithaca, NY: Cornell University Press, 1989)

Aquinas on Being, Goodness, and God (Oxford and New York: Routledge, 2015)

Jenkins, J.I., *Knowledge and Faith in Thomas Aquinas* (Cambridge: Cambridge University Press, 1997)

Jensen, S.J., "When Evil Actions Become Good," *Nova et Vetera*, English Edition, 5 (2007), 747–64

Jeynes, W. and D.W. Robinson (eds.), *International Handbook of Protestant Education* (Dordrecht: Springer, 2012)

Johnstone, B., "The Debate on the Structure of the *Summa theologiae* of St. Thomas Aquinas: From Chenu (1939) to Metz (1998)," in P. van Geest, H. Goris, and P. Leget (eds.), *Aquinas as Authority* (Louvain: Peeters, 2002), pp. 187–200

Kennedy, L.A., *A Catalogue of Thomists, 1270–1900* (Houston, TX: Center for Thomistic Studies, 1987)

Kenny, A., "Form, Existence and Essence in Aquinas," in H.A. Lewis (ed.), *Peter Geach: Philosophical Encounters* (Dordrecht: Kluwer, 1991), pp. 65–75

Kent, B., *Virtues of the Will: The Transformation of Ethics in the Late Thirteenth Century* (Washington, DC: The Catholic University of America Press, 1995)

"Dispositions and Moral Fallibility: The Unaristotelian Aquinas," *History of Philosophy Quarterly* 29 (2012), 141–57

"Losable virtue: Aquinas on Character and Will," in T. Hoffmann, J. Müller, and M. Perkams (eds.), *Aquinas and the Nicomachean Ethics* (Cambridge: Cambridge University Press, 2013), pp. 91–109

Kent, B. and A. Dressel, "Weakness and Willful Wrongdoing in Aquinas's *De malo*," in M.V. Dougherty (ed.), *Aquinas's Disputed Questions on Evil: A Critical Guide* (Cambridge: Cambridge University Press, 2016), pp. 34–55.

Kerr, F., *After Aquinas: Versions of Thomism* (Oxford: Blackwell Publishing, 2002)

Klima, G., "Thomistic 'Monism' vs. Cartesian 'Dualism'," *Logical Analysis and History of Philosophy* 10 (2007), 92–112

Kluxen, W., *Philosophische Ethik bei Thomas von Aquin* (Darmstadt: Wissenschaftliche Buchgesellschaft, 1998)

Knebel, S.K., *Wille, Würfel und Wahrscheinlichkeit: Das System der moralischen Notwendigkeit in der Jesuitenscholastik 1550–1700* (Hamburg: Felix Meiner, 2000)

Knobel, A.M., "Two Theories of Christian Virtue," *American Catholic Philosophical Quarterly*, 84 (2010), 599–618

"Relating Aquinas's Infused and Acquired Virtues: Some Problematic Texts for a Common Interpretation," *Nova et Vetera*, English Edition, 9 (2011), 411–31

Knuuttila, S., *Emotions in Ancient and Medieval Philosophy* (New York, NY: Oxford University Press, 2004)

Komonchak, J.A., "Thomism and the Second Vatican Council," in A.J. Cernera (ed.), *Continuity and Plurality in Catholic Theology. Essays in Honor of Gerald A. McCool S.J.* (Fairfield, CT: Sacred Heart University Press, 1998), pp. 53–73

Kretzmann, N., "Infallibility, Error, and Ignorance," *Canadian Journal of Philosophy* 21, suppl. 1 (1991), 159–94

The Metaphysics of Creation: Aquinas's Natural Theology in Summa Contra Gentiles II (Oxford: Clarendon Press, 1999)

Lamont, J., "Aquinas on Subsistent Relation," *Recherches de Théologie et Philosophie Médiévales* 71 (2004), 260–79

Lang, A., *Die Entfaltung des apologetischen Problems in der Scholastick des Mittelalters* (Freiburg/Vasel/Wein: Herder, 1962)

Lanza, L. and M. Toste, "The Sentences in Sixteenth-Century Iberian Scholasticism," in P. Rosemann (ed.), *Mediaeval Commentaries on the Sentences of Peter Lombard*, vol. 3 (Leiden: E.J. Brill, 2015), pp. 416–503

Laporte, J.-M., "Christ in Aquinas's *Summa Theologiae*: Peripheral or Pervasive?" *The Thomist* 67 (2003), 221–48

Lécrivain, Ph., "La Somme théologique de Thomas d'Aquin aux 16ème -18ème siècles," *Recherches de Science Religieuse* 91/3 (2003), 397–427

Leftow, B., "Aquinas on Attributes," *Medieval Philosophy and Theology* 11 (2003), 1–41

God and Necessity (Oxford: Oxford University Press, 2012)

Lisska, A., *Aquinas's Theory of Natural Law: An Analytic Reconstruction* (Oxford: Clarendon Press, 1996)

Lombardo, N.E., O.P., *The Logic of Desire: Aquinas on Emotion* (Washington, DC: The Catholic University of America Press, 2011)

Lonergan, B., *Verbum: Word and Idea in Aquinas*, D. Burrell (ed.) (University of Notre Dame Press, 1967), first published as "The Concept of Verbum in the Writings of St. Thomas Aquinas," *Theological Studies* 7 (1946), 349–92; 8 (1947), 35–79 and 404–44; 10 (1949), 3–40 and 359–93

Lottin, O., *Le droit naturel chez saint Thomas d'Aquin et ses prédécesseurs*, 2nd edition (Bruges: Beyart, 1931)

"La Loi éternelle chez saint Thomas d'Aquin et ses prédécesseurs," in O. Lottin (ed.), *Psychologie et morale aux XIIe et XIIIe siècles*, 6 vols., vol. 2 (Louvain: Abbaye du Mont César, 1942), pp. 51–67

Luna, C., "Essenza divina e relazioni trinitarie nella critica di Egidio Romano a Tommaso d'Aquino," *Medioevo* 14 (1988), 3–69

MacIntyre, A., *After Virtue. A Study in Moral Theory* (Notre Dame: University of Notre Dame Press, 1981)

"Natural Law as Subversive: The Case of Aquinas," in A. MacIntyre (ed.), *Ethics and Politics: Selected Essays*, 2 vols. (Cambridge: Cambridge University Press, 2006), vol. 2, pp. 41–63

Mahoney, J., *The Making of Moral Theology: A Study of the Roman Catholic Tradition* (Oxford: Clarendon Press, 1987)

Malet, A., *Personne et Amour dans la théologie trinitaire de Saint Thomas d'Aquin* (Paris: Vrin, 1956)

Mandonnet, P., "La canonisation de saint Thomas d'Aquin, 1317–1323," in *Mélanges thomistes, publié par les Dominicains de la province de France à l'occasion du VIe centenaire de la canonisation de saint Thomas d'Aquin (18 juillet 1323)* (Kain-lez-Tournai: Le Saulchoir, 1923), pp. 1–48

Maritain, J., *Antimoderne* (Paris: Éditions de la Revue des Jeunes, 1922)

Martin, R.M., "L'introduction officielle de la *Somme théologique* dans l'ancienne Université de Louvain," *Revue thomiste* 18 (1910), 230–39

Martin, C.F.J., *Thomas Aquinas: God and Explanations* (Edinburgh: Edinburgh University Press, 1997)

Mattison III, W.C., "Can Christians Possess the Acquired Cardinal Virtues?" *Theological Studies* 72 (2011), 558–85

McAleer, G.J., "The Politics of the Flesh: Rahner and Aquinas on *Concupiscentia*," *Modern Theology* 15 (1999), 355–65
  Ecstatic Morality and Sexual Politics: A Catholic and Antitotalitarian Theory of the Body (New York, NY: Fordham University Press, 2005).

McCabe, H., *God Still Matters* (London: Continuum, 2002)

McCluskey, C., *Thomas Aquinas on Moral Wrongdoing* (Cambridge: Cambridge University Press, 2017)

McCool, G.A., *Catholic Theology in the Nineteenth Century: The Quest for a Unitary Method* (New York, NY: Seabury Press, 1977)
  From Unity to Pluralism: The Internal Evolution of Thomism (New York, NY: Fordham University Press, 1977)
  The Neo-Thomists (Milwaukee: Marquette University Press, 2004)

McDaniel, K., "Ways of Being," in D. Chalmers et al. (eds.), *Metametaphysics: New Essays on the Foundations of Ontology* (Oxford: Oxford University Press, 2009), pp. 290–319

McDermott, T. (ed.), *Thomas Aquinas: Selected Philosophical Writings* (Oxford and New York, NY: Oxford University Press, 1993)

McDowell, J., "Deliberation and Moral Development in Aristotle's Ethics," in S. Engstrom and J. Whiting (eds.), *Aristotle, Kant, and the Stoics* (Cambridge: Cambridge University Press, 1996), pp. 19–35. Reprinted in J. McDowell, *The Engaged Intellect. Philosophical Essays* (Cambridge, MA: Harvard University Press, 1996), pp. 41–58

McGinn, B., *Thomas Aquinas's Summa theologiae: A Biography* (Princeton, NJ: Princeton University Press, 2014)

Meissner, W., "Some Aspects of the *Verbum* in the Texts of St. Thomas," *The Modern Schoolman* 36 (1958), 1–30

Mettepenningen, J., *Nouvelle Théologie – New Theology: Inheritor of Modernism, Precursor of Vatican II* (London: Bloomsbury Academic, 2010)

Michelitsch, A., *Kommentatoren zur Summa theologiae des Hl. Thomas von Aquin* (Graz and Vienna: Styria, 1924)

Milbank, J. and C. Pickstock, *Truth in Aquinas* (London and New York, NY: Routledge, 2001)

Milosz, O.W., *Miguel Mañara* (Paris: Éditions de la Nouvelle Revue Française, 1913)

Miner, R., *Thomas Aquinas on the Passions: A Study of Summa Theologiae 1a2ae 22–48* (Cambridge: Cambridge University Press, 2009)

Müller, J., *"Duplex beatitudo*: Aristotle's Legacy and Aquinas's Conception of Human Happiness," in T. Hoffmann, J. Müller, and M. Perkams (eds.), *Aquinas and the Nicomachean Ethics* (Cambridge: Cambridge University Press, 2013), pp. 52–71

Mulligan, D., C.SS.R., "Moral Evil: St. Thomas and the Thomists," *Philosophical Studies* (Ireland) 9 (1958), 3–26

Mulvaney, R.J., "Wisdom, Time, and Avarice in St. Thomas Aquinas's Treatise on Prudence," *The Modern Schoolman* 69 (1992), 443–62

Murphy, C.E., "Aquinas on Our Responsibility for Our Emotions," *Medieval Philosophy and Theology* 8 (1999), 163–205

Murphy, M., *An Essay on Divine Authority*, Cornell Studies in the Philosophy of Religion (Ithaca, NY and London: Cornell University Press, 2002)

Murphy, W.F., "Aquinas on the Object and Evaluation of the Moral Act: Rhonheimer's Approach and Some Recent Interlocutors," *Josephinum Journal of Theology* 15 (2008), 205–42

Narciso, E.I., "Alle fonti del neotomismo," *Sapienza* 13 (1960), 124–47

La Summa philosophica di Salvatore Roselli e la rinascita del tomismo (Rome: Libreria Éditrice della Pontificia Università Lateranense, 1966)

Niederbacher, B., *Glaube als Tugend bei Thomas von Aquin: Erkenntistheoretische und religionsphilosophische Interpretation* (Stuttgart: Kohlhammer, 2003)

Niemann, F.-J., "Fundamentaltheologie im 17. Jahrhundert," *Zeitschrift für katholische Theologie* 103 (1981), 178–85

"Zur Frühgeschichte des Begriffs Fundamentaltheologie," *Münchner Theologische Zeitschrift* 46/2 (1995), 247–60

Oderberg, D.S., "The Metaphysics of Privation," in R. Hüntelmann and J. Hattler (eds.), *New Scholasticism Meets Analytic Philosophy* (Heusenstamm: Editiones Scholasticae, 2014), pp. 63–88

"Divine Premotion," *International Journal of the Philosophy of Religion* 79 (2016), 207–22

Osborne, Jr., T.M., "Perfect and Imperfect Virtues in Aquinas," *The Thomist* 71 (2007), 39–64

"Augustine and Aquinas on Foreknowledge through Causes," *Nova et Vetera*, English Edition 6 (2008), 219–32

Paissac, H., *Théologie du Verbe, saint Augustin et saint Thomas* (Paris: Cerf, 1951)

Panaccio, C., "From Mental Word to Mental Language," *Philosophical Topics* 20 (1992), 125–147

Pasnau, R., *Theories of Cognition in the Later Middle Ages* (Cambridge: Cambridge University Press, 1997)

Thomas Aquinas on Human Nature: A Philosophical Study of Summa theologiae 1a 75–89 (Cambridge: Cambridge University Press, 2002)

Thomas Aquinas. The Treatise on Human Nature: Summa theologiae, 1a 75–89 (Indianapolis, IN: Hackett, 2002)

Metaphysical Themes 1274–1671 (Oxford: Clarendon Press, 2011)

Paterson, C. and M.S. Pugh (eds.), *Analytical Thomism: Traditions in Dialogue* (London: Routledge, 2006)

Peddicord, R., *The Sacred Monster of Thomism. An Introduction to the Life and Legacy of Réginald Garrigou-Lagrange, O.P.* (South Bend: St Augustine's Press, 2005)**

Pègues, Thomas, *Catechism of the "Summa theologica" of Saint Thomas Aquinas, for the Use of the Faithful*, translated by A. Whitacre (New York, NY: Benzinger, 1922; 1st French edn., 1918)

Peifer, J.F., *The Concept in Thomism* (New York, NY: Bookman, 1952)

Pelikan, J., "The Doctrine of *Filioque* in Thomas Aquinas and its Patristic Antecedents," in A. Maurer et al. (eds.), *St. Thomas Aquinas 1274–1974: Commemorative Studies* (Toronto: Pontifical Institute of Mediaeval Studies, 1974), pp. 315–36

Penelhum, T. "The Analysis of Faith in St. Thomas Aquinas," *Religious Studies* 13 (1977), 133–54

Perkams, M., *Liebe als Zentralbegriff der Ethik nach Peter Abelard* (Münster: Aschendorff, 2001)

"Gewissensirrtum und Gewissensfreiheit: Überlegungen im Anschluss an Thomas von Aquin und Albertus Magnus," *Philosophisches Jahrbuch* 112 (2005), 31–50

"Naturgesetz, Selbstbestimmung und Moralität: Thomas von Aquin und die Begründung einer zeitgemässen Ethik," *Studia Neoaristotelica* 5 (2008), 109–31

"Aquinas on Choice, Will, and Voluntary Action," in T. Hoffmann, J. Müller, and M. Perkams (eds.), *Aquinas and the Nicomachean Ethics* (Cambridge: Cambridge University Press, 2013), pp. 72–90

Perrier, E., *La fécondité en Dieu: La puissance notionnelle dans la Trinité selon saint Thomas d'Aquin* (Paris: Parole et Silence, 2009)

Philipps, R.P., *Modern Thomistic Philosophy: An Explanation for Students*, 2 vols. (London: Burns, Oates & Washbourne, 1934–35)

Pilsner, J., *The Specification of Human Actions in St Thomas Aquinas* (Oxford: Oxford University Press, 2006)

Pinckaers, S., "Virtue is Not a Habit," translated by Bernard Gilligan, *Cross Currents* 12 (1962), 65–81

Passions & Virtue, translated by B.M. Guevin (Washington, DC: The Catholic University of America Press, 2015)

Pini, G., "Henry of Ghent's Doctrine of *Verbum* in its Theological Context," in G. Guldentops and C. Steel (eds.), *Henry of Ghent and the Transformation of Scholastic Thought: Studies in Memory of Jos Decorte* (Leiden: Leiden University Press, 2003), pp. 307–26

Plassmann, H.E., *Vorhallen zur Philosophie der Schule des Heiligen Thomas*, 5 vols. (Soest: Verlag der Nasse'schen Buchhandlung, 1858–61)

Plested, M., *Orthodox Readings of Aquinas* (Oxford: Oxford University Press, 2012)

Porter, J., "The Unity of the Virtues and the Ambiguity of Goodness: A Reappraisal of Aquinas's Theory of the Virtues," *Journal of Religious Ethics* 21 (1993), 137–63

Natural and Divine Law: Reclaiming the Tradition for Christian Ethics (Grand Rapids, MI: Eerdmans, 1999)

"What the Wise Person Knows: Natural Law and Virtue in Aquinas's *Summa Theologiae*," *Studies in Christian Ethics* 12 (1999), 57–69

Nature as Reason: A Thomistic Theory of the Natural Law (Grand Rapids, MI and Cambridge: William B. Eerdmans Publishing Company, 2005)

Prouvost, G., *Thomas d'Aquin et les thomismes* (Paris: Éditions du Cerf, 1996)

Quinto, R., *Scholastica: Storia di un concetto* (Padua: Il Poligrafo, 2001)

Rahner, K., *The Trinity*, translated by J. Donceel (New York, NY: The Crossroad Publishing Company, 1999)

Ramírez, S., O.P., *De Actibus Humanis. In I–II Summae Theologiae Divi Thomae Expositio (qq. VI–XXI)*, in V. Rodríguez, O.P. (ed.), *Edición de las Obras Completas de Santiago Ramírez, O.P.*, vol. 4 (Madrid: Consejo Superior de Investigaciones Científicas, 1972)

Ramos, A., "Moral Beauty and Affective Knowledge in Aquinas," *Acta Philosophica* 13 (2004), 321–37

de Régnon, T., *Études de théologie positive sur la sainte Trinité*, 4 vols. (Paris: Victor Retaux, 1892–98)

Reichberg, G. M., "Beyond Privation: Moral Evil in Aquinas's *De Malo*," *The Review of Metaphysics* 55 (2002), 751–84

Richard, R., *The Problem of an Apologetical Perspective in the Trinitarian Theology of St. Thomas Aquinas* (Rome: Gregorian University Press, 1963)

Riley, B., "Colour for the Painter," in T. Lamb and J. Bourriau (eds.), *Colour: Art and Science* (Cambridge: Cambridge University Press, 1995) pp. 31–64

Rhonheimer, M., *Praktische Vernunft und Vernünftigkeit der Praxis. Handlungstheorie bei Thomas von Aquin in ihrer Entstehung aus dem Problemkontext der aristotelischen Ethik* (Berlin: Akademie Verlag, 1994)

"The Perspective of the Acting Person and the Nature of Practical Reason: The 'Object of the Human Act' in Thomistic Anthropology of Action," *Nova et Vetera*, English Edition 2 (2004), 461–516

Robiglio, A.A., *La sopravvivenza e la gloria. Appunti sulla formazione della prima scuola tomista (sec. XIV)* (Bologna: ESD, 2008)

Roensch, F.J., *Early Thomistic School* (Dubuque, IA: Priory Press, 1964)

Ross, J., "Aquinas on Belief and Knowledge," in W.A. Frank and G.J. Etzkorn (eds.), *Essays Honoring Allan B. Wolter* (St. Bonaventure, NY: The Franciscan Institute, 1985), pp. 245–69

Rossi, G.F., *Il movimento neotomista piacentino iniziato al Collegio Alberoni da Francesco Grassi nel 1751 e la formazione di Vincenzo Buzzetti* (Città del Vaticano: Editrice Vaticana, 1974)

Rousselot, P., *The Eyes of Faith*, translated by J. Donceel (New York, NY: Forham University Press, 1990)

Shanley, B.J., "Is Sacra Doctrina Science?," *New Blackfriars* 71 (1990), 141–47

"Thomas Aquinas on Demonstrating God's Providence," in G.T. Doolan (ed.), *The Science of Being as Being: Metaphysical Investigations* (Washington, DC: The Catholic University of America Press, 2012), pp. 221–42

Scheffczyk, L., *Theologie in Aufbruch und Widerstreit: Die deutsche katholische Theologie im 19. Jahrhundert* (Bremen: Schünemann, 1965)

Schmaus, M., *Der Liber propugnatorius des Thomas Anglicus und die Lehrunterschiede zwischen Thomas von Aquin und Duns Scotus*, 2 vols. (Münster: Aschendorff, 1930)

Schmidbaur, H.C., *Personarum Trinitas. Die trinitarische Gotteslehre des heiligen Thomas von Aquin* (St. Ottilien: EOS Verlag, 1995)

Schmidinger, H., "Der Streit um die Anfänge der italienischen Neuscholastik," in E. Coreth, W. Neidl, and G. Pfligersdorffer (eds.), *Christliche Philosophie, vol. 2: Rückgriff auf scholastisches Erbe* (Graz, Vienna & Cologne: Styria, 1988), pp. 72–82

Schmutz, J., "*Bellum scholasticum*: Thomisme et antithomisme dans les débats doctrinaux modernes," *Revue thomiste* 108/1 (2008), 131–82

"Les normes théologiques de l'enseignement philosophique dans le catholicisme romain moderne (1500–1650)," in J.-C. Bardout (ed.), *Philosophie et théologie à l'époque moderne* (Paris: Éditions du Cerf, 2010), pp. 129–50

Schoof, M., *A Survey of Catholic Theology, 1800–1970*, translated by N.D. Smith (Glen Rock, NJ: Paulist Newman, 1970)

Schröer, C., *Praktische Vernunft bei Thomas von Aquin* (Stuttgart u.a.: Kohlhammer, 1995)

Schüssler, R., 2003, *Moral im Zweifel*, 2 vols. (Paderborn: Mentis, 2003–06)

Sertillanges, A.-D., *Foundations of Thomistic Philosophy*, translated by G. Anstruther (Saint Louis, MO: B. Herder Book Co., 1931)

Shanley, B.J., "Thomas Aquinas on Demonstrating God's Providence," in G.T. Doolan (ed.), *The Science of Being as Being: Metaphysical Investigations* (Washington, DC: The Catholic University of America Press, 2012), pp. 221–42

Sherwin, M., *By Knowledge and By Love: Charity and Knowledge in the Moral Theology of Thomas Aquinas* (Washington, DC: Catholic University of America Press, 2005)

Shields, C., *Order in Multiplicity. Homonymy in the Philosophy of Aristotle* (Oxford: Clarendon Press, 1999)

Shields, C. and R. Pasnau, *The Philosophy of Aquinas*, 2nd edition (New York, NY: Oxford University Press, 2016)

Smit, H., "Aquinas's Abstractionism," *Medieval Philosophy and Theology* 10 (2001), 85–118

Sparrow, M.F., "Natural Knowledge of God and the Principles of 'Sacra Doctrina'," *Angelicum* 69 (1992), 471–91

Still, C., "'Gifted Knowledge': An Exception to Thomistic Epistemology?," *The Thomist* 63 (1999), 173–90

Stirnimann, H., '"Fundamentaltheologie" im frühen 18. Jahrhundert? Bemerkungen zum Gebrauch der Termini 'scholastische', 'positive' und 'Fundamentaltheologie', insbesondere bei Pierre Annat,' *Freiburger Zeitschrift für Philosophie und Theologie* 24 (1977), 460–76

Stohr, A., "Die Hauptrichtungen der Spekulativen Trinitätslehre in der Theologie des 13. Jahrhunderts," *Theologische Quartalschrift* 106 (1925), 113–35

Stolz, A., *Glaubensgnade und Glaubenslicht nach Thomas von Aquin* (Rome: Herder, 1933)

Stump, E., "Faith and Goodness," in G. Vesey (ed.), *The Philosophy in Christianity* (Cambridge: Cambridge University Press, 1989), pp. 167–91

"God's Simplicity," in B. Davies and E. Stump (eds.), *The Oxford Handbook of Aquinas* (Oxford and New York, NY: Oxford University Press, 2012)

Swinburne, R., *The Existence of God*, revised edition (Oxford: Clarendon Press, 1991)

The Coherence of Theism, revised ed. (Oxford: Clarendon Press, 1993)

The Christian God (Oxford: Clarendon Press, 1994)

Is There a God? (Oxford: Clarendon Press, 1996)

te Velde, R., *Aquinas on God: The 'Divine Science' of the* Summa Theologiae (Aldershot: Ashgate, 2006)

Theiner, J., *Die Entwicklung der Moraltheologie zur eigenständigen Disziplin* (Regensburg: Pustet, 1970)

Tierney, B., *The Idea of Natural Rights: Studies on Natural Rights, Natural Law and Church Law, 1150–1625* (Atlanta, GA: Scholars Press, 1977)

Torrell, J.-P., O.P., "Nature et grâce chez Thomas d'Aquin," *Revue thomiste* 101 (2001), 167–202

Initiation à saint Thomas d'Aquin, 3rd ed (Fribourg–Paris: Academic Press Fribourg–Éditions du Cerf, 1993 rev. 2008), English translation *Saint Thomas Aquinas*, vol. 1. *The Person and His Work*, translated by Robert Royal (Washington, DC: The Catholic University of America, 2005)

Aquinas's Summa: Background, Structure and Reception, translated by B.M. Guevin (Washington, DC: The Catholic University of America Press, 2005)

Toste, Marco, "The Commentaries on Thomas Aquinas' *Summa theologiae* Ia-IIae, qq. 90–108 in Sixteenth-Century Salamanca: A Study of the Extant Manuscripts," *Bulletin de philosophie médiévale* 55 (2013), 177–218

Tshibangu, T., *Théologie positive et théologie spéculative* (Louvain: Publications universitaires de Louvain, 1965)

Vagaggini, C., "La hantise des *rationes necessariae* de saint Anselme dans la théologie des processions trinitaires de saint Thomas," in J. Evrard (ed.), *Spicilegium Beccense. Congrès International du IXᵉ centenaire de l'arrivée d'Anselme au Bec* (Paris: Vrin, 1959), 103–39

Van Geest, P., H. Goris, and P. Leget (eds.), *Aquinas as Authority* (Louvain: Peeters, 2002)

Vanier, P., *Théologie trinitaire chez saint Thomas d'Aquin. Évolution du concept d'action notionnelle* (Paris: Vrin, 1953)

Verbeke, G., "L'éducation morale et les arts chez Aristote et Thomas d'Aquin," in I. Craemer-Ruegenberg and A. Speer (eds.), *Scientia und ars im Hoch- und Spätmittelalter* (Berlin: Walter de Gruyter, 1994), pp. 449–67

Vereecke, L., *De Guillaume d'Ockham à saint Alphonse de Liguori: Etudes d'histoire de la théologie morale moderne, 1300–1787* (Rome: Collegium S. Alfonsi de Urbe, 1986)

Vos, A., *Aquinas, Calvin and Contemporary Protestant Thought: A Critique of Protestant Views on the Thought of Thomas Aquinas* (Washington, DC: Christian University Press, 1985)

Wald, B., "*Rationalis naturae individua substantia*: Aristoteles, Boethius und der Begriff der Person im Mittelalter," in J. Aertsen and A. Speer (eds.), *Individuum und Individualität im Mittelalter* (Berlin and New York, NY: Walter de Gruyter, 1996), pp. 371–88

Waldschmidt, P.E., *The Notion and Problems of Credibility in St. Thomas and the Major Commentators* (Washington, DC: Holy Cross College, 1955)

Weisheipl, J., "The Revival of Thomism as a Christian Philosophy," in R. McInerny (ed.), *New Themes in Christian Philosophy* (Notre Dame: University of Notre Dame Press, 1968), pp. 164–85

Weisheipl, J.A., "The Meaning of *Sacra Doctrina* in Summa Theologiae I, q. 1," *The Thomist* 38 (1974), 49–80

Westberg, D., *Right Practical Reason. Aristotle, Action, and Prudence in Aquinas* (Oxford: Clarendon Press, 1994)

"Good and Evil in Human Acts (Ia IIae, qq. 18–21)," in S.J. Pope (ed.), *The Ethics of Aquinas* (Washington, DC: Georgetown University Press, 2002), pp. 90–102

White, V., *God the Unknown* (London: Harvill Press, 1956)

"Prelude to the Five Ways," in B. Davies (ed.), *Aquinas's Summa Theologiae: Critical Essays* (Lanham, MD: Rowman and Littlefield, 2006), pp. 26–44

Williams, C.J.F., *What is Existence?* (Oxford: Clarendon Press, 1981)

"Being," in P.L. Quinn and C. Taliaferro (eds.), *A Companion to Philosophy of Religion* (Oxford: Blackwell, 1997), pp. 223–28

Williams, Scott. "Augustine, Thomas Aquinas, Henry of Ghent, and John Duns Scotus: On the Theology of the Father's Intellectual Generation of the Word," *Recherches de Théologie et Philosophie médiévales* 77 (2010), 35–81

Wippel, J.F., "Thomas Aquinas and the Axiom 'What is Received is Received According to the Mode of the Receiver'," in R. Link-Salinger et al. (eds.), *A Straight Path: Studies in Medieval Philosophy and Culture: Essays in Honor of Arthur Hyman* (Washingon, DC: The Catholic University of America Press, 1988), pp. 279–89. Repr. in J.F. Wippel, *Metaphysical Themes in Thomas Aquinas II* (Washington, DC: The Catholic University of America Press, 2007), pp. 113–22

"Thomas Aquinas on Demonstrating God's Omnipotence," *Revue Internationale de Philosophie* 52 (1998), 227–47. Repr. in J.F. Wippel, *Metpahysical Themes in Thomas Aquinas II* (Washington, DC: The Catholic University of America Press, 2007), pp. 194–217

The Metaphysical Thought of Thomas Aquinas: From Finite Being to Uncreated Being (Washington, DC: The Catholic University of America Press, 2000)

"Thomas Aquinas on Philosophy and the Preambles of Faith," in G.T. Doolan (ed.), *The Science of Being as Being: Metaphysical Investigations* (Washington, DC: The Catholic University of America Press, 2012), pp. 196–220

Wittgenstein, L., *Tractatus Logico-Philosophicus*, translated by D.F. Pears and B.F. McGuinness (London: Routledge & Kegan Paul, 1991)

Zahora, T., "Thomist Scholarship and Plagiarism in the Early Enlightenment: Jacques Echard Reads the *Speculum Morale*, Attributed to Vincent of Beauvais," *Journal of the History of Ideas* 73/4 (2012), 515–36

Zeller, W., "Lutherische Orthodoxie und mittelalterliche Scholastik," *Theologie und Philosophie* 50 (1975), 527–46

Pre-1900 Works

Abelly, Louis, *Medulla theologica, ex sacris Scripturis, conciliorum pontificiumque decretis et sanctorum Patrum ac doctorum placitis expressa* (Paris: George Josse, 1650)

Alamanni, Cosmo, *Summa philosophiae D. Thomae*, 4 vols. (Paris: Pierre Billaine, 1639)

Antoine, Paul Gabriel, *Theologia universa speculativa et dogmatica*, 7 vols. (Paris: Jacques Clousier, 1736)

Arnauld, Antoine, *Lettres*, vol. 7 (Nancy: Joseph Nicolaï, 1727)

Averroës, *Commentarium magnum in Aristotelis De anima libros*, F.S. Crawford (ed.) (Cambridge, MA: The Medieval Academy of America, 1953)

Aristotle, *Nicomachean Ethics*, translated by W. D. Ross (Oxford: Oxford University Press, 1925)

The Complete Works of Aristotle: The Revised Oxford Translation, J. Barnes (ed.) (Princeton, NJ: Princeton University Press, 1984).

Aquinas, Thomas, *Opera omnia, iussu Leonis XIII edita cura et studio Fratrum Praedicatorum* (Rome: ex typographia polyglotta S. C. de Propaganda Fide, 1882–)

Quaestiones Disputatae De Anima, in Quaestiones Disputatae ad Fidem Optimarum Editionem (Paris: P. Lethielleux, 1884), vol. 2, pp. 163–278

Scriptum super libros Sententiarum magistri Petri Lombardi Episcopi Parisiensis, P.F. Mandonnet (vols. 1–2) and M.F. Moos (vols. 3–4) (eds.) (Paris: Lethielleux, 1929–47)

Le *"De Ente et Essentia" de S. Thomas D'Aquin*, (ed.) with introduction and notes by M.-D. Roland-Gosselin, O.P. (Paris: Librairie Philosophique J. Vrin, 1948)

Summa Theologiae, translated and edited by T. Gilby et al., Blackfriars translation, 60 vols., (London/New York, NY: Eyre and Spottiswoode/McGraw Hill, 1964–76)

Quaestiones de Quodlibet, vol. 25 of *Opera Omnia*

Babenstuber, Ludwig, *Philosophia Thomistica Salisburgensis* (Augsburg and Dillingen: Georg Schlüter and Johann Samuel Melso, 1706)

Bañez, Domingo, *Scholastica Commentaria in Secundam Secundae* (Venice: Pietro Maria Bertano, 1602; Douai: Borremans, 1615)

Baronius, Cesare, *Martyrologium Romanum* (Rome: Ex typographia Dominici Basae, 1586)

Cajetan, Thomas de Vio, O.P., *Commentaria in Summam theologiae Sancti Thomae Aquinatis*, printed together with the *Summa theologiae* in Aquinas, *Opera omnia* (1882-), vols. 4–12

Camblat, "Opusculum secundum de perpetua doctrinae S. Thomae Aquinatis in scholis et in ecclesia authoritate," in *Institutiones theologiae angelicae sive in auream summam S. Thomae Doctoris Angelici (...). Tomus primus* (Paris: Gilles Blaizot, n.p., 1663)

Collegium Conimbricense, S.J., *Commentarii (...) in tres libros De Anima Aristotelis Stagiritae* (Coimbra: António de Mariz, 1598)

De' Medici, Girolamo, *Formalis explicatio Summae theologiae D. Thomae Aquinatis Doctoris Angelici tribus partibus absoluta* (Venice: Ambrosio e Bartolomeo Dei, 1614–22)

Dorsche, Johann and Georg, D., *Thomas Aquinas exhibitus Confessor Veritatis Evangelicae Augustana Confessione repetitae* (Frankfurt/M.: sumptibus J.W. Ammonii, apud Nicolaum Schumannum, 1656)

Duns Scotus, John, *Doctoris subtilis et mariani Ioannis Duns Scoti Ordinis Fratrum Minorum Opera omnia*, C. Balić et al. (eds.) (Rome: Typis Vaticanis, 1950-)

Échard, Jacques, *Sancti Thomae summa suo auctori vindicata* (Paris: Jean-Baptiste Delespine, 1708)

Échard, Jacques and Jacques Quétif, *Scriptores Ordinis Praedicatorum, notisque historicis et criticis illustrati (...) Tomus primus* (Paris: J.-B.-Christophe Ballard & Nicolas Simart, 1719)

Eustachius a Sancto Paulo, *Summa philosophiae quadripartita* (Paris: Charles Chastellain, 1609)

Gazzaniga, Pietro Maria, *Theologia dogmatica in systema redacta* (Vienna: J.T. von Trattnern, 1777)

Girolamo, da Montefortino, *Duns Scoti (...) Summa Theologica ex universis eius operis concinnata*, 5 vols. (Rome: Giorgio Plachi, 1728–34)

Goudin, Antoine, *Philosophia iuxta inconcussa tutissimaque D. Thomae dogmata*, 4 vols. (Lyons: Antoine Jullieron, 1670)

Gravina, Domenico, *Totius Summae theologicae S. Thomae Aquinatis compendium rhytmicum* (Naples: Lazaro Scoriggio, 1625)

Hardouin, Jean, *Censura summae theologiae Thomae Aquinatis*, 4 vols., Paris BNF, Ms. lat. 3421, 1717

Jansenius, Cornelius, *Augustinus, seu doctrina sancti Augustini de humanae naturae, sanitate, aegritudine, medicina, adversus Pelagianos et Massilienses* (Louvain: Zegers, 1640)

St. John of Damascus, *Saint John of Damascus, Writings*, translated by F.H. Chase, Jr., vol. 37, *The Fathers of the Church Series* (New York, NY: Catholic University of America Press, 1958)

Kant, Immanuel, *Critique of Pure Reason*, translated and edited by P. Guyer and A.W. Wood (Cambridge: Cambridge University Press, 1998)

Labbé, Pierre, "Elogia utriusque Doctoris Angelici et Subtilis," in L. Bail (ed.), *Supplementum Theologiae Affectivae* (Paris: P. de Bresche, 1663) pp. 637–40

Launoy, Jean de, *Veneranda Romanae Ecclesiae circa simoniam traditio* (Paris: Edmond Martin, 1675)

Le Gendre, Louis, *Les mœurs et coutumes des François* (Paris: Briasson, 1753)

Luther, Martin, *Table Talk* (1531/32), edited and translated by T.G. Tappert, in *Luthers's Works*, vol. 54 (Philadelphia, PA: Fortress Press, 1967)

Maldonado, Juan, "De constitutione theologiae," in T. Idígoras and J. Ignacio, "Metedología teológica deMaldonado: Estudio de su 'De constitutione theologiae'," *Scriptorium Victoriense* 1 (1954), 226–55

Marandé, Louis de, *La Clef ou Abbregé [sic] de la Somme de S. Thomas* (Paris: Michel Soly, 1649)

Mariales, Xante, *Bibliotheca Interpretum ad universam Summam theologiae divi Thomae Aquinatis* (Venice: Combi & La Nou, 1638)

Massoulié, Antonin, *Divus Thomas sui interpres de divina motione et libertate creata. Tomus secundus* (Rome: Giuseppe Vannacci, 1693)

Meisner, Baltasar, *Philosophia sobria*, vol. 2 (Wittenberg: Martin Henckel & Andreas Rüdinger, 1611)

Morhof, Daniel Georg, *Polyhistor litterarius philosophicus* (Lübeck: Peter Böckmann, 1714)

Muratori, Ludovico Antonio, *Riflessioni sopra il buon gusto nelle Scienze, e nelle Arti* (Cologne [in reality Naples]: Francesco Ricciardo, 1721; 1st edn 1715)

Ochoa, Juan de, *Omnes primariae conclusiones omnium et singulorum articulorum Summae Divi Thomae* (Rome: apud Antonium Bladum, 1564)

Ortega, Cristóbal de, *De Deo uno. Tomus primus controversiarum dogmaticarum, scholasticarum de essentia, attributis non vitalibus, de scientia, de decreto concurrendi cum causis liberis (...). Editio novissima* (Lyon: Pierre Chevalier, 1671)

Penon, François, *Hymnus angelicus, sive Doctoris Angelicis Summae theologicae rythmica synopsis* (Paris: J. Piot, 1653)

Philippus a Sanctissima Trinitate, *Summa philosophica ex mira principis philosophorum Aristotelis et Doctoris Angelici D. Thomae doctrina, iuxta legitimam scholae thomisticae intelligentiam composita* (Lyons: Antoine Jullieron, 1648)

Plato, *Complete Works*, J.M. Cooper (ed.) (Indianapolis, IN: Hackett, 1997).

Porphyry, *Introduction [Isagoge]*, translated by. J. Barnes (Oxford: Clarendon Press, 2003)

[Pseudo-] Dionysius, *De divinis nominibus*, Greek text and Latin translation in C. Pera (ed.), *Thomae Aquinatis In Librum beati Dionysii De divinis nominibus Expositio* (Turin–Rome: Marietti, 1950)

Reiser, Anton, *Vindiciae evangelico-thomisticae* (Ulm: Kühn, 1667)

Roselli, Salvatore Maria, *Summa philosophica ad mentem angelici doctoris Thomae Aquinatis*, 6 vols. (Rome: Octavio Puccinelli, 1777)

Serpilius, Georg, S., *Commentatores in Psalmos Davidis, darinnen über DC Autores, so die Psalmen erläutert (...) beurtheilt werden* (Regensburg: J.Z. Seidel, 1716)

Serry, Jacques-Hyacinthe, *Historiae Congregationum de auxiliis diuinae gratiae sub Summis Pontificibus Clemente VIII et Paulo V libri quatuor, quibus etiam data opera confutantur recentiores huius historiae deprauatores* (Louvain: Gilles Denique, 1700)

Simplicius, *Commentaire sur les Categories D'Aristote*. Traduction de Guillaume de Moerbeke, A. Pattin, O.M.I. (ed.), Corpus Latinum Commentariorum in Aristotelem Graecorum, 2 vols. (Louvain–Paris: E. J. Brill, 1971/1975)

Sixtus Senensis, *Bibliotheca sancta ex praecipuis Catholicae Ecclesiae auctoribus collecta* (Venice: Francesco De Franceschi, 1575; 1st ed., 1566)

Soto, Domingo de, *Commentariorum in quartum Sententiarum tomus primus* (Salamanca: Juan María de Terranova, 1561)

Touron, Antoine, *La vie de S. Thomas d'Aquin* (Paris: chez Gissey, Bordelet, Savoye, 1737)

Valla, Lorenzo, "In Praise of Saint Thomas Aquinas," translated by M.E. Hanley in L.A. Kennedy (ed.), *Renaissance Philosophy* (Den Haag: Nijhoff, 1973) pp. 13–27

Van Malderen, Jan, *In primam secundae D. Thomae commentaria* (Antwerp: ex officina Plantiniana, 1623)

Van Mastricht, Peter, *Theoretico-practica theologia* (Utrecht: Sumptibus Societatis, 1714)

Voetius, Gisbert, *Exercitia et bibliotheca studiosi* (Utrecht: Jan van Waesberghe, 1651; 1st ed. 1644)

Volpi, Angelo, *Sacra theologiae summa Ioannis Duns Scoti Doctoris Subtilissimi et commentaria quibus eius doctrina elucidatur, comprobatur, defenditur*, 12 vols. (Naples: apud Lazarum Scorigium, Anelli Cassetae, Camilli Cavalli, 1622–46)

Werner, Karl, *Der heilige Thomas von Aquin, vol. 3: Geschichte des Thomismus* (Regensburg: Manz, 1859)

Index

.

CPSIA information can be obtained
at www.ICGtesting.com
Printed in the USA
LVHW052048060220
646086LV00013B/1374